The excellence of play

Edited by
Janet R. Moyles

Open University Press
Buckingham · Philadelphia

Open University Press
Celtic Court
22 Ballmoor
Buckingham
MK18 1XW

email: enquiries@openup.co.uk
world wide web: http://www.openup.co.uk

and
325 Chestnut Street
Philadelphia, PA 19106, USA

First Published 1994
Reprinted 1994, 1995 (twice), 1996, 1998, 1999

Copyright © The Editors and Contributors 1994

All rights reserved. Except for the quotation of short passages for the
purpose of criticism and review, no part of this publication may be
reproduced, stored in a retrieval system, or transmitted, in any form or by
any means, electronic, mechanical, photocopying, recording or otherwise,
without the prior written permission of the publis
her or a licence from the Copyright Licensing Agency Limited. Details of such
licences (for
reprographic reproduction) may be obtained from the Copyright Licensing
Agency Ltd of 90 Tottenham Court Road, London, W1P 9HE.

A catalogue record for this book is available from the British Library

ISBN 0 335 19068 5 (pb)   0 335 19069 3 (hb)

Library of Congress Cataloging-in-Publication Data
The Excellence of play / edited by Janet R. Moyles.
        p.   cm.
    Includes bibliographical references (p.   ) and index.
    ISBN 0-335-19069-3
    1. Play. 2. Early childhood education - Curricula.   I. Moyles,
Janet R.
LB1140.35.P55E93   1993
372.21 – dc20   93-25317
                                                    CIP

Typeset by Graphicraft Typesetters Ltd, Hong Kong
Printed and bound in Great Britain by
Biddles Ltd, Guildford and King's Lynn

0172288

SM99006700
3.2000.
£13.99.

JJN
(Moy)

The excellence of play

WITHDRAWN

WITHDRAWN

WITHDRAWN

CARLISLE LIBRARY
SUPPORTING SERVICES LTD.

033 519 0685

Contents

Notes on the editor and contributors

Lesley Abbott is Principal Lecturer in Early Childhood Education at the Manchester Metropolitan University. She has a particular interest in the role of play in the education of young children and was a member of the Rumbold Committee of Inquiry into the quality of educational experiences for three- to four-year-old children. She is co-editor, with Nigel Hall, of *Play in the Primary Curriculum* (Hodder and Stoughton) and is at present involved in research on identifying quality experiences for young children and their families.

Angela Anning is Lecturer in Early Years/Arts education at the University of Leeds where she is a teacher trainer. Formerly a Headteacher, she has a wide range of teaching experiences particularly in inner-city primary schools and her particular interest over many years has been the education of young children. Her current research interest is Key Stage 1 Design and Technology and, in addition to several articles, she is the author of *The First Years at School* (Open University Press).

Tony Bertram is a Senior Lecturer in Early Childhood Education at Worcester College of Higher Education and works on the postgraduate and inservice courses. Formerly a Headteacher, he worked for fourteen years in first schools. He is secretary of the European Early Childhood Education Research Association.

David Brown is a primary Headteacher in Leicestershire. Having completed an MA on play area culture, he is currently extending these studies towards a PhD in which he is examining the relationship between play area play and the culture of childhood.

Tina Bruce was formerly Director of the Centre for Early Childhood Studies at the Froebel Institute. She received the award 'International Outstanding Woman Scholar in Education' at the Virginia Commonwealth University, USA, in 1989. She is the author of *Early Childhood Education* (Hodder and Stoughton, 1987) and *Time to Play in Early Childhood Education* (Hodder and Stoughton, 1991). She has recently directed the Froebel Blockplay Research Study, a collaborative venture together with research assistant Pat Gura and the Froebel Blockplay Research Group.

Audrey Curtis was formerly a Senior Lecturer at the Institute of Education, University of London, and is now working as an educational consultant. She has lectured widely both nationally and internationally and has acted as a consultant for UNESCO and UNICEF and is Vice President of the European Region of OMEP (The World Organization for Early Childhood Education). Her publications include *A Curriculum for the Preschool Child* (NFER/Nelson) and she has undertaken continuing research in the areas of child development and early childhood education.

Rose Griffiths is currently Lecturer in education at the University of Leicester. Starting as a mathematics teacher with a particular interest in working with children who find maths difficult, she has worked with under-fives, with adult students, in playschemes and parents' groups and was previously head of mathematics at a comprehensive school. Her publications include several books for parents and teachers and she also enjoys writing books for children. The latter include *Mice Maths, The Puffin Times Tables Book, Calculator Alligator* and a series of books for younger children called *Simple Maths*.

Nigel Hall is Senior Lecturer in the School of Education at the Manchester Metropolitan University. He is a specialist in literacy in the early years and has published widely in this area. His publications include *The Emergence of Literacy, Writing with Reason* and *Literacy in Action*. He is the co-editor with Lesley Abbott of *Play in the Primary Curriculum*. He is currently directing 'The Punctuation Project', co-directing a project on play and writing, and writing a book on play and literacy.

Peter Heaslip is now an early childhood Consultant working in England, Europe and the USA, having formerly spent considerable time in teacher education. He has cooperated in producing a Directory of Teacher Education in European Countries and is currently Chair of the Early Years Working Party of the Association for Teacher Education in Europe (ATTE).

Jane Hislam is currently Lecturer in early years/primary education at the University of Leicester, having been an advisory teacher for English. Her research interests are particularly focused in the areas of children's literature, oral storytelling, gender issues and equal opportunities and she has lectured widely in her field. Her publications include two books in the Black's Primary Language Project series (*Myths and Legends, Out and About*) and several articles on aspects of story.

Victoria Hurst is currently a Lecturer at Goldsmiths' College, University of London, where she teaches on a range of multi-professional courses. She is the author of *Planning for Early Learning* (Paul Chapman) and has also written on partnership with parents and on assessment in nursery education. She founded, and currently chairs, the Early Years Curriculum Group, and has contributed to its publications. Her research interests are in educational evaluation in early years education for both adults and children.

Neil Kitson lectures in primary education at the University of Leicester. He has worked for several years in early years education both as teacher and later as advisory teacher for drama. He has published and broadcast widely in both drama and socio-dramatic play. He is currently researching the role of the teacher in encouraging quality experiences in drama and socio-dramatic play.

Janet Moyles is Senior Lecturer in Education at the University of Leicester where she is responsible for initial and inservice education relating to early childhood education. Formerly a nursery/first school Headteacher, she is committed to establishing and providing quality experiences for young children. She has written and lectured widely on children's play and issues related to the management of learning and her books include *Just Playing?* (Open University Press), *Play as a Learning Process* (Mary Glasgow) and *Organizing for Learning* (Open University Press). Her main research interests continue to be in play and learning – and all that entails.

Christine Pascal is Reader in Education at Worcester College of Higher Education. She taught in infant schools in Birmingham for ten years before becoming a lecturer and researcher. Her work takes her all over the UK and, increasingly, abroad. A member of the Rumbold Committee of Inquiry, she has a strong commitment to raising the status and quality of education for young children.

Roy Prentice is Chair of the Department of Art and Design at the Institute of Education, University of London. Before that he was an art adviser in East Sussex, working across primary and secondary education. His main research interest is in the role of art and design in teacher education. He is a practising painter.

Jeni Riley is Course Tutor for the Primary postgraduate certificate in education at the Institute of Education, University of London. She has taught infants and been an advisory teacher in Oxfordshire. Her main research and doctoral thesis has been into the development of literacy in the first year of school. She is currently evaluating different modes of initial teacher education.

Jane Savage is Lecturer in primary education at the Institute of Education, University of London, having previously worked as a teacher, deputy headteacher and advisory teacher. Her research and publications are in the areas of science planning, assessment and whole school policy, and school development plans and planning.

Peter K. Smith is Professor of Psychology at the University of Sheffield. He has carried out research on children's play and development for many years. He is co-author (with Helen Cowie) of *Understanding Children's Development* (Blackwells) and editor of *Play in Animals and Humans* (Blackwells) and *Children's Play: Research Developments and Practical Applications* (Gordon and Breach). He is currently examining the issue of school bullying and how best to reduce it.

Acknowledgements

I should like to credit the title of this book to Melanie McCombe with whom I worked for a brief but pleasurable time in Cheshire. Credit is also due to the contributors for their perseverance in sticking to deadlines, and particularly to Peter Heaslip who permitted me the luxury of selecting several of the photographs used in the book from his delightful collection. I should also like to thank the many teachers and others who may recognize within the text aspects of their own practice which they have so willingly, and perhaps unwittingly, shared, in particular Sue Greet and Jean Allen and the staff of Humberstone Nursery/Infant School, Leicester.

Introduction

Janet R. Moyles

Plate 1   *The excellence of play – but how do we prove it?*

Plate 2   There is no doubt that young children need to be actively involved

Plate 3   Children play what they know!

Sarita is four. She is playing in the water tray where she has a small plastic bucket, a funnel with a thin, clear, plastic tube attached and a squeezy bottle holed at various points in its vertical surface: the water is green. As she pours the green liquid from the bucket into the funnel from whence it enters the thin tube, she looks puzzled. She tries again – and again. 'Look!' she says to no-one in particular. 'The water's not green any more in there.' [the tube] She plays some more in just the same way and looks satisfied as she clearly confirms her earlier thinking.

Sarita moves on to the squeezy bottle and quickly recognizes that the thin stream of water pouring out from the sides equally looks clear, rather than green. She peers into the top of the bottle 'It's green in there,' she says. She calls to the adult and explains what is happening: 'It's because the water's gone thin!' she asserts. Together they put a thin layer of green water on a small white tray; the colour is barely visible. She fetches other containers and is able to explain convincingly that the 'thickness' or 'thinness' of the water determines whether the colour will be clearly visible or not.

Wayne is seven. He has entered the greengrocer's shop area in the classroom and donned the apron which indicates that he is the shopkeeper. He quickly tidies the trays of play fruit and vegetables and brings an immediate appearance of 'order' to the area. He checks the till for money, counts each set of coins, recounts the single pennies (discovering only three) and rehangs the paper bags on the hook on the wall. He calls across the classroom for a 'customer' and a peer obliges. Wayne hands his customer a bag saying, 'Good morning. This shop's self-service – you can 'ave wot you wants but you 'ave to pay me.' The customer duly takes a bag, fills it with apples and hands it to Wayne. 'Them's good for ya teeth,' he suggests, adding, '6p each, that's 24p . . . please madame. Can ya give me it right 'cos I ain't got much change today!'

Talking to various adults about these and similar activities, there is comprehensive agreement that the children are 'playing'. There is usually equal agreement that a) they are 'learning' – or at least giving evidence of previous learning, of 'playing what they know' (Schwartzman 1982); and b) there is a level of 'excellence' represented in these experiences for children.

Quality links between play and learning seem obvious to many practitioners and parents: yet the dilemma still exists as to whether play can provide any kind of 'excellence' in relation to 'real' learning in early years educational contexts. With a nationally prescribed curriculum apparently overtly favouring written activities and threatening to overwhelm everyone concerned in a sea of paper, the burden of proof in relation to what play has to offer children and teachers lies with committed early years practitioners in various fields (Fisher 1992). What must also be remembered and stressed is that 'proof', in relation to quality learning from paper and pencil activities, has still to be given; indeed there is research indicating obverse effects on young children (Bennett *et al.*, 1984; Desforges and Cockburn 1988; Meadows and Cashdan 1988). The NC documents themselves within the programmes of study equally give credence to children's active involvement in their own learning, though rarely mention the word 'play' *per se*.

It cannot be denied that the dilemmas for teachers are quite fundamental. The National Curriculum is a power coercive model: it emphasizes a mechanistic view in which children and teachers are not valued for themselves but for what they 'produce'. Similarly, the thrust of what is also an 'economics' model of curriculum is that it operates from a very surreal view that we can get 'quality' regardless of human strengths and weaknesses – or, paradoxically, financial constraints! In play activities production may or may not be important; the emphasis is on children and their ownership of, and active involvement in, curriculum processes and on what they *bring* to learning which forms the foundation of knowledge, skills and understanding – all of which appear to effectively place play in direct confrontation with the current model of curriculum.

Must this be so? This book is primarily intended to generate and enhance further thoughts and inform debate on all these issues. It has been written by a wide-ranging group of people who have given extensive thought and time to the fascinating, if sometimes frustrating, study of play, specifically in relation to children's learning and development, and issues of quality provision in educational philosophy and practice.

The title *The Excellence of Play* in itself indicates the main stance taken by contributors. Each of them, in very individualized ways, gives value to both the concept and reality of play. Despite play being a very natural phenomena all over the world, especially for the young, play continues to defy a single, rational definition (Smith 1984). Each of the contributors has examined the concept from several different angles and given their own definitional propositions. What they have in common, however, adds up to a very powerful argument for the 'excellence of play', based on a firm belief that practitioners should be advocating strongly in support of a greater understanding of the potential contribution of play to children's development and learning.

The book is intended for practitioners across the three- to eight-year-old age range. Mainly geared towards teachers, it nevertheless recognizes the extent of the 'educator' role so beautifully expressed by the Rumbold Committee (1990) and acknowledges that, whenever and wherever possible, any divisions, actual or imagined, must be overlaid by multi-disciplinary understanding and coherence, if only for the sake of the children.

The arguments about play, in general, centre round a number of issues which it is worth examining briefly as they provide a basic overview of the contents of the main contributions.

Play and play behaviours

Grappling with the concept of play can be analogized to trying to seize bubbles, for every time there appears to be something to hold on to, its ephemeral nature disallows it being grasped! Because of its diversity (Fisher 1992), it continues to defy attempts at quantification.

Even examining general usage in English, play can be deemed to be a noun, verb, adverb, adjective – the play or a plaything, as in drama and toys; to play in relation to method or mode; to undertake something playfully; or to be described as a 'playful child'. Even at this basic level, it is not easy to distinguish any one meaning which might be attached to 'children's play', for it is likely to be a combination of many of these. Garvey (1991: 7) has suggested that 'several layers of significance may be present simultanteously' and, as I have argued elsewhere (Moyles 1989 and 1991), it makes more sense to consider play as a process which, in itself, will subsume a range of behaviours, motivations, opportunities, practices, skills and understandings.

The work/play arguments and similar polarizations are singularly unhelpful, for, as most of us will acknowledge, it is possible to play at one's work and work at one's play. In any case, as Pellegrini (1987: 201) rightly suggests:

> A child's playful behaviours can be categorized according to the number of dispositional criteria met. As a result, play can be categorized as 'more or less play', not dichotomously as 'play or not play' . . . Simply put, acts should not be categorized as 'play' or 'not play'; they should be rated along a continuum from 'pure play' to 'non-play'.

If as adults we are really 'hooked on children', we have to be hooked on play as a process across this continuum of experiences – and agree that the full range is valid in relation to a broad, balanced and relevant education. Most people seem to agree that every child has a right to play – indeed Article 31 of the United Nations Convention on the Rights of Child makes this quite explicit (Newell 1991). What seems to be at issue is whether they have the right to do so in *educational contexts*.

Justifying play in educational contexts

Somewhere on the 'back-burner' in all of us there appears to be a feeling that if it doesn't hurt it can't be doing us any good! Therefore, something like play with its high levels of motivation and potential enjoyment appears, in some way, not to be appropriate in institutional settings. This is perhaps surprising considering that we all, on the whole, enjoy being with motivated people of all ages, who approach tasks readily and willingly, who are open and responsive to learning, who will

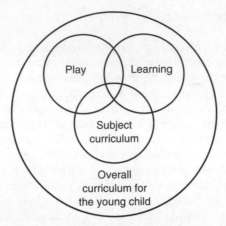

Figure I.1   A simple model of early years curriculum

'have-a-go' at things unfettered by anxiety: in other words, those who have a playful attitude. The motivational qualities of play are accentuated throughout this book, as is the concept that play in educational settings should have *learning* consequences. This is what separates play in that context from recreational play – educators need to show quite clearly that, and what, children are learning through play. This needs to occur *in* the educational setting, rather than in clinical trials (as has so often been the case) because play in the 'to order' sense will put it at a different level on the play continuum and will, therefore, effectively change it. Studies by Gura (1992) and Athey (1990) have taken an initially more qualitative approach to evaluating play episodes through observations and analysis and contribute potentially the best way forward.

Anyone who has observed play for any length of time will recognize that, for young children, play is a tool for learning and practitioners who acknowledge and appreciate this can, through provision, interaction and intervention in children's play ensure progression, differentiation and relevance in the curriculum. The sense of children actively seeking to construct their own view of the world and the contribution of quality interactions with others, both adults and children, is now widely accepted as a suitable approach to early years curriculum. Work versus play arguments can become honed upon academic versus practical skills' polarizations. As indicated above, we must not allow this to happen, for, as Angela Anning in Chapter 5 insists, to be a whole, balanced person we all need to use both kinds of skills and related thinking.

The simple model of early years curriculum (represented in Figure I.1) indicates that there really need be no conflict of interest as each element readily interweaves with the rest. The excellence and quality of this process constitutes the main thrust of the arguments in this book.

Ensuring excellence and quality in play provision

. Can play actually *raise* standards in early education? As several writers suggest, there is much evidence to indicate that play-based curricular experiences for children can initiate and give momentum to the raising of standards generally in early childhood education and beyond. There appear to be three main strands to the argument: the quality of provision, the value associated with play processes and the involvement of adults. These elements, particularly the latter, are emphasized by all contributors to this book. No-one, however, is suggesting any of these things are easy! When adults actually begin to approach the provision of high quality play and their involvement in it, it does not usually take long to find out that it is really hard work for adults to play with children!

Striving to understand children in their play, many educators have turned to Corinne Hutt's (1979) model of play (shown in Figure I.2). The essential argument that, in epistemic play children explore the basic properties of materials and gain knowledge and handling skills and that this is a vital prerequisite to developing further knowledge, skills and understandings, is implicit within many of the chapters of this book. The ludic play elements, including as they do socio-dramatic play contexts, subsume more opportunities for language play and creativity and constitute opportunities for rehearsal and practice. Games-play occurs at increasing levels of difficulty and 'rule-boundness' and incorporates simple social games, children's own attempts at rules, riddles, number games and so on, until 'fairness' is established as a concept and competition enters the arena. According to Kohl (1977: 78) games for young children provide:

> occasions for repetition and therefore enable children to master certain academic skills in a setting where learning is combined with play.

Perhaps one of the greatest attributes of play is the opportunities it affords for learning to live with *not knowing*, for it is readily recognized that we all learn more effectively through trial and error (Holt 1991) and play is a non-threatening way to cope with new learning and still retain self-esteem and self-image. Knowing children's learning needs also enables adults to encompass the notions of Vygotsky (1978) and Bruner (1978) respectively in relation to the 'zone of proximal development' from which 'scaffolding' by the adult will enable progress in learning to proceed from a point of current understanding. These propositions are extensively cited in the chapters of this book and practical implications and applications discussed. In itself this will constitute new thinking for many practitioners for, as Tharp and Gallimore (1988: 57) suggest, although 'assisted performance' is found commonly among parent/child relationships, it is rarely found in schools.

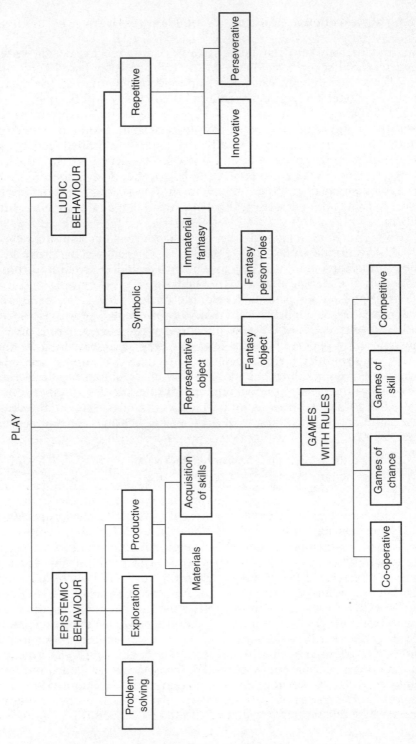

Figure 1.2 A taxonomy of children's play (after Hutt 1979)

The sensitivity of educators to children's play cannot be over-emphasized. We all need to remember that:

> to maintain its status as a play activity, it is necessary for the activity to remain player-centred, i.e. initiated, paced and stylized by the child.
>
> (Johnson and Ershler 1982: 139)

Deep involvement by children is necessary and must be allowed and encouraged by the adults if the play is to be really challenging and contribute fully to the learning process (Monighan-Nourot *et al.*, 1987).

This book constitutes an attempt to relate play theory to practice in an on-going, continuous and straightforward way. Throughout, examples of specific practices are given: play with the ideas and make them your own! It is possible to dip into the book at almost any point, for each chapter can be read as a discrete unit or viewed as part of a whole, the writers all operating from different but interrelated standpoints.

Part 1 sets the scene by exploring the value of play as a cross-cultural concept as well as one rooted in the Westernized world. Concepts of play, and therefore values associated with it, are intrinsically bound up with the way it is viewed by societies. Peter Smith argues for a level-headed approach to considering the values to be associated with play in Western culture and in curriculum provision for young children. Audrey Curtis uses her wide experience of play in different cultures and concepts of childhood to emphasize the similarities and differences in types of play and the values attached to them across the world, relating this firmly back to Western culture. Equal opportunities for both boys and girls are emphasized in Jane Hislam's chapter where, through the medium of domestic play, she explores how ostensibly 'established' gender identity can dominate classroom practice and how variation in provision can influence and transform the play. Children's own culture, including gender issues, is the focus of David Brown's chapter, wherein he examines in detail the ways in which play-area spaces in schools are utilized by children to create a very different kind of world of play 'beyond the classroom door'.

In stark contrast to the way children play and perceive play in different cultures, are the passionate arguments Angela Anning puts forward in the first chapter in Part 2, Play, schooling and responsibilities, regarding corporate views of play in education. Most early years practitioners will empathize with Angela's view that *children* are at the heart of the curriculum and that play-based, holistic learning opportunities must be central to early childhood learning and teaching. Ensuring the personal and professional commitment of educators to children's play as a distinct feature of learning is the theme of Lesley Abbott in Chapter 6. She emphasizes the demanding nature of making good quality provision and suggests a number of staff development issues which practitioners will need to address in order to monitor their approaches to play provision and its outcomes. Although traditionally, adults have felt somewhat uneasy attempting to enter the children's play arena, Neil Kitson, in Chapter 7, extends the responsible practitioner argument by making a striking case for direct adult intervention in children's socio-dramatic play. He argues, from a psychological basis, for both the importance of this type of pretend play and adults' responsibilities in extending and enhancing children's learning through structuring and modelling. The final chapter in this section by Peter Heaslip recapitulates on some of the previous discussions presented, arguing for both a revision of what is meant by 'the basics' in curriculum terms for young children and the case to be made to parents, politicians and others for 'bottom-up' educational provision which gives the child, rather than a prescribed curriculum, centrality.

The previous sections' discussions lead neatly into Part 3, Play and the early years curriculum, in which the four writers examine the provision of a subject curriculum through play. While not denying that many other 'subjects' are readily subsumed within the early years curriculum framework (particularly within cross-curricular approaches) language, art, science and maths are acknowledged as 'basics' in any early years subject curriculum and these respectively form the focus of Part 3. Nigel Hall in Chapter 9, talks of 'the extraordinarily rich potential of play' in relation to developing children's literacy, and uses role play in various stimulus area settings as the basis for exploring and extending quality in children's reading and writing experiences. In Chapter 10, Roy Prentice argues that play, creativity and art go hand-in-hand, projecting a clear view that integral to all three are skills, attitudes and activities which emphasize 'the nature and quality of an individual's engagement with ideas, feelings and materials'. Roy's practical suggestions for creating appropriate conditions for initiating children into art as a way of knowing, and the process/product dilemmas for practitioners, are insightful. Jeni Riley and Jane Savage follow on in Chapter 11 with a discussion about the role of play in children's development of scientific understanding. They give clear indication of the direct and incontrovertible need for children to play with the materials and concepts of science if real learning is to ensue, a firm stance also taken in the following chapter. All those who learned mathematics with difficulty will appreciate Rose Griffith's stance in Chapter 12. Her playful approach to mathematics teaching and learning, her emphasis on skills and gaining sound mathematical knowledge through games, pinpoints alternative and exciting ways of learning abstract, symbolic systems. Rose's argument that more advanced mathematics can be achieved through play approaches than by didactic methods bears close scrutiny by educators and politicians alike.

The final part of the book, Assessing and evaluating play, has three chapters written respectively on evaluating and improving the quality of play, observing play and the individual child and play. In Chapter 13, Christine Pascal and Tony Bertram emphasize the need for quality in play provision but assert strongly that the concept of 'quality' can only be defined by the 'shared reflections and agreement of experienced practitioners'. They offer within the chapter a sound theoretically-based framework for practitioners through which the quality of their own particular play provision can be identified, evaluated and monitored. As observation is the key both to making quality provision for play and in understanding children's learning through play processes, Victoria Hurst (Chapter 14) turns her attention directly to methods of observation and outcomes in relation to greater understanding about play and children through assessment. Both chapters offer productive and valuable contributions, given the clear need to 'prove' to the world at large (as well as occasionally to ourselves) that play is worthwhile and valuable for young children's learning and development. In terms of the individual child, any persisting doubts about the value of play are dispelled in the final chapter by Tina Bruce, who offers her unique view of 'free-flow' play and its contribution to children's education. Tina argues that children in industrialized societies may not be so 'privileged' as it might appear in being subjected to highly formalized education, but would benefit from a vision of the future which includes ready opportunities to free-flow play.

There is, of course, much more that could have been included, for that is the diverse and flexible nature, indeed the excellence, of play.

Part 1
The culture of play and childhood

Plate 4   Different socio-dramatic play themes generate different types of social play

Plate 5   The principle that children can learn through play and that play activities should be part of the early childhood programmes is accepted among educationalists in most countries

1 Play and the uses of play

Peter K. Smith

Few people interested in young children doubt the fascination of play. Whether it is physically exuberant play, mock fighting and chasing, the scripted pretend and role-play games mimicking the world of adults, elaborate constructive play with objects, or perhaps play with words and verbal conventions, play conjures up a carefree world of childhood for adults who feel themselves pressured by the responsibilities of work. Indeed, play is often seen as the opposite to work – an activity done for its own sake, without external constraint. Conflicts and coercion can occur in play, as in most other activities, and there has perhaps been a tendency to idealize play, particularly among educationalists, over the last half-century (Sutton-Smith 1986): a theme I shall return to. Nevertheless the fascination is a real one.

Play is something of an enigma. Just how important is it in development? It is certainly enjoyable, but is it vital? Some people argue in the affirmative, but it is difficult to prove. Anyway, does it matter? And should we leave children alone to play, or try to 'structure' and 'improve' it by adult intervention? These are some of the themes to be discussed in this opening chapter.

Types of play

Play is very characteristic of children in the age range two to six years. This is the major developmental period for symbolic play. Piaget (1951) distinguished between 'practice play', 'symbolic play' and 'games with rules'. Practice play includes the sensorimotor and exploratory play of the young infant – especially six months to two years; symbolic play the pretend, fantasy and socio-dramatic play of the preschool and early infant school child, from about two or three to six years; games with rules characterize the activities of children from six or seven years onwards.

Much of the play of the preschool child will be *symbolic*. Children pretend that an action or object has some meaning other than its usual, real-life meaning; for example if a child rotates his arms, goes 'poop-poop', and gives out pieces of paper, he is pretending to turn a steering-wheel, sound a horn and give out bus tickets. If these actions are sufficiently well-integrated, we can say that the child is in *'role play'* (in this case, pretending to be a bus driver). If two or more children are engaged in role play together, this is *'socio-dramatic play'* (explored further in Chapter 7). Such forms of play, according to Piaget, appear to increase with age, then decline, through the three- to seven-year age period.

Piaget's scheme was changed slightly and augmented by Smilansky (1968). She added a category of *'constructive play'*, in which objects are manipulated to construct or create something. Many teachers do indeed regard such constructive activities as play. Piaget (1951), however, believed that 'constructive games . . . occupy . . . a position halfway between play and intelligent work, or between play and imitation', stating this because he thought that the goal-directed nature of constructive activities meant it was 'accommodative' – the child adapting his/her behaviour to fit reality – whereas symbolic play was 'assimilative' – adapting reality to fit the child's own wishes.

Certain kinds of play do not fit well into the schemes of either Piaget or Smilansky (Takhvar and Smith 1990). For example, *physical activity play* (running, climbing, sliding, swinging and other gross muscular play) and *rough-and-tumble play* (playful fighting, wrestling and chasing) are very characteristic of young children, especially in outdoor play areas (Chapter 4). But they are not constructive, and they are not necessarily symbolic. These kinds of play have been somewhat neglected by psychologists and educationalists, who have paid most attention to constructive play and symbolic play, especially in discussions of nursery and infant school curricula.

Play behaviour is one useful way in which the child can acquire developmental skills – social, intellectual, creative, physical. First, much play is social. Socio-dramatic play and rough-and-tumble play necessarily involve coordination of activities with one or more play partners. Such forms of play can form a primary mode of social interaction at this age range (including gender identity, as discussed in Chapter 3). This is less true of constructive play, which can, but need not be, social. Most forms of play occur naturally between like-aged children, but play can also foster child-adult relationships if the adult engages in a play activity with the child (explored in Chapter 8).

Second, many theorists claim that play has intellectual benefits. Socio-dramatic play may foster language and role-taking skills, while constructive play may encourage cognitive development and concept formation. Such aspects of cognitive development may overlap with, though are not identical to, school-based criteria of academic achievement.

Many theorists and practitioners believe that play experience is the optimal way of enhancing creativity and imagination (Roy Prentice, for example, explores art and play in Chapter 10). This is because children have the freedom to try out new ideas in play and can express themselves in their own way, especially in socio-dramatic and fantasy play where they can invent roles and develop a story as their imagination leads them. Finally, much play is physically active. Constructive play may practise fine motor skills, while gross physical play and rough-and-tumble play can provide whole-body exercise and motor coordination.

It seems plausible and likely – as both Angela Anning and Tina Bruce argue (Chapters 5 and 15 respectively) – that playful activities can advance most of the aims of early years education in all main aspects, social, intellectual, creative and physical. Still, it is important to keep a sense of perspective on this. The aims of early education can also be advanced by many other more structured or didactic activities, organized games, physical exercises, story-telling, and real-life tasks such as preparing food (cultural aspects are discussed by Audrey Curtis in the following chapter), and tidying the classroom. These activities are not necessarily 'play' (unless we broaden the definition of play quite unacceptably, to include all behaviour of young children!). Any benefits of play must be considered against any benefits of non-playful activities.

A free play curriculum

If play is useful in development, how should it be made use of in the early years curriculum? One view is that children should just be provided with a variety of good, suitable playing materials and props, and then be left free to play according to their own needs and inclinations. Many Western European educators have believed that such a free play curriculum is the ideal form of preschool experience. Like most ideas, this has a history. Play was not seen as educationally valuable when nursery and infant schools began to be introduced in Western Europe in the eighteenth and nineteenth centuries. Children were believed to need instruction and, in the case of religious doctrines, redemption from sinful behaviour. However, a number of writers and educators, such as the Czech writer Comenius, the Swiss writer Rousseau, and early social reformers and educators such as Owen (UK), Pestalozzi (Switzerland), Froebel (Germany) and Montessori (Italy), began to emphasize the value of the child's own spontaneous growth, and the image of the child as naturally 'good'. From this viewpoint, spontaneous play was seen as having some importance. In addition, the value of active teacher involvement was often stressed, though with considerable variation in the types of activities recommended. Montessori, for example, favoured constructive play activities using specifically designed materials, but did *not* encourage fantasy or socio-dramatic play.

An even more positive attitude to the value of spontaneous play and dramatic play came to the fore in the twentieth century, especially in the period 1930 to 1970, at least so far as many Western European writers on early education were concerned. Spontaneous play was thought to be not only important but actually an essential component of the child's social and intellectual development and of creative and personal growth. This viewpoint can be termed the *'play ethos'* (Smith 1988). Susan Isaacs (1929: 9) summed this perspective up when she wrote 'play indeed is the child's work, and the means whereby he or she grows and develops'. It is found again in *The Plowden Report* (DES 1967: 193): 'we now know that play – in the sense of "messing about" either with material objects or with other children, and of creating fantasies – is vital to children's learning and therefore vital in school. Adults who criticize teachers for allowing children to play are unaware that play is the principal means of learning in early childhood.'

The play ethos – this particularly strong evaluation of free play – seems to have come about for several reasons. It could be supported by arguments from theoretical perspectives such as psychoanalysis (suggesting the role of play in expressing emotions and working through personal conflicts), and evolutionary biology (suggesting the value of play throughout mammalian species). Also, broader socio-economic changes in Western Europe and North America (such as smaller families, reduced child mortality, the separation of work from home life, and the growth of the toy industry) led to the greater concentration on children as a distinct group with separate needs from adults.

Although originating in the 1920s and 1930s, the play ethos has had a continuing influence on early years education. Writers such as Singer, and Smilansky, have argued that play has great cognitive or social benefits; although Piaget's writings are more ambivalent on this issue, they have not infrequently been reinterpreted to support these arguments. The resulting emphasis was on respecting the child's spontaneous play, and the initiative the child makes, rather than on the adult structuring or directing the child's play.

Surprisingly, there has not been a great deal of firm evidence to support this very positive view of spontaneous play. Some experimental studies in the 1970s did seem to point to the superiority of free play over structured activities in problem-solving tasks, but these studies have subsequently been shown, by quantitative methods, not to be valid (Smith 1988). These studies did not adequately represent the real nature of children's spontaneous play, and were often distorted by 'experimenter effects'. More valid evidence comes from play-tutoring studies, though as we shall see the recent evidence is mixed in its conclusions (Smith 1988). Many educators and child psychologists remain somewhat divided and uncertain about the importance of spontaneous play in development, and the role of the adult. While the 'play ethos' remains influential, there has been some shift back to more structured curricula activities in Western Europe, particularly since the advent of the National Curriculum under the Education Reform Act 1988.

Structuring play by means of adult involvement

Despite the fun and learning that can come about through free play, some play can become very repetitive. It has, therefore, been argued that educators have a key role to play in helping children develop their play; the adult can, as it were, stimulate, encourage or challenge the child to play in more developed and mature ways.

To some extent this can be done by providing structured materials which children are encouraged to use. A familiar example is a jigsaw; the design of the jigsaw means that the child is challenged to get it right – all the adult has to do is provide a jigsaw of the right level of difficulty. (Adult and child games as a feature of mathematical learning are discussed by Rose Griffiths in Chapter 12.)

Besides structuring by materials, adults can also provide structure and challenge by joining in the child's play. Smilansky (1968; Smilansky and Shefatya 1990) argues that socio-dramatic play is very important for the development of social, cognitive and language skills in young children. She gives a high priority to increasing the amount and complexity of socio-dramatic play in those children, especially from disadvantaged backgrounds, whom, she believes, seldom engage in such play in early years settings. Smilansky (1968) has tried several methods of encouraging such play, and found that the most effective method was for the adults or teachers to initiate role play with small groups of children and help them to sustain it and develop it for a period of time. She calls this 'play-tutoring'. Her ideas have also been quite widely used in the USA. Four variants of this method are used by Smilansky and others:

- Modelling – The teacher participates in the play, joining in, and by acting out a role demonstrates how it can be performed effectively. For example, in acting out a 'doctor' role, the teacher could pretend a doll is a baby and pretend a pencil is a thermometer. This demonstrates both fantasy transformations, and some real parts of the doctor's role, to the children. The teacher could help develop an extended sequence of play, for example, asking a child to go and get some more 'medicine' for her.
- Verbal guidance – The teacher does not join in but makes comments and suggestions to help the children develop the roles they are in, for example, reminding a child playing 'mother' to wash the baby before bedtime.

- Thematic-fantasy training – Children are helped to act out familiar story-dramas. Since the plot is usually known in advance, this is a more structured procedure than the previous two.
- Imaginative play training – The teacher trains children in skills which focus on make-believe activities. For example, they are trained to use finger puppets, or practise using facial expressions to represent different emotions. Or, children might sit under a large sheet of grey paper and pretend to be outside on a rainy day. This kind of training focuses on fantasy and does not usually involve role playing.

Smilansky found that such forms of adult encouragement and training *do* increase the amount and complexity of fantasy and socio-dramatic play in young children, especially if they do not show much of this play initially. Furthermore, some increase in spontaneous socio-dramatic play is maintained even when the play training is stopped. This finding has been confirmed by other researchers, in the UK, the USA and elsewhere.

Do the children benefit from play tutoring in other ways? This would be expected, if the increased spontaneous play has the benefits that Smilansky, and other advocates of the 'play ethos', believe. Studies have suggested that there are strong benefits to fantasy and socio-dramatic play. Children involved in play training improved on social, cognitive and language skills more than the children in control groups.

However, it is not necessarily the case that the play-training children have improved more because of the increase in socio-dramatic play. This is because of the nature of the control groups in these studies. In these control groups, an adult was usually present but only in a fairly passive way. The children in the fantasy play-training groups probably received much more extra adult conversation and encouragement. Thus, the greater gain they made could be due *either* to the increase in fantasy or socio-dramatic play, *or* to the extra adult involvement. To choose between these alternatives, a better control condition is needed.

Some studies have been done using better control groups. These have compared fantasy play training with skills training. Skills training involves an equal amount of adult involvement, but *not* in a fantasy context. Rather, children might be encouraged in shape and colour matching, jigsaws, picture dominos, and so on. In one such research study (Smith *et al.*, 1981), the play training or skills training each lasted for a full nursery school term. Observations confirmed that the play and skills groups received about the same amount of adult contact and verbal communication, though of course the nature of this varied, with very much more fantasy content in the play-tutored groups. In general, the outcome on cognitive and language assessments was very similar, whichever kind of training the children received.

Similar studies (Christie and Johnson 1985; Hutt *et al.*, 1989) have confirmed that, when equated for adult contact, the fantasy play training and the skills training conditions are about equally effective. So far as cognitive and language skills are concerned, children in either condition make gains, irrespective of which condition they experience. Although the earlier play-tutoring studies have been defended by Smilansky and Shefatya (1990), in my opinion the research to date suggests that it is adult involvement which is the crucial factor, not the encouragement of fantasy – a point taken up by many contributors to this book.

Fantasy and socio-dramatic play training is enjoyable for children and teachers, and is one way of promoting active adult-child involvement. It may assist many aspects of children's development, but probably no more so than other kinds of involvement which do not involve fantasy or socio-dramatic play. Its particular appeal may be that it can increase adult-child interaction and communication, without detracting from child-child interactions, which adult intervention can so often do.

Another example of increasing adult involvement in play was the Manning and Sharp (1977) project. This reflected a belief that play of any kind, while educationally valuable, can be made more so by some degree of adult involvement. Adult involvement may involve participation and initiation. Participation involves playing either with or alongside the children, while initiation means developing an existing play situation or devising a fresh one, identifying problems, advising about solutions. For example, if a child is playing with sand, pouring it into a container, the adult might join in nearby and provide some more containers of different sizes, thus providing an opportunity to talk about size, and concepts such as 'half-full', 'twice as large'; or if the child is pretending to make cakes from moist sand, the adult could help develop this into making different types of 'cakes', encourage other children to join in, and perhaps use the opportunity to develop counting skills by seeing how many cakes of different kinds have been made. In all cases, the idea is that the adult observes the child's spontaneous play and acts to develop that – rather than organizing activities for the children from the start. This project has been felt to provide many valuable ideas for preschool teachers, though it has never been systematically evaluated.

Another model of ways to structure play is provided by the High/Scope Curriculum, developed in the USA (Hohmann *et al.*, 1979) in which adults and children plan and initiate activities and actively work together. Originally developed with disadvantaged black preschoolers in Ypsilanti, Michigan, it is now used in some preschools in a number of countries including the UK and China. Classroom experiences revolve around 50 'key experiences' intended to promote intellectual and social development; for example, distinguishing between 'some' and 'all'; expressing feelings in words; comparing time periods. Adult help is guided by a 'plan-do-review' cycle. Adults encourage children to choose and plan an activity, then to carry out the plan, and then to reflect on why some things went right and others wrong. There are materials and games for number concepts, spatial relations, representation, classification, seriation, and time. Children learn about these concepts through active exploration and experiment, then reflect on them through discussion with adults and peers. A follow-up of the effects of this curriculum in the USA has claimed long- and short-term beneficial effects, especially in social adjustment and cognitive gains (Schweinhart *et al.*, 1986).

Part of the emphasis in the High/Scope curriculum is that the adult should not be *too* intrusive; children should not be surrounded with adult talk or dominated by instructions but given scope to develop their own ideas and succeed or fail. Some of the ideas would be similar to what is commonly done in many UK schools with five- to six-year-olds. For example, many infant schools use the idea of 'themes' to help organize activities over a week. Themes also often provide an opportunity to bring in relevant materials, or experiences, from their home environment to share in the group. This kind of programme may be particularly suitable for older preschoolers, i.e. four- to six-year-olds.

As well as a range of play activities covering a wide curriculum, as shown in other chapters in this book, adults can also organize cooperative games for children (Masheder 1989). These can range from expressive and fantasy activities (such as Smilansky also encouraged), through storytelling, singing and sound games, and actual cooperative, social games which can develop awareness of others. For example, in the 'mirror game' children face each other in pairs, and each has to do exactly what the other does.

Highly structured activities

At the opposite extreme to the free play curriculum are approaches in which adults provide a great deal of structure for children; the children do not exert much choice themselves but follow closely the rule structure of the activity or imitate what the adult has modelled. Some kinds of games are actually highly structured in this sense, for example 'picture dominoes' in which a child must match a domino with the same number as that shown on the table; especially if the adult also structures it socially so that children must follow the rules and take turns at the activity. Some 'skills-tutoring' approaches are along these lines and the children's choice is quite closely constrained.

More structured still are programmes where children, often in a whole class, are required to join in a prescribed group activity, or imitate what the teacher demonstrates or answer the teacher's questions. For example, there might be drill in particular exercises, or song and movement routines; or rote learning of number bonds, or the meanings of certain words; or a child might be required to construct a copy of a given model. In the USA, the curriculum of Bereiter and Englemann (1966) is along these lines. Many preschool activities in African countries, and in Asian countries such as China, Korea and Japan, often use rote learning or drill techniques very widely.

Rote learning and drill are not looked on very favourably by many Western educators. This may reflect the influence of the 'play ethos' and the greater emphasis on individualism, and hence individual freedom and choice, compared to perhaps more collectivist values elsewhere. I must say that I do not totally share this negative view of drill and rote learning. Depending on the circumstances, it can be enjoyable – learning a physical exercise or dance routine, for example. It can also be an effective way of learning when what is to be learnt is definite factual material or associations, as in number bonds. As mentioned, rote learning is used considerably in Oriental countries, and the generally high level of academic achievement found there (Stevenson and Lee 1990) hardly suggests that it is a disaster. The learning of songs can also be educational; the rhyming and alliteration often present in children's songs have been shown to be a useful early reading activity (Bryant and Bradley 1985).

Having said that, it is also unlikely that drill and rote methods are going to help develop independent and creative thinking and planning; they are not designed to do so. Also, drill can at times be very mechanical and unenjoyable, forcing on a large group of children tasks which many may not properly understand. Drill methods were highly used in UK infant schools at the turn of the century, but the insensitivity with which they were applied probably helped fuel the reaction to more child-centred methods and the 'play ethos'.

Quite which choice is made among all these sorts of curriculum approaches is, of course, very much a matter of circumstances, local traditions, parental expectations and societal needs and values. The latter is now forcefully expressed in the NC, a contentious issue discussed by Angela Anning in Chapter 5. All can provide a caring, stimulating and enjoyable environment; and much of the research in the UK and USA suggests that all can have positive effects on children's development (Miller and Dyer 1975; Osborn and Milbank 1987). There is obviously scope for variety, both between different schools and also within schools. There is no reason why a particular early years setting should not, at various times through the day or week, use *all* the methods outlined above – and, indeed, most do!

The role of the adult in assisting children's development

I have said a lot about the role of the adult in developing children's play and activities. The importance of this has been particularly emphasized by two influential psychologists and educators: Vygotsky in Russia and Bruner in the USA. Their ideas provide some contrast to those of Piaget whose writings have provided a basis for our expectations of what children can do on their own, and for understanding the active nature of the child in learning about the world.

What Piaget does not stress very greatly is the role of the adult and the social community in supporting learning. This is where the ideas of Vygotsky, and of Bruner, can be especially enlightening: not so much in opposition to Piaget but rather as complementary. These ideas are especially relevant for educators and for the curricula ideas we are considering.

Vygotsky (1978) argued that the adult has a key role in helping children learn. He advanced the idea of the '*zone of proximal development*' (ZPD). The idea is that the child may have developed a certain level of competency in a skill, which can be performed independently and unaided. This Vygotsky calls the *actual* developmental level. However, if assisted by an adult, this ability can be stretched slightly so that something a bit harder can be attempted. It obviously cannot be stretched too far, else the child just could not understand what the adult was getting them to do. This Vygotsky calls the *level of potential development*. The difference between these two is the ZPD – the area of development which the child can cope with and understand *with adult help* (or with the help of more capable peers).

For example, suppose a child is playing with wooden blocks, and is able to make a tower by placing three or four blocks on top of each other. The adult could suggest to the child that he or she makes two such towers near each other; and then ask how we could make an archway, if necessary hinting that a long block across the top would help. In this way the child could come to understand how to make an archway (and what the term means). This was not something they could have done unaided at the time, so it is in the ZPD. However, if the adult were to try and get the child to build or copy a complicated house structure with a roof, this would be outside the child's ZPD. Even if the child could follow the adult's instructions, they would not really understand what they were doing, or be able to do it themselves, unaided, afterwards.

Somewhat similar ideas are advanced by Bruner in his concept of '*scaffolding*' (Wood *et al.*, 1976). A scaffold is a structure used to help gradually construct a building from its foundations; the scaffolding grows as the building gets higher; eventually, the scaffolding can be taken away. Here, the construction of the building is an analogy to the development of the child's abilities; and the scaffolding is an analogy to how the adult can support this. The support should be matched to the child's current level of development, and can be reduced or removed once the child has mastered that particular task. Particular aspects of scaffolding may be:

- directing children's attention to relevant aspects of the situation;
- helping children break a task down into a sequence of smaller tasks which they can manage;
- helping them orchestrate the sequence of steps correctly.

The ideas of the ZPD, and of scaffolding, can be used to help implement most of the ideas for the curriculum discussed earlier, with the exception of the totally free play curriculum in which the adult does not take an active role.

The curricula which emphasize structuring children's play, or play tutoring, involve the adult interacting with children either individually, or more probably in small groups. If the adults have previously observed the children's play, they will know the kind of level at which they currently function and can then gauge participation at the right level. They want to avoid telling children obvious things which they know already; and equally need to avoid talking above their heads, using vocabulary or concepts which children cannot understand. Ideally, adults will interact in the children's ZPD, scaffolding a slightly more complex task so that children can achieve and subsequently do it themselves. As we have seen, this 'slightly more complex task' might take many forms: a more advanced wooden block construction; a more elaborate game in the sand pit; reflecting on other properties of objects being played with; acting out a story with a more complete story line, or with more characters, and so on. The adult is best placed to do this if she or he has noted the children's current level of activity and understanding.

More structured activities such as skills tutoring, cooperative games, drill and rote learning activities can also use these concepts. Obviously the tasks which the child is being asked to do should be within their competence when a model is provided for them to copy. Indeed, someone using rote-learning activities to teach, say, a dance routine, probably will use scaffolding principles. They will teach part of the routine first; then, when this is learnt, build on this with the next sequence, and so on.

Two difficulties with rote learning should be noted here. One is that it is characteristically used with large numbers of children – perhaps a whole class or preschool group. This *does* provide economy of time and effort for the teacher, and give a feeling of whole-group involvement for the children. However, as children will vary in developmental levels, then the learning provided may be easy for some, just right for others, and too difficult for still others. Not all children of the same age have the same ZPD for a given skill.

The other limitation is this: in rote learning, the adult usually provides a complete model (or a complete part of a model) for the child to imitate or learn; for example, a number bond such as $2 + 2 = 4$; or a verse of a song. This task should be within the child's ability, and, indeed, often is. However, the child has a passive role in this. It is not so much that the child's learning is being scaffolded for the child itself to build; rather, it is as if the child was presented with a bit of a building to incorporate. The child does not have the same degree of initiative. In rote learning there is a danger of too much help being given so that the child's contribution is lost. Whether these are serious drawbacks will depend on many factors: what is being taught, the size and composition of groups, staffing resources and cultural traditions and values.

Final statement

The ideas of Vygotsky and Bruner are valuable for the preschool educator, in pinpointing how adults can most effectively enhance and support children's play and development. Whatever the value of either free-play curricula on the one hand, or of structured drill and rote activities on the other, there should also be a place for adults to work with children individually or in small groups, structuring their play or activities in developmentally appropriate ways.

2 | Play in different cultures and different childhoods

Audrey Curtis

'When I use a word,' Humpty Dumpty said in a rather scornful tone, 'It means just what I choose it to mean – neither more nor less.'
'The question is,' said Alice, 'Whether you can make words mean so many different things.'
'The question is,' said Humpty Dumpty, 'Which is to be master – that's all.'

(Lewis Carroll 1871)

It is unlikely that any of the readers of this book will query the contribution made by play to the development of young children. Although play appears to be the dominant activity of children in all cultures, our perception of play is closely associated with our own societal beliefs and values. As Whiting and Whiting (1975) point out, play is not only affected by cultural influences, it is also an expression of culture.

Definitions of play are many and varied, but most will include the idea of play as a pleasurable experience, that has no end product and is intrinsically motivated (see the previous chapter by Peter Smith). Underlying such an interpretation is the philosophy of the work/play dichotomy, which permeates much of the thinking in Western societies. The idea that work can be a playful experience and that some play involves work is alien to the thinking of many in our society, although anthropologists have long known that there are many non-industrialized societies where there is no such distinction.

There are many early childhood educators, including myself, who wish that this rather artificial dichotomy could be abandoned so that we should not always be trying to convince politicians and others that when young children are playing they are also learning. Maybe we should adopt Humpty Dumpty's approach to the meaning of a word!

The child's right to play was first universally accepted in the United Nations Declaration of the Rights of the Child in 1959 (section 7) and reiterated on 20 November 1990, when the United Nations adopted the Convention on the Rights of the Child. Article 31 stated that:

> State parties recognize the right of the child to rest and leisure, to engage in play and recreational activities appropriate to the age of the child and to participate freely in cultural life and the arts.

However, as Peter Newell (1991) points out, children's rights to play are not recognized in the legislation of the UK. He argues that parents and others concerned with young children should consider carefully whether we do in fact provide for this right.

The need for all children to be allowed to play has been officially recognized, but its value as an educational tool is not necessarily accepted by all cultures. In this chapter I intend to explore a number of issues relating to adult attitudes towards play in differing societies and to look at how play is used as a medium for learning in early childhood settings throughout the world.

Play with infants and toddlers

Visitors from an alien planet could be forgiven if they thought that all that mattered for a young child living in an affluent Western society was that they had mobiles hanging from their prams, stimulating toys which made strange noises when shaken or chairs which bounced them up and down to keep them happily distracted. The media, with its widescale advertising, naturally does not concentrate on infants and adults playing 'peek-a-boo' or babies being walked around the home or the streets strapped to their mothers. Yet this is the early experience of the majority of the world's population.

Brazelton (1977) in his study of Mayan infants argued that opportunities for play were restricted because of the custom of swaddling babies, an observation which I also made during my recent visit to that society. It is interesting that the children are totally enveloped in the cloth which binds them to their mothers or elder sisters, with no possibility of seeing anything of the outside world. However, around one year of age, it seems that the head covering is taken off and they are then to be seen peering from the shoulders of their carriers. In African societies, where I have seen mothers carrying their babies in slings strapped to their hips or on their backs, the child finds something to play with, albeit the mother's jewellery or hair adornments.

A neat study carried out by Rabain-Jamin (1989) compared the culture and early social interactions of mothers and infants in African and native French families. In comparing the interactive styles of French and African mothers (living in Paris) in an object-play situation, it was found that early education in traditional African families places prime importance on the infant's motor and social behaviour. Children need to learn from an early age their role in the social structure and to observe kinship position and recognize sibling rank order. To this end the African children receive greater physical contact from their mothers than French children.

The cultural effects of the home environment cannot be overlooked as they have a considerable influence upon children's later play and behaviour patterns. The presence of other adults and older siblings must effect the development of young children and the way they play. For example, Lewis and Ban (1977) found that infants in the former Yugoslavia are held less than their counterparts in the USA, even though the two groups of mothers spend similar amounts of time playing with them. One wonders what it is about these early play patterns that makes Yugoslavian children more able to spend time in quiet play during infancy compared with American children of the same age.

Hale-Benson (1982) has pointed out that black American children, like their counterparts in Africa, receive more handling and feeding contact with their mothers, which tends to make them more people oriented as opposed to the object orientation of white American children. Generally, both Afro-Caribbean and African children have a greater interest in people. Another reason for this may be due to the fact that they grow up in large families with a high degree of human interaction. In Africa, and sometimes in the UK, they grow up not only with their brothers and sisters, but are in close physical contact with other extended family members. These living patterns undoubtedly have an effect not only on child-rearing practices, but also upon the play patterns that develop. The practices will also affect their orientation to educational settings, a factor which is sometimes overlooked.

Children's representational play

There has been some considerable discussion among researchers as to whether children in certain communities have limited ability to play imaginatively. Some, like Le Vine and Le Vine (1963) and Feitelson (1977), have argued that children from some traditional cultures are deficient in imaginative play abilities. On the other hand, Bloch and Pellegrini (1989) have demonstrated that, given sufficient time to observe the children, it is possible to see imaginative play even in an area where there is a paucity of toy materials and equipment.

Most researchers will agree with Schwartzmann (1978) and Feitelson (1977) that four factors are important for the development of imaginative play in early childhood. They argue that children must have:

1 adequate materials for imaginative play;
2 an extended period of time;
3 space;
4 a favourable 'attitude' i.e. encouragement and modelling, expressed
  by the adults in the setting.

However, it seems that the specific toys and materials associated with
imaginative play in our culture are not necessary for good representational play to occur.

Children in rural communities in Africa become independent at an
early age as they are allowed to roam freely, and, by the age of two,
many children have left their mother's sides and made their way to the
houses of other family members. Living as they do in compounds, they
first venture alone to the central area of the compound and then from
compound to compound and finally as far as the ground immediately
outside the village, generally in the company of their older peers. Bloch
(1989) reported this in her study of Senegalese children and I witnessed
Gambian children playing in the villages under the direct or indirect
supervision of their numerous relatives.

That children of three years upwards can wander around their villages
with safety and security is something which those of us coming from the
urbanized Western world find difficult to comprehend. Although Bloch
saw both Senegalese boys and girls playing in the open spaces, in Gambia I found that the girls were expected to carry the midday meal to the
women working in the fields and, from the age of four to five years, acted
as baby-sitters for the toddlers who did not accompany their mothers.

However, when the women returned from the fields in the late afternoon the girls could be seen playing with materials found on the streets.
Bloch found that although children in these societies do not have many
toys and the amount of junk material available is limited, nevertheless
the children played with the remains of store-bought household materials.
Used baskets, discarded gourds and old cardboard cartons were among
the makeshift materials used to support their play. In Gambia, children
used empty coke cans to make drums and sometimes small cartons were
converted into pull-push toys. The only manufactured toys were the
occasional ball or sometimes a plastic doll.

Bloch described how she had seen girls pretending to 'cook' the evening
meal using leftover bits of grain and improvising with leaves and such
like. In Sri Lanka, Prosser *et al.* (1986) saw children acting out a home
sequence with a boy taking the role of the father who was supposed
to be going to work. The girl, taking the role of the mother, gave instructions like, 'You must serve the father first and a lot of food must
be given to him.' Here is an instance of the father's role being clearly
defined, reflecting the cultural values of that society.

Bloch also tells of boys making home-made sling shots out of tree
branches to practise catching birds or snakes and of little girls carrying

corn cob or plastic dolls slung over their backs like their mothers. When some researchers commented that African girls had few dolls, it was pointed out to them that they did not need dolls as they had the younger members of the family to practise on. A similar observation can be made about little girls from most parts of the world where there are large families and the girls are expected to participate in the up-bringing of their younger siblings.

Much of the imitative play that we see among children in Great Britain, like ironing and washing, is not necessary for young children in some cultures as one sees little girls fetching water from the wells at a young age or doing the family wash in the streams. They do not need to 'play out' the activity, they learn to do it for real!

In some societies dolls, human images, are not permitted and it is important to be aware of this. In some religious groups, even if dolls are not explicitly banned, there is an implicit understanding that girls should not be encouraged to play with them. They stay on the shelves in the kindergartens untouched. Interestingly it is only in Western societies that it would be considered appropriate to offer these toys to boys (see Jane Hislam's discussion in the following chapter).

Children increasingly practise adult roles and activities as they grow older and approach the age when this would be part of their real life responsibility. Sutton-Smith (1972) points out that in African rural communities, the children appear to have few toys designed to promote cognitive or creative play, or language development, but nevertheless their use of commonly available materials encourages them to be creative and innovative in their play. As Bloch and others have suggested, the materials available in these communities support children in their creative play. They have the space – they can wander throughout the compound and as they get older, the village. They have the time, particularly the boys. They also have adult models all around them, who, when they have time, are willing to help and encourage them.

My own observations in Gambia indicated that young children are still inventive and can enjoy fairly complex representational play activities if the materials available are multi-purpose or adaptable. Without toys, boys in Gambia appeared to engage in a great deal of rough-and-tumble play, a finding which I believe would be replicated in many parts of the world (as indicated in the work of Peter Smith, Chapter 1).

Although it can be argued that too few toys or other challenging materials may lead to little or no socio-dramatic play, we need to question whether children need so many. An interesting study by Ishigaki (1987) compared the numbers of toys owned by Japanese and Israeli children. Israeli children boasted an average of eleven toys per head, whereas the Japanese felt they were deprived if they had around 45 toys. But if, as has been suggested, creativity has been linked to toys and materials of low structure like blocks and junk materials then it is not the quantity of toys but the quality of the materials that are required.

If this is the case, then children from the traditional rural communities should be able to engage in stimulating, imaginative play activities.

Schwartzmann (1978) and others have demonstrated clearly that children do this, often integrating their play with the work requirements of the adults (Tina Bruce, in Chapter 15, discusses this kind of 'apprenticeship' model within free-flow play). Fortes (1970) gives a vivid description of the Tallensi children's play while carrying out their 'work' tasks. Although I could not understand their language, I observed little Mayan girls sometimes playing together while carrying their younger siblings on their backs, although it was mainly the boys that seemed to be playing the most.

A feature of much representational play in Western societies involves dressing up and it is a very familiar sight in many early childhood institutions to see young children wearing clothes other than their own in order to take on another role. In this country and many other European countries, young girls and boys dress up and 'become' a variety of people, like brides or nurses or police persons. We believe that this practice enables children to understand more readily various societal roles (in Chapter 7, Neil Kitson expands upon this). However, in some societies dressing up is not regarded as appropriate and may bring bad luck. For instance, in parts of Southern Africa it would be considered very unlucky for all the family if a little girl dressed up as a bride.

What do parents think about play?

Throughout the world parents accept that their young children play, but few of them really consider that it is their child's way of learning. In reflecting upon the lives of many children of infant school age, I realize that they have little time for free play and movement after they have attended ballet classes, gym classes or music lessons. Attendance at these activities is not just the prerogative of middle-class children in industrialized countries like Japan, Germany and the USA, but in places like China there is also a strong emphasis upon children attending extra-curricular activities at a very young age.

One wonders whether this feeling by many parents that children must be kept fully occupied all the time, is a reflection upon their attitudes towards play. If they see play as time-wasting and these other activities as learning experiences, is this one of the ways in which the work/play dichotomy is being continually reinforced? (Lesley Abbott takes up these issues in Chapter 6.)

Recently, I have been involved in an investigation into the use of the microcomputer in the nursery classroom and one of the issues raised is related to parental attitudes towards microtechnology as part of the nursery curriculum. Without exception, parents commented upon its value as they could understand that their children were mastering skills when using the equipment, whereas they found it difficult to appreciate the value of traditional play activities. Parents from Asian cultures were particularly enthusiastic about its use, as they frequently have difficulties in accepting the traditional nursery-school curriculum with its opportunities for freedom of choice.

Although in India and Pakistan there are opportunities for play in the more progressive kindergartens, the majority offer children structured activities with little or no free choice. Under these circumstances it is not surprising that Asian parents see play differently from early childhood educators in our country.

When parents tell their children to 'go and play', they normally expect them to engage in some form of pleasurable activity, which is self-initiated and which does not involve adult participation or too much supervision. Children will no doubt interpret such a command as an opportunity to get out of the adult's way while the grown-ups are doing something more important. In fact much of the language which is used in encouraging children to play gives the impression of undervaluing the activity.

There are, however, interesting cultural differences concerning the value of toys. The shops in industrialized societies are full of educational toys designed to teach children certain skills and develop cognitive understanding. Few Western parents will admit that they give children specific toys for pure fun. However, the attitude of some cultures is summed up by the remark of the African mother quoted by Rabain-Jamin (1989: 298): 'We give toys [to children] to play with. You give them toys to teach, for the future. We feel that children learn better when they are older.'

Children not only need time and space to play and to practise skills, but they also need parents who are willing to help them learn these skills. Both Singer (1973) and Dunn and Wooding (1977) argue that parental play involvement is related to intellectual and emotional development. Swadener and Johnson (1989), in reviewing studies on parental attitudes and beliefs towards play, concluded that the involvement of parents in their children's play will raise levels of play. Overall it appears that where parents have positive attitudes towards play, children are likely to become involved in high levels of imaginative and creative play.

In playing with their children, it seems that parents are helping them to learn how to play with their peers. Parental involvement in this way may be not only desirable, but necessary in our society where the family size is small and the child is frequently isolated from others during the first two or three years of life. However, parental involvement may not be so crucial in non-industrialized communities, where children from a very early age are exposed to others. Furthermore, in rural communities the adult female population, who are the usual interactors with young children, are so involved in the 'business of living' that they have little or no time to spare for playing with the children. However, this does not necessarily reflect a negative attitude toward play, rather a pragmatic approach to life.

Play and education

Play as a tool for learning and as part of the educative process is regarded by early childhood educators in this country as essential for young children, as several writers in this book emphasize. As long ago as 1933, Susan Isaacs was writing of 'play as education', stressing the importance of play for the development of manipulative skills and growth in discovery and reasoning. More recently, Bruner and Sutton-Smith, to name but two, have emphasized the role of play in children's learning. However, in my experience, although play is regarded as an important part of the kindergarten curriculum in many countries, in practice it may be interpreted differently in the various cultures. For example, in Eastern Europe, where the influence of Russian psychologists, like Vygotsky, is apparent, although play is part of the curriculum, the approach is very different when compared with Britain.

My first experience of this difference of interpretation came almost a decade ago when I attended a UNESCO seminar in Bulgaria. Arrangements were made for all the seminar participants to visit selected nursery schools and early childhood institutions where we were able to see the various 'national curriculum' in action. The newly implemented programme included opportunities for imaginative play and, in my naïvety, I imagined that I would be watching children playing spontaneously involved in their own world of make-believe.

What I saw was to me a drama lesson. The children were dressed up and acting out parts which they had rehearsed beforehand. The script was flexible, but none the less was based upon the written word. I am not making any judgement upon the inclusion of this type of exercise in the kindergarten curriculum, but quote it as an excellent example of how 'play' is interpreted according to our own cultural experiences. Examples of socio-dramatic play as suggested by Smilansky (1968) can be found in our preschool settings, but I do not believe that schools which put on a performance for parents and others believe that the children are engaged in imaginative play.

Such an approach to play can be found in many parts of Eastern Europe. There exist set times for 'free play' during the school day but the pedagogues do not see the same role for play as we do. This may be the reason why El'Kounin (1971) has stated that he did not see any evidence of children's imaginative play in Russia; rather the children were only engaged in imitative activities. I saw several instances of this in both Russia and Poland, where the 'play sessions' were highly structured and followed a prescribed pattern.

Imitation is also part of the curriculum in the kindergartens of the United Arab Emirates. Here, during the social studies programme, children dress up and participate in traditional cultural activities. For example, the girls wear their national dress and practise presenting dates and other sweetmeats, while the boys pretend to smoke the traditional pipe (hookah). A kindergarten supervisor referred to the children as 'playing out' the roles which they will take on in later life. During my visit I did not see any imaginative play, as we understand it, taking place in the classrooms, although there was some evidence of it during the official 'play time' (as evidence in David Brown's research in the UK in Chapter 4). Later, during discussions with my interpreters, I realized that there was no doubt that young Arab children play imaginatively, but not in school.

Except in a few experimental kindergartens, play is not seen as part of the educative process in China. The curriculum allows children opportunities to dance and act out songs and stories but does not seem to permit them to engage freely in activities of their own choice. However, in the past few years there have been radical changes made in the kindergartens in selected parts of China; and in Nanjing I saw children playing as freely and with as much enthusiasm and concentration as I have seen anywhere in the UK.

If we look at play and its role in education in Europe we shall see a number of differences. In Denmark the approach is in many ways similar to our own and children are allowed to select their own activities and use time, space and materials according to their own needs and wishes – in the words of Tina Bruce in Chapter 15, to free-flow play. The adults encourage and facilitate young children's learning, taking their lead from the children. There is no structured programme and activities arise from the interests of the children. Play is regarded as the prime medium for children's learning in that society.

Play is also regarded as having an important role in the learning process in German kindergartens but there is not necessarily the same amount of freedom of choice and movement given to the children. As each of the states is autonomous, the interpretation of play in the curriculum varies from the totally unstructured to the relatively structured approach, a point discussed in the previous chapter by Peter Smith.

Throughout Europe there is a strong commitment to play as part of the nursery school curriculum: nevertheless each country's approach is affected by its philosophy, culture and environment. As a result there are considerable differences in the ways in which play is interpreted.

Conclusion

In this chapter I set out to raise some of the more important issues relating to attitudes towards play in various parts of the world. In particular, parental attitudes towards play have been considered as well as the more fundamental question of what is meant by play. However, from the illustrations given it can be appreciated that, although play as an activity of childhood is accepted in all societies, its importance is not acknowledged to the same extent throughout the world. Similarly, the principle that children can learn through play and that play activities should be part of the early childhood programmes is accepted among educationalists in most countries, although the understanding and interpretation of the concept may differ.

Play is, and should be the right of every child, but, as has been shown, in some societies young children, particularly girls, have less opportunity to exercise that right than children in the industrialized world. In most cultures, including our own, the majority of parents find it difficult to accept that during play children are learning many skills and concepts. For most of them play is seen as something that children do to keep them busy while the adults are engaged elsewhere. Even those who understand its value and spend considerable periods of time playing with their children, find it difficult to understand that it has an important place in the early years curriculum.

Educationalists see play, especially imaginative play, as having a crucial role in developing such abilities as problem-solving, creativity and flexibility in young children. We believe that through play, children can practise skills and come to understand the world around them. The differences among the professionals relate not to whether play is or is not an important way to develop abilities and skills in young children, but rather whether the approach is child initiated or more teacher directed.

The more I visit other educational systems, the more I am convinced that considerable misunderstanding can arise as a result of the terminology. I wish that we could find another word which more clearly defines this amorphous concept. At present it often seems as though it means what the speaker wants it to mean, a real Humpty Dumpty approach, which is, in my opinion, highly unsatisfactory for such an important aspect of young children's development.

3 Sex-differentiated play experiences and children's choices

Jane Hislam

From an astonishingly young age it seems that children develop ideas about sex-appropriateness. For example, their preferences for certain kinds of play and playthings often appear to be gender-related (Serbin and Connor 1979; Pitcher and Schultz 1983). We know, too, that young children exhibit these preferences on entry to school and that they already have distinct ideas about sex-roles by the age of five (Paley 1984). What is less clear is whether parents and other educators should be concerned about this and what interventions, if any, are appropriate.

In this chapter, I shall discuss gender issues in relation to children's play, particularly in the home corner area. Questions will be raised about how adults might interpret the play, create a climate for play and make decisions about appropriate interventions.

My interest in gender issues and play began as a classroom teacher but was brought sharply and somewhat painfully into focus when I became a parent. As a teacher, I had been able to pass responsibility for children's stereotyped views and behaviour neatly backwards on to parents and earlier school experiences. As a parent I heard my own daughter tell me that 'men can't be nurses' despite the fact that she had just been treated by a male nurse; and that she didn't want to play with cars because 'that's what boys do'. Similarly, Grabrucker (1988) was horrified to hear her child reproduce narrowly stereotypical viewpoints despite her ambitions for her daughter to receive an open and unbiased upbringing. Parents may attempt to shield their children from limiting stereotypes. They may be shocked to discover at first hand the extent to which children want to work out for themselves what differentiates the sexes, so that they can more readily conform to the appropriate behaviour. At around five and six years of age, children's ideas of what is sex-appropriate may seem worryingly exaggerated to the adult, but this appears to be a stage which is unlikely to last. Children are not 'sponges' soaking up stereotypes, but are trying on roles and trying out ideas in order to categorize and make sense of the world and their own place within it (as Neil Kitson explores in Chapter 7).

In my work as teacher educator, I am constantly reminded of the need to examine the evidence critically and to try to resist jumping to hasty conclusions about the way children perceive and construct the world in relation to gender.

Children, gender and play

The literature which supports this field reflects a gradual change in emphasis away from ideas of passive conditioning towards a view of children as active participants in the construction of a social world. Social learning theories, especially in the 1970s and early 1980s, concentrated on the acquisition of sex-roles and the learning of sex-appropriate behaviour through children imitating and modelling adult and peer behaviour. Included in many studies and research reports were accounts of the supposed influence of toys, games and television and how these influences might be manifested in children's play. Numerous studies (e.g. Maccoby and Jacklin 1974; Serbin *et al.*, 1979; Schwartz and Markham 1985) concluded that children's play reflects the socialization patterns of children into sex-roles which are stereotypical.

In some quarters the argument is still powerfully made that toys and play materials are important in shaping the ideological outlook of children (Dixon 1990). Many parents and teachers continue to feel troubled about the ways in which the media, particularly television, manipulate children's choices of playthings according to their sex, through constant bombardment from advertisers to consume images of gender alongside products. Advertisements for children's toys and games contain direct messages about sex-appropriateness not just in content but also in their construction, for example in the use of colour, soundtrack or even camera shot (Greenfield 1984).

Latterly, however, a view of children as passive consumers has been seen as an inadequate explanation of the ways in which they actively engage in the construction of their own reality through their play and other experiences (e.g. Steedman 1985; Barrs 1988; Davies and Banks 1992). We need to look beyond the idea that children soak up ready-made stereotypes to a view of children as busily working out for themselves what is appropriate and acceptable.

Children inhabit a social world which is organized, to a large degree, according to gender, as evidenced in Audrey Curtis' work in the previous chapter. The expectations and responses of significant adults exert a subtle but powerful pressure on boys and girls to behave in sex-appropriate ways. It is likely, and perhaps inevitable, that children will explore gender boundaries and identity in socio-dramatic play as they seek to come to terms with who they are as individuals. Their play will therefore render valuable information and offer insights to educators who wish to understand children better in order to enrich their development and to meet their needs as individuals within a social context. The home corner, in early years settings, offers an especially interesting situation for adult observation since, in this setting, children in school and preschool contexts will be most likely to practise and explore gender-roles as part of spontaneous play. Girls seem to be readily attracted to domestic play and may receive more encouragement from adults. It is important not to jump to hasty conclusions in interpreting the evidence, but even a cursory glance is likely to prompt questions about gender:

1 Is the area itself predominantly a male or female domain?
2 Do children play differently according to whether they are boys or girls?
3 What kinds of choices do children make about their play and what do they have to say about these?
4 How significant are adult perceptions of gender issues in this context?
5 Can – and should – adults actually exert any influence on children's play patterns?

The home corner – boys or girls?

The use of language in naming the play area itself is clearly a significant factor. The home corner might be considered to be an improvement on the 'Wendy house', although possibly not much of one. Both terms are still in use and implicitly appear to suggest to children, if not to adults, that girls mainly play there. Talking to children about their play has led me to believe that they often hold strong views about the sex-stereotyped nature of the play area: the way the area is described and introduced to children affects play patterns. When I asked a six-year-old boy if he liked playing in the 'Wendy house', for example, he shook his head vigorously and grimacing replied, 'Girlish!' 'Why is it girlish?' I asked. 'It's dumb. Only GIRLS play in there.' Later, with the minimum of change in play provision but a new name, the same child told me that the police station was, 'Great, you can arrest anyone you like!' 'Is it girlish?' I asked. 'No, it's boys,' was the response.

This conversation with Peter, aged six, took place shortly after the Wendy house in his classroom became a police station. He had not been alone in expressing the view that a Wendy house was only for girls and could be dismissed therefore as a boys' play area. Teachers are often surprised by the discovery that only a small minority of the boys enter the play area. In this instance the area was almost entirely inhabited by girls, and yet the extent of the sex separation had not struck the teacher before systematic observation revealed it to be the case. If teachers are working from the premise that socio-dramatic play is a valuable part of the children's experience, it is alarming to discover that only around half the children appear to be engaging in it at any one time.

D'Arcy (1990: 83) comments:

> The play area or play house is a largely female domain and children often assume stereotypical roles on entering it. Girls are pleased to act out stories and situations. However, boys seem unhappy in deferring to the girls in this context and I have often observed boys changing roles to become animals, introducing elements of aggression, noise and disruption to the situation.

During observations in a class of six-year-olds it was possible to confirm, by recording who went into the play area, that girls greatly outnumbered boys. On several occasions boys went into the area, but they were usually chased out by the girls, who could be heard complaining to the teacher that the boys were 'messing things up'. In other domestic areas I have seen boys recruited as 'animals' and occasionally as 'babies'. These roles appear to be more acceptable than being father or some other family member.

Initial observations indicated that boys were rarely involved in socio-dramatic play. But further examination revealed that play was not necessarily confined to the home corner itself. There appeared to be a high level of general awareness of domestic scenarios by children in other parts of the classroom. For example, if the play involved the 'baby' having to be taken to hospital, this was soon common knowledge throughout the classroom. On several occasions children who were sitting doing maths or making models were temporarily engaged in discussions concerning the play. Play at this level frequently involved many of the boys. Later, when the play area became a police station, this 'corridor' of play across the room extended. Sometimes it involved actual movement of the play action itself, as in a chase for the 'jewel-thief'. In a subtler form, children outside the area became part of the action as 'bystanders' and commentators.

These interesting insights on the use of play space both in and outside the home corner challenged an assumption that boys were not involved in socio-dramatic or fantasy play or that there were few interactions between the boys and the girls. It appeared that there were several layers of play in operation but because the domestic area was specifically marked out as a 'girls' area, boys, who tend to 'care more about boundary lines than do the girls' (Paley 1984: 54) would not go into it. Significantly, these discoveries highlighted the value of focused observation. Admittedly, this is not easy, but much domestic play passes without remark, partly because less value is usually attached to it than other classroom activities.

Interpreting the play

A voluntary or assigned division by sex will be familiar to teachers in a range of play situations. In the use of construction materials, for example, there have been numerous accounts of differentiated and segregated play. Home and school expectations and attitudes will affect the range of play observed; the account above perhaps represents an unusually exaggerated sex distinction. Dunn and Morgan (1987: 280) report that 'both sexes used things in the home-corner equally'. However, they were differentiated in the *ways* in which they used it. Many educators have observed that boys, in particular, are less likely to use opposite-gendered toys. Adults often exert subtle pressure on boys to conform to narrow expectations: disapproval or even hostility may be expressed towards boys who dress up in 'female' clothes or play with dolls. Differences before schooling in peer and adult attitudes, for example where boys are punished for playing with 'girls' toys (Langlois and Downs 1980), are assumed to play an important part here. It is unlikely that teachers themselves feel completely neutral about these issues, much as they might wish to, because censorship in this area is so strong. Much that is written about the importance of educators giving 'free choice' to children fails to address these problems or the inner conflicts which can arise for the responsible adult. It is not always easy for adults to make counter-stereotypical interventions in real-life situations.

In the classroom described, different uses of the area and the playthings within it became most obvious after a change of status. Following visits of police personnel to the school during police week, the domestic area became a police station. In addition to the existing telephone and other resources, helmets, a typewriter and a pot plant were installed. The effect was dramatic. Boys flooded into the area immediately. All the previously heavy users of the area remained, although some of the girls were clearly rather bewildered at first. Very quickly different patterns of use became established. The typewriter and the telephone were immediately appropriated by a few boys. As were the helmets which were, unfortunately, replicas of the old fashioned 'bobby's' hat and resembled neither of the actual hats seen worn by the real police officers. Items were also found and adapted for use, most notably some makeshift handcuffs which were a central prop.

After a brief period of exploration and orientation, an elaborate game began to develop whereby each person had a role, or even several roles to play. From time to time the play action spread into the main area of the classroom and the excitement level was noticeable. The range of roles was extended and, interestingly, many domestic roles were retained. A number of girls continued to make tea and put people to bed, just as before. The improvised 'cells' gave an added dimension to this and the cushions became beds as several 'robbers' were brought in and summarily stretched out. The boys certainly became involved in aspects of the play previously owned by the girls and, although not called fathers or children, they assumed roles within a loosely domestic framework. At first glance, the girls appeared to be almost literally 'swamped' by the boys. There was an increase in noise-level and much broader and larger movements involved in the play.

Later, and on reflection, it was felt that the boys had been subsumed into the girls' patterns of play more than previously supposed: together they had established a territory where negotiations could take place. One girl appeared to take a general managerial role in relation to the play, and was often heard in director-role, telling other children to be 'so-and-so' or not to go out until they had had their tea.

Significantly, the language altered and became adjusted to the situation. One child was overheard 'on the telephone', saying, 'Hello. Is P.C. Parker there?' and then holding the telephone casually away from his ear, he added in an aside to another child, 'He's a nice guy.' In many of these exchanges there was an unselfconscious but quite deliberate adoption of adult roles in which children were exploring the kinds of things that people say, their intonation, the way they interact and their body movements.

Children playing in the police station were literally acting out the experiences of their own lives as well as their vicarious knowledge of the world (Moyles 1989). They also drew on images from television and books: the police station gave a different scope for this. In the home corner the boys may have felt that they had nothing to play out which related to recognizable elements of their own life experience now or to come. However, Paley (1984) came to the conclusion that children are not necessarily as caught up with the surface features of play as we might imagine, and that we must be careful to differentiate between their desire to conform to gendered roles and their involvement in an inner and personal world of exploration. Not only do children explore social roles but they also 'play' with states of mind or feeling states in which they are able to experiment with situations they are not actually feeling or experiencing. Caution must always be exercised before imputing that children are 'playing things out' in either a conditioned or a therapeutic sense. It is always likely that at some level children's play acts as a kind of personal mirror and that through play children are coming to grips with their own realities (Tina Bruce asserts this strongly in Chapter 15). Through play they may be getting to know themselves a little better and finding out how to negotiate relationships with their peers and with adults in the here and now, rather than rehearsing for an uncertain future.

It was clear that the development of the police station had an effect on the children's play. Most significantly, the boys entered the play area and acted out a range of roles within it. It was tempting to interpret these changes along narrow sex-stereotyped lines. In fact, there was evidence that the new area offered a wider range of possible roles *including* most if not all of those that had been previously enjoyed by the girls.

Challenging assumptions

However striking the differences are between groups of children, the individual with a distinct personal history will be acting from a basis of uniquely various and complex motivations. In comparisons between groups, the actual picture may be obscured by a significant difference displayed in only a minority of children. This point was illustrated in a study of rough-and-tumble play (Maccoby and Jacklin 1974) in which highly significant differences were recorded between the behaviours of boys and girls but, in fact, only a few boys were outstanding 'rough-and-tumble players'. The majority of the boys were in the same range as the girls. Thus the sex differences recorded were large but not demonstrated in *all* the boys.

As adults we rarely watch with a completely open mind and may be unaware of why we select certain aspects as significant and overlook others. Our preconceptions make a difference to the way we view things. To a certain extent we see and hear what we want to see and hear. Therefore what we think and expect needs to be placed constantly under review and we must interrogate our own *assumptions* as well as what we read and hear, looking closely at the evidence before us.

It is often assumed, for example, that girls play more imaginatively than boys in the home corner. Is this actually the case? Singer (1973) questioned such a distinction and could find no significant differences between the sexes according to his criteria. The adult observer can be tempted into explaining what is seen according to a particular 'formula' – that girls may be passive and boys aggressive, for example, whereas the play is likely to be far more fluid than such labelling allows. In their play, children are making the rules as well as acting them out. The roles children adopt may not be constant but are subject to change 'mid-action'. Sustained observation often reveals that, below the surface features, children may be exploring issues of central concern, for example in their acting out and exploration of feelings associated with being jealous, punished or unfairly treated. They may be exploring what it feels like to be in the position of a powerful person, somebody who controls rather than being controlled. Such speculations on what children engage in through play are far removed from ideas that children passively submit to and play out their domestic roles in limited domestic settings (e.g. the traditional home corner). Paley (1984) paints a vivid picture of a five-year-old's world where children are acutely aware of sex differences and are busily playing out their stereotyped roles. The observer's assumptions about these stereotypes are easily reinforced, if, for example, the little girl is busy making tea and the little boy busy knocking it over. In this picture, however, there is little that emerges as passive or imposed behaviour. Indeed, the reverse appears to be the case. Here children make choices which highlight an active desire to explore and embrace their gender differences and establish a strong gender identity. 'They think they have invented the difference between boys and girls and, as with any new invention, must prove that it works' (Paley 1984: ix). What is more, they are able to reflect on the nature of their gender roles and explicitly resist or challenge what does not fit.

Young children are often said to blur fantasy and reality but it is adults who tend to confuse the two. Adults are apt to take too literally what is actually a far more flexible and non-literal process (Rubin *et al.*, 1983). Children may be moving from one plane of 'reality' to the other. Certainly, in their socio-dramatic play children seem to be acting out significant events and feelings almost as though they are deliberately taking on a different point of view.

'Now *you* have a broken leg and *I'll* make it better,' my daughter exhorted her friend as they repeatedly reworked the scenario in the wake of a real broken leg event. At least in part play is a rehearsal of the known and also an exploration of possibilities. Just as stories have a range of possible endings, children quite deliberately develop storylines and explore possible solutions in play situations. Like narrators, they can be both in and outside of the action, able to comment and judge as well as move the action forward from within (as Nigel Hall ably explores in Chapter 9). Unfamiliar with this complex arrangement, the adult observer is liable to be perplexed by how readily children will move in and out of a scenario and adopt a range of roles in succession or even simultaneously.

Creating an appropriate climate for gender-free play

In indirect ways, educators have an enormous influence on the parameters within which children will play. Through other activities and simply through ways of talking and being, children will pick up signals about the extent to which the early years setting is a place where it is alright to pretend; where children and adults can engage in frank exchange; where different roles can safely be assumed without fear or favour; where possibilities can be explored and taken seriously by the adults. Through drama, storytelling and reading, the agenda can be set for extending ideas and challenging attitudes.

Stories in particular can be powerful in indirectly affecting the climate of the classroom. By encouraging children to take on board a range of options through fiction, teachers will extend the range of possibilities for play. It has been argued that in this way stories can be directly influential on children's attitudes towards gender roles (Ashton 1978 and

1983). Stories may supply children with 'a substantial and detailed manifestation of the culture' (Davies and Banks 1992: 5). They should be chosen deliberately to extend and develop children's knowledge, giving a broad representation of gender roles and introducing children to ideas of control and choice.

Adults need to become 'tuned into' certain kinds of information from children's play, as Tina Bruce asserts in Chapter 15. Tuning-in allows adults to gain insights into how children are seeing and constructing their own world, including what they have to say about sex-appropriateness. Sometimes this can provide puzzling information, as it did when my own daughter, at three years of age, confidently informed me that, 'Mummies don't drive.' (I was driving at the time!)

When children are playing imaginatively they rarely address themselves to an adult audience and so it is usually a case of observing and overhearing their talk as their play is in progress. A child of six, dressing a teddy, exclaimed, 'I'm going to put him in his party dress . . . (pause) . . . her, I mean.' Listening to children in the police station play revealed: Bhavesh: 'I'm not going to be a police lady. I haven't got long hair. I haven't got a dress,' or: 'We play mummies and daddies, babies and cats.'

This last remark is made in response to questions (Constantine 1992) about what a group of Year Two children liked to play in the home corner. The researcher came to the conclusion, from interviews and observations of 40 children, that they were often assigned limited roles within the traditional domestic area. She also revealed an explicit awareness by children of those who cross the boundaries into counter-stereotyped roles; several children described a boy who 'always wants to be a ballet dancer and he's a boy. Hayley wants to be the dad and she's a girl. Once she wore torn things to be a cowboy.' Significantly, and regrettably in Constantine's view, the teacher had drawn attention to the boy (though not the girl) with adverse affects on the child's freedom to play. Although the teacher had not directly intervened in the play itself, she had affected negatively the climate within which play happened for that child.

Teacher interventions and participation

More positive discussions with the children may take place outside the immediate context of the play area by encouraging children to think about the underlying issues (Paley 1981; Thomas 1986), and encouraging reflection upon their own views of sex-appropriateness. In this way adults will actively stimulate a wider range of possibilities. Such interventions, however, are likely to have repercussions and could promote conflict.

Interventions may also need to take the form of directly challenging *damaging* stereotypes, as one would in a case of racism within the class-room, although as we have seen in examples above, children are often able to present these challenges for themselves in play. This is also a delicate decision to make, especially with younger children, since in the context of socio-dramatic or fantasy play, they may be engaged in the dramatic rehearsal of ideas rather than expressing their own viewpoints.

In the context of the play area, there are many reasons why educators should themselves sometimes be participants in the play. The mere presence of the adult near or in the play area acts as a signal to children that a value is attached to the play. Increased adult interaction can provide a new direction or give fresh impetus to the play. Sometimes it is appropriate to take on a role and so sustain and extend what is taking place. This needs to be done with sensitivity and should never cross in-to an appropriation of what is, after all, a part of the children's culture (a very powerful factor, as discussed by David Brown in Chapter 4). Sometimes children will weave adults into their play, as parents and adults in the home context can testify. A wonderful example of this is the account of Myra Barrs (1988) of an adult who unwittingly became a key player in Ben's game, while the child retained control of the direction of the play.

Lastly, but crucially, adults act as *models* for children, by implicitly assigning values to certain kinds of play, and not others, but also in the way they themselves model behaviour and attitudes towards the two sexes. Children will undoubtedly be affected and pick up these attitudes from teachers, whether or not they are exhibited at a conscious level.

Essential to the process of affecting the quality and range of imagina-tive play are the decisions made by practitioners not only about when it is appropriate to intervene more directly in children's play but in the actual provision of materials and the modelling of their use by peers and adults.

In terms of the things we place in front of children, we know that young children already have preferences for certain play based on gendered choice in their preschool years and that, in experimental situations at least, they will choose sex-appropriate toys (Singer 1973). Experience has taught us that even if we place Technik or Lego in front of girls they will not necessarily play with it, or use it in the same way as boys.

In toy shops, sex-stereotypes are often rigidly and crudely reinforced both in the marketing of toys and the nature of the toys themselves. It has been well-documented that distinctions are made from birth on-wards in the choice of toys (Belotti 1975) and that certain toys are not given to children if they are thought to be inappropriate to their sex. It is not always the parents who apply this early pressure. As the mother of a preschool daughter, I wanted to purchase a Briomec for her and was subjected to cross-examination by the shop assistant who enquired,

'Is it for a boy or a girl?' When the reply indicated a girl, the assistant was anxious to protect me from possible embarrassment. 'Will her mother mind?' she enquired. '*I am* her mother,' I replied, at which she shrugged her shoulders and assumed an air of resignation.

The commercial pressures on the consumer, whether child, teacher or parent, have been well-documented and the overriding theme is gender distinction. Nearly all toys are deliberately marketed according to sex. Hasbro claimed (Dixon 1990: 30) that 82 per cent of four- to nine-year-old girls owned at least one My Little Pony in 1986. Many of the toys at the sharp end of these heavy sales are avoided in the classroom. Rarely have I seen Sindy, My Little Pony or Rambo in the play area, though these are often brought in by children to play with at breaktimes. Adults within school and preschool settings instinctively separate themselves from the commercial toy world, believing that Barbie and Darth Vader have little intrinsic educational value, and may be positively harmful. Dixon (1990) and Sutton-Smith (1986) both believe that these kinds of toys invite ritualistic rather than creative or spontaneous play. However, Dixon urges that teachers acquaint themselves with toys and games which form such a major part of the dominant ideology of childhood.

Conclusion

The home corner offers interesting insights into children's play and the formation of ideas about gender and sex-appropriate behaviour. At first glance, it would appear that many narrowly stereotypical behaviours are reproduced, including the decision by many boys not to play there at all! There is also evidence that teachers and other adults may sometimes limit play opportunities by failing to question their own assumptions about sex differences. This may have a subtle and damaging effect on children's self-image so that play patterns are inhibited and may even cease to occur.

It is important to recognize that children are far from strait-jacketed into predictable or conditioned roles. They are, in a very real sense, acting out a whole range of possibilities and attempting to make sense of their world, including their place within it as a girl or as a boy. By becoming more aware of the many facets of children's play in domestic area settings, educators can learn a great deal about children's thinking, motivations and desires.

In relation to gender and play, educators should consider the need to:

- vary the context of the play (see Moyles 1989, for an extended list of stimulus area ideas);
- involve children in choosing, discussing and planning for the play;
- build in 'real-life' experiences and draw on children's experience of the real world;

- appreciate that play is not always physically contained within the socio-dramatic area;
- ensure that domestic area provision, with traditional props, is still provided as the site of children's most recognizable and relevant experience;
- acknowledge the role of adults in recognizing and participating in children's play;
- listen and observe carefully;
- continue to challenge personal and professional assumptions about gender.

4 | Play, the playground and the culture of childhood

David Brown

A school provides a number of very different contexts within which play takes place. Within the structured setting of the nursery or class area, the stimulation to play, the physical environment and, to an extent, the progress of the activity will be under a degree of adult control and supervision. Indeed, it is desirable that this should be so, as Peter Smith argues in Chapter 1, as the justification for play in education must be that it helps to promote children's learning. It will also follow that the teacher will have taken decisions as to the area of learning which is appropriate to the child and the appropriate form of play which will support that learning. So the 'free' play of the nursery or class area is substantially within the domain in which adult control and supervision prevails.

Outside the school building lies an area in which the writ of adults plays a less decisive part. The assumption, on the part of many teachers, is that the activities which take place here are largely recreational, in contrast to the purposeful play of the classroom. Certainly the nature of much of the activity in the play areas around schools is very different from that which takes place inside. If, however, play-area play can be shown to have an influence on individual children's development, our view of the value of such activities and of the period we call playtime may change. If the activities of play areas can also be shown to constitute a constructive part of children's social development, moves to limit playtime in school, because such times pose problems of supervision or finance, may be counter-productive and short-sighted.

The purpose of this chapter is to set play-area play in the framework of children's learning and explore evidence about the context as an educational and cultural forum.

Play areas and children's play

Evidence suggests that the amount of time during which children play in groups with their peers has declined considerably. The street, park and field are seen as areas where children are at risk. Children are more likely to be escorted by adults from school, and so less likely to linger in play. In England over the last 20 years the proportion of seven- and eight-year-old children returning from school unaccompanied by adults has fallen from 80 per cent to 9 per cent (Hillman *et al.*, 1990: 45). Once home, the increase in traffic has made many roads unsuitable for play. So children are frequently limited to play in homes and gardens where adult supervision is more influential. In addition the solitary attraction of video and computer games has reduced time for group and other out-of-doors activities. For many children, therefore, the play areas of the primary school provide the only social setting for play in which they are able to operate in large groups and beyond the immediate surveillance of adults.

In this setting, children are able to gain experience of determining their own play activities and to exercise choice of activity with few restrictions other than those of their own making. The supervision of patrolling adults can usually be circumvented with ease and only activities resulting in violence and physical harm stimulate adult intervention. Davies (1982: 33) describes zones in children's play areas which tend to attract games which are outside adult definitions of acceptability. Given the limited ability of the supervisors of playgrounds to observe more than a small proportion of the activities before them, these zones may form a significant majority of the play areas of school. As a result, the play areas provide a setting in which the possible function of play activities in a child's development can be considered relatively free from the influence of adults.

Observing play-area play

Studying play-area activity is complicated by the range of observable activity and the speed with which it changes. However, even quite young children are able to respond to questions about their behaviour and to offer their own explanations. This helps in the understanding of the complex series of multiple interactions which can be observed (plate 4.1).

Tinbergen (1963: 29) identified four aspects of particular relevance to studies of animal behaviour generally. These concern:

- the motivation or causation of the behaviour;
- its development;
- its function for the individual and for the species;
- its evolution.

Plate 4.1   There may be a complex range of observable behaviour

These are of equal importance to the study of the play of children as to the study of other playing species. A methodology which combines the use of observation techniques, surveys and interviews can help to provide a basis for exploring these questions. The use of video recording not only enables repeated observation of an episode of play-area activity, so helping to unravel the complex strands of behaviour, but also makes it possible to discuss the activities with the participants.

These techniques have formed the basis of my study of the play areas in two county primary schools in Leicestershire (Brown 1991), the underlying assumptions of which are that play activities serve a functional need for children and that a greater understanding of these activities will promote a greater understanding of the complexity of children's social development.

For at least 100 years, popular views of play-area play have indicated a supposed decline in the range and quality. A *Times* leader was written on the subject as long ago as 1909. Such views are frequently based upon the contrast between adults' idealized memories of the games of their childhood and upon their often limited understanding of the games which children are currently playing. Some traditional games have disappeared but many may have been replaced by new forms. My initial surveys of play areas began with consideration of the children's perception of their playtime. Children of different ages were asked to identify the activities which they took part in during these times and, perhaps surprisingly, the surveys revealed a large range of activities. In initial

Figure 4.1   Main categories of games played

Ball games	(including football, queenie queenie, marbles, donkey)
Running or chasing games	(including various forms of tig, ice cream, grannie, footsteps)
Games using rhymes	(including skipping and clapping games)
Narrative games	(including turtles, aliens, my little pony, doctors and nurses, mums and dads)
Rough-and-tumble games	(including play fighting, piggie-back fighting, bulldogs)

surveys the children were able to identify over 100 different games and activities. The activities recorded fall into five main categories (see Figure 4.1) and most could be categorized under the general heading of 'games with rules' (see the Hutt model in the Introduction).

In addition, many activities take place during any session of 'playtime' which do not take the form of actual play. Among these, 'talking with friends' and 'interfering with skipping' provide examples which suggest a need to allow for both social and antisocial activities as distinct categories of play-area behaviour.

Some of the games identified by the children could be included in two or more categories of activity. For example, narrative games, in which the children act out a story, frequently evolve into rough-and-tumble activities and occasionally into antisocial activities like real fighting and bullying.

After the initial survey, play periods were recorded on video and examples of the categories of behaviour sought. It was apparent that games form only a part of the playtime experience of children. Many episodes of play are very brief and may be preceded by longer periods during which children engage in activities which can be seen as 'preparing for play'. Some of these preparations may have rules of their own. Choosing activities or 'dips' clearly serve the function of allowing selection while minimizing conflict. Other preparations appear less structured. A large part of children's time appears to be spent in a search for a place to settle.

In order to explore the children's perception of the range of activities, the video recordings were shown to groups of children and to participating individuals, their comments being tape recorded and later analysed. There was a high degree of agreement between the children in their interpretation of the activities shown on the video. They were also able to interpret activities which were not clear to adult observers. For example, the viewing children were able to observe the point, during a recorded episode of rough-and-tumble play, when the activity began to

Figure 4.2   Factors which will influence a child's choice of play activity

Personal factors	Environmental factors
Age	Available space
Sex	Type of 'place'
Status	Equipment
Group membership	Weather
Knowledge and skills	Supervision

Cultural factors
Range of activity within play-area culture
Conventions of behaviour
Fashion
Season

change into the bullying by one child of another. They identified the changing gestures and expressions of the participants which went unnoticed by adult viewers. An understanding of body language appears to be a critical ability for children during playtimes and is learned in the play-area context.

The context of play-area play: environmental and cultural influences

The absence of direct adult supervision and stimulus does not, perhaps surprisingly, mean that children operate without constraint. The interaction of the many factors which influence children's behaviour is complex. Darvill's (1982) deceptively simple equation of play behaviour suggests that a child's play behaviour is a function of the relationship between the playing child and the play environment. Each factor of this equation is variable. Though not perhaps a tool for prediction, the equation does serve to emphasize the interrelationship of factors which drive a child's choice of activity (see Figure 4.2).

Children identified the search for an available space as a major influence upon their choice of activity. If a 'place' for ball play or for skipping is available, these are included in the range of available activities. Such places, however, may have been taken by an earlier group. Consideration of place goes some way to explain why a number of children, observable on any play area, are apparently wandering aimlessly. In reality, their conscious aim is to explore the available possibilities for activity. Some children rarely move from this searching activity and this in turn has consequences for the forms of playground behaviour which they might adopt.

The influence of 'place' can be very strong. Children play some games in only one 'place' although others look equally suitable to the less-discerning adult eye. Identical games may have continued in the same place for many generations of school children. A game called 'Round and Round the Stew Pot' was reported as having taken place in the time of parents and of grandparents in one school.

The environment also includes personal and social factors. The availability of other children and the size of group are strong influences on play-area behaviour, as are factors relating to the gender of the participant players and the relationship between them.

The culture of the play area in which the children operate provides what is possibly the strongest influence upon the playground behaviour of children. This body of shared understanding will include a knowledge of games within the group repertoire and of the acceptable forms of behaviour and its limitations. The culture will embody sanctions which the children will be prepared to impose upon those who do not operate within the accepted forms of behaviour. These factors of play areas may work in direct opposition to the culture of the school in which they are sited. The most common example of this may be the accepted response to a 'hurt', whether accidental or deliberate: the school culture will encourage restraint and forgiveness, with an ultimate appeal to an adult supervisor. The children's culture, on most playgrounds, suggests a more immediate and retaliatory response. Similarly, play-area activity will include play of a nature which runs contrary to the expressed values of schools: the many forms of the game of 'dare' or 'chicken' provide examples of this. The excitement of such games appears to arise, in part, from their opposition to the safety consciousness of the school.

Clearly the culture of play areas is not that of the adult community within a school but resides within the community of children. In my studies, children demonstrate a shared understanding of their life in and on the play areas. They are able to explain their own behaviour and to interpret that of others in a way which sees the individual in a social and cultural context. For example, children will be seen by their peers as having high status within the play area because they understand the rules of play and the correct forms of behaviour. Equally, others who do not have these attributes will be viewed as of lower status. These rules will not necessarily reflect those of the school.

Bruner (1986) describes culture as a forum within which it is possible to create and to recreate meaning. The play spaces of schools provide children with a physical setting for this forum. Erikson (1950: 182–218) suggested that play was a form of the human ability to deal with experience by creating model situations and to master reality by experiment and planning. Play provides a means for the mastery of current reality, allowing experimentation and planning. Huizinga (1949) suggests that play is able to create order: play, and the activities associated with play, provide order within children's culture. They give a structure which allows children to develop relationships, practise competence and measure status, three themes which Woods (1983: 100) identified as embedded within the culture of children. Conversely, the apparently random activities which an observer of a playground will see, can best be put into ordered place by an understanding of the relationship of each activity to the culture of childhood.

Patterns of playtime activity

The notion of play as the 'work' of the child can be applied particularly to the games with rules in playground play. Just as an adult may frequently be identified and defined by their occupational role, so children in the play area may be categorized by association with a game activity. Some children will play games only intermittently, their choice depending upon environmental or social factors. Others will spend most of their play periods at the same activity. In many school playgrounds football provides a major focus for activity. In this case the factors which make up the play-area equation are strongly determinant: if the playing child is a boy of seven plus years, who is with a group of similarly aged boys on an open play area where balls are allowed, there is a strong possibility that the game chosen will be football. Boys may then be seen as 'football playing' or 'non-football playing' by other children. Those who play regularly are perceived by their peers as less likely to follow such unsocial activities as interfering with skipping or taunting girls. The relationships which these football players make are based upon the group of fellow football players, their competence as football players is practised daily within the same endless game and their status is measured by their peers in terms of their performance at football.

Within such a culture, a child who is seeking a football-playing identity and who is last to be chosen for teams by the current high status holders, is awarded low value in terms of relationships, competence and status among his peers.

Most children do not follow such a narrow approach to their playtime activity. The aspect of choice will consequently be a more significant feature. Children interviewed described the approach which they would take to the choices available in similar ways. This can best be summed up by the series of questions:

- Who is available to play with?
- What places are available for play?
- What shall we play?
- What are the rules we shall play by?

Other considerations – the weather, the existence of a 'season of play', like conkers – will be influential in the choice of game, but the availability of appropriate players and of a suitable place appear to be the driving factors.

At the beginning of each play period, children may have answered these questions before they leave the school building. The footballers will almost certainly only begin this sequence should a place to play football not be available or if, for some reason, ball play is not allowed. Other children may have planned a particular game during a previous play period or during their time in school. There are children, however, who enter the play area with all the questions unanswered. As a consequence the beginning of a play period is a time of much apparent confusion. Some children emerge in groups and head purposefully for a particular part of the play area and begin play. Others will form pairs or groups as they meet suitable collaborators. A period of searching and consultation will follow and eventually an activity will begin. Still others will enter the play area alone and will remain searching or standing and watching throughout the play period, observing but making no attempts to join an activity. Children in this last category may be only temporarily isolated: perhaps their regular partner is away from school. One or two, however, may be repeatedly isolated from the activity of their peers and are, in consequence, unable to build relationships, develop competence or gain status within the children's culture.

The pattern of play-area activity does not remain constant. Some episodes of play are only very brief and groups will form and reform several times during a play period. The periods of game-playing may be interspersed with social activity. Pairs of children who are walking and talking are perhaps the most common features of play-area social behaviour but, when the weather conditions are appropriate, larger seated groups of children will develop. This form of grouping will often be accompanied by grooming actions, by stroking and manipulating each other's hair while talking (plate 4.2).

The children who are not included in social groups or play may not remain totally isolated from their peers throughout a play period. They may make repeated attempts, which are rebutted, to join with others. This in turn may lead to conflict as the isolated child tries more and more forcefully to enter the play of others. Occasionally this will result in acceptance but, more frequently, the group of players will make their rejection of the individual clear, possibly by the use of violence.

Other disruptions to the ordered flow of playground activity will result from conflicts of place. Groups inevitably overlap in their use of play space. The frequency of collisions and the room to play unhindered affects the rate of conflict. Large open play areas with few features and protective barriers would appear to be designed to provoke the most conflicts over space: the lack of protected areas denies children the option for undisturbed social activity. Though apparently easy for supervisors to oversee, the conflicts of interest caused by different groups of children competing for space may raise the levels of aggression in the play area.

Plate 4.2   'Places' for social activity

The games played by children will reflect this higher level of conflict and for the children the cultural acceptance of violence as an acceptable form of behaviour will be greater. Provision of sheltered areas may well reduce this trend (plate 4.3).

Bengtsson (1970) uses the term play 'rooms' in connection with outside play areas. Children themselves define the use to which particular 'rooms' will be put (plate 4.4).

The games played on the open play areas are those of a robust nature: football is the dominant form but vigorous forms of 'tig' 'and 'bulldogs' are also common. The smaller play areas are used for a variety of activities. Corners and seating areas attract children in groups or pairs in conversation. Children playing narrative games use similar corners as 'bases' from which to begin their play. Small sheltered spaces are chosen by children playing clapping games and small group or individual skipping. Some places have developed very strong associations for the children. A tree which stands in a relatively quiet and sheltered spot is used almost as a friend. Solitary children find comfort by holding on to this tree, often leaving it only when they have found a real friend (plates 4.5a and b).

The patterns of conflict generated by each area would seem to be different. On the open playground, conflicts are frequent but usually quickly resolved by the children themselves. All the participants in these games expect to bump into one another from time to time and, therefore, take it fairly calmly. The smaller sheltered spaces generate fewer conflicts: groups of children occupying each of these areas tend to follow the same activity and conflicts between groups are rare. Within groups, most conflicts are resolved by the members of the group. Children consider

Plate 4.3   Use of play 'rooms' is determined by the players. Open play area with football the dominant activity

Plate 4.4   Small play 'room'. Note the gender contrast with the previous photograph. Both were taken during the same play period

Plates 4.5a and b   A friendly tree

the monitoring of group behaviour to be a part of the game and only in extreme circumstances is a participant ejected from the group and only then after repeatedly refusing to abide by the game's rules.

Certain children may be considered arbiters of good behaviour and are appealed to in the event of disagreement. Others gain such status temporarily if they are the owners of an article which is necessary for play. The child who provides the rope or ball is given such enhanced status only for that period of play.

The pattern of activity, group-forming, decision-taking, subsequent activity and group-reforming, is broken only by the end of the play period or by conflicts which cannot be resolved by participants or by other child arbiters. In this latter case, it is at this point that children feel that adults may properly be involved.

The influence of age and gender on play-area play

This generalized view of the pattern of play-area play has made few references to the gender of the participants or to their age. This is not to imply that these are inconsequential factors, for they are perhaps the leading elements which determine the nature of the play activity to be chosen.

The play-area culture contains a wide repertoire of activities transmitted as part of an oral tradition centred on each play area. It also contains many values which are part of the wider community. Many activities are seen by children as gender specific. A negative aspect of the play of children may be that the culture, in which the children operate, conserves the stereotypes of the wider community. Narrative games provide an example. The occupational themes taken by girls tend to relate to office work, hairdressing and family care. The boys choose themes which are adventurous, more likely to evolve into rough-and-tumble and perhaps even simulated or real violence. The distinction made by Sutton-Smith (1971) between play and games and their relationship to power is perhaps illuminating in this respect. Contest games like football and those narrative games, which result in a trial of strength between individuals, test the power of one individual over another. Contests tend to be the preserve of boys' play; tests of cognitive ability – like the learning, repetition and adaptation of rhymes – tend to be the preserve of girls.

The limitation of play as a cultural means whereby children can create and recreate their worlds may be that it is unlikely to challenge the values which children bring to the culture – as Audrey Curtis has shown in Chapter 2. As the play-area culture of schools will develop only among children of five and older, the notion that certain forms of activity are suitable only for boys or girls is already well-established in many children's value systems. Challenges to stereotypes of gender, which are undertaken by most schools, will therefore not only conflict with the messages which many children receive while outside school, they will also conflict with the daily messages which they receive on the play areas. Jane Hislam has explored this in the context of classrooms in the previous chapter. Similarly, conservative aspects of the nature of play-area culture may also influence attitudes to race.

The age of the children is similarly a major determinant of the form of play-area activity they will follow. There is a progression observable in the development of children's chosen activities. Some categories of game will not be played by children of a particular age. Ball games are rarely played by children of five and six, for example. Others activities will evolve as the children who are playing them grow older. Narrative games appear at all ages but use different themes. The practice of the play will also change. The statement, 'Look, I'm Batman,' may be the extent of the narrative for four- or five-year-old children. Nine- and ten-year-olds may undertake the development of a complex plot of family life lasting for several play periods (Lesley Abbott and Nigel Hall both reflect this in Chapters 6 and 9 respectively). This changing repertoire may provide some indication as to the possible function of different categories of play, both for the individual and for the group.

Play-area play can be seen to operate on a number of functional levels. Some games may be seen to meet the immediate functional needs of individual children. Martin (1984: 74) describes these as weak functions, strong functions being those which influence an individual's survival and ability to reproduce. Most play-area activity can be seen to serve areas of weak function in that they help the individual to operate within the context of childhood. Narrative games are loosely structured, but allow the children to role play and to rehearse responses to the situations which they expect to face in reality, thereby creating and recreating meaning.

Children's narrative play at seven or eight is frequently of a physically demanding nature. The themes which link their narratives are often taken from television viewing. As well as encouraging cooperative planning and exercise, such games are also a means by which status can be gained or lost. The ability to develop the story of the game, and to lead the other participants through it, enhances the status of the individual in the group (Paley 1990). This in turn enhances the individual's attractiveness as a play partner. The physical tests which are often incorporated into such play, perhaps in rough-and-tumble form, provide a means of establishing a place in the hierarchy of strength or speed.

The prevalence of games with rules in play-area play may indicate that a function is served for the wider society. Such games necessitate levels of cooperation and shared understanding. This will have functional benefit beyond that of the individual acting in the society of children. The ability to operate within self-imposed and regulated limits may also later enhance the individual's success within adult society.

Distance and deviance

The ability to operate successfully within the society of children can be seen to depend upon performance in play and its associated activities. Functional benefit for the individual and for the group will be gained only if this performance is acknowledged to be satisfactory by other members of the society.

For many children, successful integration into the society is hindered by difficulties at each stage of the cycle of play activity. Some children find difficulty with the accepted techniques used to join groups or to establish partnerships. Others find that performance of the chosen activity is judged unsatisfactory by the group, or that their repeated breaking of the rules leads to eventual expulsion. The sense of rejection felt by those who have been occasionally isolated is intense.

Children who are temporarily excluded from play, games or the social activities with which they are interspersed, may seek to distance themselves from the activity. They may adopt a searching or questing posture which indicates that they are no longer interested in the activity but are seeking something better. This pose is also adopted by children who are newly arrived on the play area and is as distinctly recognizable as the 'play face' (plates 4.6, 4.7a, b and c).

Distancing may also take the form of ridiculing the activity vocally, particularly if more than one child is excluded. Less frequently, the excluded child will seek to disrupt the activity by imposing another conflicting activity into the same place and claiming right of prior occupancy. Distancing and disturbance techniques allow the excluded child to reject the low status implied by the exclusion and will usually extend only for that particular episode of play.

Plate 4.6   Play faces

Plate 4.7a, b and c   Searching posture

A minority of children repeatedly fail to gain acceptance into the groups of players or to those involved in social activity. For these children the building of relationships, the development of competence and the establishment of a high status position within the society of children is denied. Goffman (1963: 129) suggests that when individuals are denied (or believe themselves to be denied) the means to succeed within a society, they may seek to alienate themselves from the means by which success is judged within that society and eventually from the society itself. Those children who are continually rejected by their peers during

Plate 4.8   Cultural exchange in the society of children

playtime are in just this position. Their rejection by the society of children leads them to seek status other than by accepted means. So, as the successful performance of a game leads to high status within the society, the ability to disrupt and disturb to great effect provides status for those rejected by the society. Such individuals may be the focus of conflicts which the regulatory powers of the children are unable to control. At its most extreme, groups of rejected children may form coalitions whose unifying purpose is to provide status for its members resulting from their power to disrupt and disturb. Such groups frequently adopt bullying and violent tactics to ensure recognition by other children. This violent behaviour can, in turn, becomes the 'play' activity around which a children's sub-culture may form.

Conclusion

The suggestion by Lee (1977: 340), and many others, that play is the main business of a child's life is nowhere more apt than in the play areas of schools and in those other spaces where children are able to play in self-regulatory groups. Play and games activities form the basis around which the social and cultural activities of childhood revolve (see Tina Bruce, Chapter 15). Individual children's ability to establish themselves within a game-playing or social group will determine their ability to build relationships, to develop greater competence and consequently to gain status. The transmission of cultural knowledge relating to play and the maintenance of cultural values is within the control of the children on the play area. These values may, at times, be in conflict with the values of the school.

Play areas provide a setting for a cultural forum within which the children can create and recreate meaning from the sum of their experiences. The activities, play, games, social and antisocial behaviours provide a means by which the culture can find expression and by which individual children can seek to meet functional needs. I do not believe that they primarily provide a rehearsal for later adult society, nor recreation from the 'real' work of the school, but they serve an immediate purpose for the children in their own present society (plate 4.8).

Part 2
Play, schooling and responsibilities

Plate 6   The modelling of symbol systems is a significant source of empowerment for children

Plate 7   Play is ace!

Plate 8   Observing the socio-dramatic play of young children can be a most delightful experience

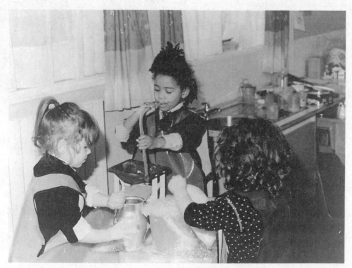

Plate 9   What are the basics of early learning for a young child?

5 | Play and legislated curriculum
Back to basics: an alternative view

Angela Anning

Every education system functions within a social context and a set of political imperatives. So it is with the Educational Reform Act (ERA) in schools in England and Wales in the 1990s. The version of the National Curriculum and related assessment procedures documented in the serried ranks of ring files dominating the staffroom shelves of schools in England and Wales, has a particular genesis. It was constructed around concern to 'raise educational standards' and deliver an effective workforce for the economic recovery in the UK. The ideologies underpinning the paper NC model are based on concepts of value for money in a market-led economy, and a return to disciplined behaviour and competence in 'traditional' school subjects in classrooms in the maintained sector – with an emphasis on the basics of literacy, numeracy and scientific knowledge at primary-school level.

The adequacy of this as a model of curriculum for young children is, at best, questionable. As I shall show in this chapter, there are alternative and superior models which use play and creativity as the basis of an early years curriculum designed around children's learning needs and encouraging a love of learning.

The existing framework

The value system of the dominant political power group of the past decade – mostly men, mostly educated within the independent sector, mostly deeply uncertain about women – have determined the policies for which they have legislated under the terms of the Educational Reform Act. For them, *play* is a frivolous and low-status activity associated with the long hair, beads, and the hedonism of The Sixties Generation or with women and children in church halls. Acceptable play may take place only in competitive team games or on the golf course. A few comments from their public announcements will serve to illustrate the point. Michael Fallon, a previous Minister within the DES, criticizing the use of project work, said: 'At worst this kind of practice turns the primary school into playgroups where there is much happiness and painting, but very little learning.' Kenneth Clarke, in a brief period of opportunism, claimed that 'child-centred' education was failing to deliver: 'At its weakest there is a lot of sticking together of egg boxes and playing in the sand.' Finally, my favourite quotation comes from Tim Eggar, at that time minister with responsibility for women within the DES, trying to justify the lack of women in public positions: 'Women tend not to be in our networks; the chaps we know are not always women!'

Their appointees, the senior administrators at the now defunct National Curriculum Council, the Schools Examination and Assessment Council and now the School Curriculum and Assessment Authority, have mostly had politically correct business credentials and, latterly it seems, connections with the Church. The language they use – of accountability, quality assurance, a market-led economy, value for money, preparation for work – and a morality based on the Puritan work ethic, discipline and trouble-shooting 'commando style' units, are designed to intimidate. NCC, SEAC (or indeed SCAA) staff dealing directly with curriculum or classroom-based policies, are almost all drawn from higher education or secondary-school backgrounds. Representation, even at working party level, from the primary-school sector has been limited, and, from early years education, scandalously deficient. Despite (or perhaps because of) this, the generality of many of the Orders as they stand at present, gives plenty of scope for Key Stage 1 teachers to use practical, experiential learning as the basis for much of their curriculum planning and still fulfil their legal obligations to teach and assess the Orders.

The so-called 'Three Wise Men' (Alexander *et al.*, 1992) were charged by the Secretary of State with reviewing available evidence about the delivery of education in primary schools in order to 'make recommendations about curriculum organisation, teaching methods and classroom practice appropriate for the successful implementation of the National Curriculum particularly in Key Stage 2'. They suggested that primary schools should introduce children to subject disciplines – 'some of the most powerful tools for making sense of the world which human beings have ever devised'. They were critical, on the basis of empirical research evidence, of classroom organization in which children are 'working on too many different activities of subject simultaneously'. It is, of course, significant that the brief was to focus on *Key Stage 2* (the education of seven- to eleven-year-olds) but inevitably, since the Discussion Paper was entitled Curriculum Organisation and Classroom Practice in *Primary* Schools, it was assumed that Key Stage 1, though scarcely mentioned in the text, was also included in the discussion. Consequently, a critique of the discussion paper by 'Three Wise Women' (David *et al.*, 1992) argued that the paper had neglected the specific needs of organizing the learning of four- to seven-year-olds and ignored evidence from research (Campbell and Neill 1991) that infant teachers have found ways of integrating content from the Programmes of Study into themes in ways which are meaningful to young children.

Designing an alternative early years curriculum

Eisner (1982: 49) wrote:

> The kind of nets we know how to weave determine the kind of nets we cast. These nets in turn determine the kinds of fish we catch.

The 'nets' woven by those determining policy for the education of four- to seven/eight-year-olds currently bear little resemblance to those traditionally woven by the early years educators who are charged with the 'delivery' of the National Curriculum.

The value system espoused by *practitioners* emphasizes beliefs in the value of play as a powerful vehicle for learning, the importance of experiential learning, the education of 'the whole child' within both their family and school contexts, the significance of physicality, the vital role of developing literacy and numeracy as tools for learning and the importance of fun and enjoyment as sources of motivation. (Many chapters in this book bear witness to these values.) Their nets are significantly different shapes, sizes and colours. Practitioners feel deskilled and dispirited with the unfamiliar, brand new, 'official' nets, designed with scant reference to their established craft knowledge, thrust into their hands. These unfamiliar nets will not catch the kind of fish they say they value.

Yet early years educators must accept equal responsibility for what has happened. We are a female-dominated profession, socialized into taking a passive role in public decision-making. By inclination we have chosen to sit back and wait for 'them up there' (usually men) to tell us what to do, and then struggled to make models, designed without grass-roots knowledge, work effectively. We have had a poor record in researching, documenting and articulating our professional thinking. We have lacked the confidence to engage in public debate and offered no convincing alternative to the NC framework for the education of young children.

Where might we start to weave an alternative net that has some strength? I believe that research into how children think and learn has given us insights into what such an alternative might look like. But we need a boldness of vision to argue for a radical reappraisal of what constitutes 'basics' for the education of young children. So it is to some of the more visionary research that I have turned for inspiration.

Left and right brain hemisphere functions
Early years educators have always argued the case for educating 'the whole child' and for the importance of recognizing links between the emotions, the intellect and the body in learning. Research summarized by Brierley (1987) on left and right brain hemisphere functions alerts us to the importance of understanding the biological basis of learning processes.

Information comes to the brain via the five senses: sight, hearing, touch, smell and taste. Information is taken on board visually, auditorily or kinesthetically (i.e. physically experienced or related to feelings). There is a processing system to prevent information overload, a sort of switchboard system, within the brain. Information which invokes an emotional response, or with content relating to self-preservation, ranks high in the editing process for selective attention. All information is processed through the left or right hemispheres of the brain. Both are capable of similar functions but they have particular propensities. The left brain emphasizes language, logic, mathematical formulae, linearity, sequencing: in general, analytical aspects of thinking. The right hemisphere emphasizes forms and patterns, spatial manipulation, images, things of the imagination, rhythm and musical appreciation. The right hemisphere appears to have the capacity to process faster more holistic aspects of thinking and learning. When the right side of the brain is processing data, it triggers pleasurable responses and chemicals are released which give the learner a sense of heightened awareness and well-being. This positive feedback encourages the learner to repeat the action.

Csikzentmihalyi (1979) likens the absorptions and sense of total involvement which characterizes children involved in sustained bouts of play to a 'flow' state (see Tina Bruce, Chapter 15). Adults can recapture this 'flow' state – characterized by a loss of self-consciousness but at the same time an awareness of being in control of one's absorption in an activity – through highly motivating activities which may be work or leisure related. But for the adult and the child, a 'play' context allows the learner the freedom to experiment without the fear of expensive or potentially embarrassing error. As Bruner wrote, 'Play provides an excellent opportunity to try combinations of behaviour that wouldn't be tried under functional pressure' (Bruner 1972: 82).

Such research can help us to understand what we instinctively know about the power of play as a vehicle for young children's learning and to legitimate proper attention being paid to resourcing and supporting play-based activities. Many teachers feel under pressure to justify time spent in interacting with children engaged in play (as Vicky Hurst suggests in Chapter 14). They feel guilty about being seen to be 'wasting' time; about being seen to have fun.

Alternative forms of intelligence
Infant teachers talk about the need to educate 'the whole child' and take the argument forward as a justification for an integrated approach to

curriculum planning based on topics. Now, aspects of the content of Programmes of Study from the core and foundation subjects are slotted into topic webs so that planning the Key Stage 1 curriculum has become like completing an ingenious jigsaw of Attainment Targets (ATs) and New Attainment Targets (NATs). Fitting all the pieces together is a complex and time-consuming task.

In their original overview of the curriculum (DES 1985), Her Majesty's Inspectorate (HMI) listed nine Areas of Experience as the basis for planning: the aesthetic and creative, the human and social, the linguistic and literary, the mathematical, the moral, the physical, the scientific, the spiritual and the technological.

Two years earlier, in the US, Howard Gardner (1983) argued from a more radical standpoint that a curriculum should be designed around the need to educate eight 'forms of intelligence':

1 linguistic – dealing with language and words;
2 logical/mathematical – abstraction and numbers;
3 musical/auditory – rhythm and sound;
4 visual/spatial – patterning and imagery, knowing the environment;
5 kinesthetic – physical skills, reflexes and timing;
6 interpersonal – sensitivity to others' emotions and needs;
7 intrapersonal – self-knowledge and inner focusing;
8 intuitive/spiritual – flow states and feelings.

I think that these are the kinds of domains of 'the whole child' of which early years educators are aware, but which they find hard to define.

Gardner (ibid.) argues that the education system of the Western world concentrates too narrowly on the first two forms of intelligence – the linguistic and logical/mathematical. Moreover, in the context of schooling most information is passed on through the *auditory* mode. Little emphasis is placed on the *visual* mode and, as the child progresses through the education system, even less on the *kinesthetic* mode of learning. Gardner cites evidence that some people have a natural propensity to learn through verbalizing, others through visualizing and others through 'doing'. When I talk to educators they can usually fit the children they know, and themselves, into one of these categories. Our system favours those who learn most effectively through the auditory mode, fails to accommodate the needs of those who learn most effectively through the visual mode, and increasingly creates an apartheid for those who persist in a preference for learning through the kinesthetic mode.

Donaldson (1978: 83) quotes Whitehead's famous maxim, 'In teaching you will come to grief as soon as you forget that your pupils have bodies.' Yet our education system encourages the myth that those who chose to work with their hands are of less intelligence than those who deal in abstractions. Clever children are filtered into groups where 'academic' subjects are taught. Dull children are sent to the workshops. The concept of 'the intelligent hand' is not part of our cultural heritage. Yet as Whitehead argued, 'It is a moot point whether the human hand created the human brain, or the brain created the hand. Certainly the connection is intimate and reciprocal' (ibid.).

When we listen to the rhetoric of infant teachers, we would anticipate that they at least would pay careful attention to structuring and supporting children's learning in practical work across the ability range in art and craft, technology, block play, role play, small figure play, sand and water and so on. Research evidence from infant classrooms (Bennett and Kell 1989; Tizard *et al.*, 1988) indicates, however, that teachers actually spend most of their teaching time with children engaged on seat-based literacy and numeracy tasks. For the children the status activities in the class-room are marked by where their teachers, driven by pressure from the world outside schools, spend their time (a point also taken up by Jane Hislam and Lesley Abbott in Chapters 3 and 6 respectively). Practical, play-based learning activities are seen as low status and occupational, mainly for far less able children; something to do when you have finished your work, or have time for a bit of a laugh.

Every time infant teachers make a clear distinction between the 'important' aspects of learning (the 'real work' of learning the basics of literacy and numeracy) and the low status of practical activities (the 'play' or 'choosing time' activities) they are beginning the process of focusing on a narrow range of intelligences of the children for whom they are responsible. They are negating, by their actions, their claim to want to educate the whole child and beginning to shut down potential areas of growth. They are laying the foundations of the apartheid separating the academic from the practical.

To design a curriculum around a framework such as Gardner's eight intelligences would take courage, but would educate children with a truly grounded set of basic skills for life. Those would be some impressive fish to catch!

Delivering the curriculum

The Piagetian paradigm of the child as a lone scientist learning about the world from direct experimentation has been challenged by Bruner (1966) and Vygotsky (1962). In their models, learning is perceived as a social process. The child is held within the culture of the family, community or school (see David Brown, Chapter 4) and works towards mastery of the genres within each context. We know that children learn as much by observing and imitating the behaviours of those around them as they do by active engagement in tasks. But the Vygotskian model implies an interventionist model of teaching and learning. Instead of waiting for the child to accumulate enough experience to move on to the next stage, the adult or more experienced child supports the learner's progression. (For a fuller discussion see Peter Smith, Chapter 1.)

For early years educators these models of how children learn imply a much more active role for teachers than their training may have indicated. They are no longer relegated to the status of hovering, full of uncertainty, above the child waiting for them to 'move on'. From all the implications of research into learning through play straddling the Keele project, the team (Hutt *et al.*, 1989: 194) highlighted the role of the adult:

> If there is a single message that comes through . . . it is the import-ance of the caring adult both in directing the child's play in an appropriate way at the appropriate moment and in gauging the child's mood and state and deciding in which circumstances it is appropriate to intervene.

In order to achieve an appropriate match of task to learner, the teacher must be closely involved with children as they work and play, able to listen rather than talk at children, and skilful at observing and analysing evidence of learning. Clearly this applies as much to practical, play-based activities as to teaching reading or mathematics.

One way in which the adult can scaffold the child's learning is to ensure that the tasks presented to them are meaningful. Donaldson (1978: 18) draws the distinction between tasks embedded in the here and now of children's current interests and concerns, calling this 'present moment embedding'. Children gradually shift, supported by increasing linguistic competence, towards concerns about the past and future, but generally still with a core focus on their own concerns – 'own-life em-bedding'. The final shift is towards thinking and learning about things beyond the child's immediate concerns. As Donaldson points out, suc-cess in schooling depends on developing competence in 'disembedded thinking'.

> It is on this kind of development that the achievements of logic, mathematics and science depend. These achievements are, however, hard won. They call for a mental discipline and self-control which does not come easily to us. We do not readily relinquish the support for thought which an embedding context provides (Donaldson 1978: 106).

For many children the switch from a domestic culture of play based on real life problem-solving to the 'peculiar' school tasks of worksheets, sorting plastic shapes and playing in waist high containers of sand and water, can be traumatic. Teachers are often so socialized into perceiving these school-based activities as 'the norm' that they neglect to ex-plain to children their purposes. There are ways of making the transition to the genres of school learning more humane, without resorting to what Egan (1988: 200) has dismissed as 'the mild babysafe school', where expectations of children are low and the diet offered patronizingly limiting.

The modelling of symbol systems is a significant source of empower-ment for children to help them move towards increasing levels of abstraction. Research done by, for example, Hall (1987) on emergent literacy, Hughes (1986) on the acquisition of understanding of mathematical symbols, and Gardner (1983) on the use of drawing to make sense of the world, give plenty of support to the notion of modelling these tools for thinking through play-based activities. For educators, there is real excitement in observing children accruing knowledge and understanding of these tools. Each one is a separate code to crack and for young children, in a well-structured, active learning environment, cracking the codes can involve personal adventures rather than stacks of worksheets to complete!

Egan (1988), Wells (1987) and Nigel Hall (in Chapter 9) have argued for the power of narrative in building bridges from the particular or concrete to the general or abstract.

> Constructing stories in the mind – or storying as it has been called – is one of the most fundamental means of making meaning; as such it is an activity that pervades all aspects of learning.
>
> (Wells 1987: 194)

Egan believes that we should turn the content of the curriculum for young children topsy-turvy. He argues that young children are not necessarily turned on by a diet of trivial, and often sentimental, stories:

> programmed reading schemes, and the absence of powerful emotional, dramatic, and intellectual content . . . typify many primary classrooms . . . Disney-esque sentimentality is the exact emotional equivalent to intellectual contempt.
>
> (1991: 199)

He argues that children should be introduced instead, through stories, to the universal human emotions of love, hate, fear, anger and jealousy which are the source of their earliest understandings of the world. Such universal concepts can often be encapsulated in bi-polar opposites – good/evil, diligent/lazy, cruel/kind – and he argues that an early years curriculum should be developed around such themes. He labels the years birth to seven as the Mythic Phase and believes that during this time children should recapitulate the main features of the myths of oral cultures. Like Gardner, Egan pleads for serious attention to be paid to sound as a way of promoting development. He argues that young children's intellectual lives are most attuned to an oral culture – sounds rather than words – and that by introducing 'the technologies' of writing and reading at too early a stage, we impoverish their intellectual lives by forcing them to operate with tools for thinking which actually depress their powers of reasoning and slow them down.

Conclusion

I have argued that we have research evidence available to us which could provide frameworks for a radical alternative to the NC for young children. Such an alternative curriculum would aim to empower children with tools for thinking, giving them the capability to explore a whole range of ideas, experiences, feelings and relationships. (Chris Pascal and Tony Bertram argue this strongly in their treatise for quality play provision in Chapter 13.) It would also introduce children to the cultural tools – print, mathematical symbols, graphicacy, rhythms, rhymes, communication through speech, metaphors, fine and gross motor control – which they see being used all around them, rather than constraining them within a straitjacket of 'school' learning.

Much of the learning would be based on well-structured and resourced play-based activities. Our infant-aged children are, by many other cultural standards, still at a kindergarten stage of education: school starting ages of six and seven are more common in other societies. If the curriculum was genuinely designed around children's learning needs, perhaps then we would encourage a generation of children with a love of learning rather than groups of anxious and dispirited 'beginning readers' already feeling that they are inadequate.

Bronowski (1958) quotes Newton in the *Ascent of Man*:

> I do not know what I may appear to the world, but to myself I seem to have been only like a boy playing on the sea shore and diverting himself and then finding a smoother pebble or a prettier shell than ordinary while the greater ocean of truth lay all undiscovered before me.

It would be a real achievement to educate young children who became adults with such a sense of curiosity and playfulness.

6 | 'Play is ace!' Developing play in schools and classrooms

Lesley Abbott

Recognizing play and acknowledging its role in children's learning is not necessarily a problem. Several educationalists and researchers (referenced in many places throughout this book) give countless examples and a range of evidence that play is the child's way of learning, and that to neglect or ignore the role of play as an educational medium is to deny the child's natural response to the environment and indeed to life itself! As most educators will readily acknowledge, children *will* play in spite of, rather than because of, any planned provision for them to do so or real acceptance on the adults' part that it *can* play a central role in the curriculum. (There is equally real uncertainty about the value of play among some theorists, as Peter Smith clearly acknowledges in Chapter 1.)

If, as educators, we *are* committed to play as an important process in children's learning, there is no doubt that in the present climate we will be called upon to justify the provision made for play and indeed to define, and sometimes defend, the use of the word in educational contexts. Nor should the role of play in the primary curriculum be the concern of individual educators: discussion among professionals in a shared context is essential in order to develop shared beliefs, mutual understanding, coherence and a consistency of approach.

As *Starting with Quality: The Report of the Committee of Inquiry into the Quality of Educational Experience offered to 3- and 4-year-olds* (DES 1990) points out, 'play underlies a great deal of young children's learning. For its potential value to be realised a number of conditions need to be fulfilled' (1990: para 90). These conditions include adults who are sensitive and informed, careful organizing and planning for play, assessment which allows for continuity and progression and, above all,

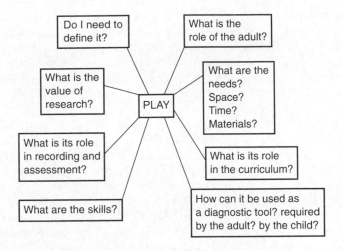

Figure 6.1 Play in the primary school – some considerations

commitment to the view that play is a high status activity in the education of young children.

The aim of this chapter is to put a general perspective on some of those issues and questions which confront educators attempting to introduce and justify quality play experiences within the classroom context, which includes:

1 defining play;
2 the value of research in informing and enriching practice;
3 observing, assessing and recording play experiences;
4 the role of play in the curriculum;
5 the role of adults in play provision.

Several of these, it will be recognized, are recurring themes throughout this book and raise questions which practitioners at all levels need to address repeatedly when making decisions about play in educational settings. The questions, shown in Figure 6.1, are intended to provide a focus for staff-development sessions on play within the wider context of curriculum planning. What follows in this chapter is an exploration of my considered views on the points identified above, and the associated questions. There is no doubt that in responding to these issues, staff will raise even more questions but this is useful in that it helps to reshape thinking and challenges preconceived views.

Do we need a definition of play?

Defining play within an educational context can, for some teachers, be problematic since many of the characteristics we associate with play –

freedom, spontaneity, exuberance, fun, ownership – do not sit happily or naturally within a context geared to prescriptive programmes, long-term planning or summative testing. Yet those practitioners who remain committed to play and who acknowledge its centrality in their curriculum find no problem in defining play because they do so on *their* terms and within the context in which they, the children and the parents operate.

Most people would accept that the child squealing with delight in popping bubbles in the water tray or dressing up as mum or dad in the home corner is playing. Where they may experience difficulty is in recognizing and acknowledging that the child, deeply engrossed in completing a time-sheet in the stimulus area set up as a 'factory' or writing a cheque in the 'travel agent's' is also playing.

There are as many definitions of play as there are ways of playing, as Janet Moyles argues in the introduction, and there is no way that any one definition will encompass all the views, perceptions, experiences and expectations that any one of us will bring to the word. This is simple to say but the full impact is extremely difficult for many people to acknowledge!

In 1977 Manning and Sharp asked 500 teachers for their definition of play; the result was as many definitions as there were teachers in the study. What is important is that, because play is 'context related', those who share that context also share a definition of play which covers the kinds of experiences that players will have there. Children's own views and definitions of play are important and worth exploring. In an interesting study undertaken in Sweden, in which children's perceptions of play were investigated, Karrby (1989) found that young children had a clear definition of play and were able to differentiate play from other activities that are often called play by adults. For children, it transpired, play is a complex mental activity, not easily observed and interpreted by parents and teachers.

Although attempting to reach a consensus definition of play is problematical, the discussion process itself is a valuable and rewarding one – at both the individual and group level. Indeed, if children are to experience consistency, coherence and quality in provision and in their interactions with adults, then discussion about what play is, and can be, is essential. It is equally valuable in a search for quality experiences to explore also what play is *not*: for example, play is not simply everything the child does.

In the same vein, Webb (1974: 59) raises important questions about the concept of 'worthwhileness'. Acknowledging the considerable debt owed to the work of Peters (1966) in defining 'worthwhile activities', she claims that to be worthwhile the activity should be 'worthy' at any level of pursuit. This is an important maxim to be borne in mind when considering a definition of play and attempting to identify 'quality' characteristics (for a discussion of this, refer to Chris Pascal and Tony Bertram,

Chapter 13). Webb also claims that to be worthwhile an activity must be 'infinitely extendible' (1974: 61): there are implications here in relation to considerations of developmentally appropriate play provision (Bredekamp 1988). Play provision must differ in relation to the age and stage of the child and continually be extended for those children making speedy progress.

In any discussion about what play is and how it is defined, it is essential that the views of the players themselves are sought. These are often ignored, and yet they are central to any development if concepts such as ownership and shared values are held to be important (Tina Bruce, Chapter 15). The involvement of parents, not only in discussions about play and its role in the classroom but in the activity itself, would help to raise its status and to provide a shared focus for discussion. There is much more chance that children, parents and educators will be using a common vocabulary if some attempt at reaching a working definition has been made (see also Peter Heaslip, Chapter 8). It would also guard against the 'just playing' syndrome when parents ask children, 'What have you been doing in school today?' A knowledge of the context in which the activity has taken place, the value placed upon it and the range of potential learning experiences to be encountered, can only be helpful to all those involved.

When asked for their views about play, one eight-year-old replied that, 'Play is ACE!' – and indeed it was in his particular school and class-room. There was a real commitment to, and a recognition of, play as a high status activity. Its centrality in the curriculum was not in dispute – the staff shared a common view, a play coordinator was appointed, and a policy document drawn up, of which parents, children and staff shared common ownership. They were justly proud of what children were achieving in play. Play was 'upfront' and there was no attempt to bow to pressure and to reduce the status of the activity by calling it something different, such as active learning, simulation or, indeed, 'work'.

Discussion about what play is *within the context in which children and adults are working* is essential if the status of the activity is to be upheld. It may be that a definition remains elusive (Smith 1984) but an explanation and justification must be sought and agreed in principle and in practice.

What is the value of play research?

Tina Bruce (in Gura 1992) asks the question, 'Are we researchers, practitioners or educators?' It is heartening that, in both initial and inservice training, the emphasis is now on the teacher as active learner and reflective practitioner and, therefore, as Tina Bruce later claims, 'an educator is a researcher and practitioner combined' (1992: 11).

There is a wealth of research in this book and elsewhere which challenges and informs our views about play, yet there is still some way to go before research finds its way into classrooms and really influences in positive ways how adults and children work together.

As an example, the particular influence of Corinne Hutt's research (several dates) bears specific mention here, as in other chapters. Hutt argued (see Figure 1.2 in the Introduction) that exploration and play are distinct behaviours, both giving expression to different forms of learning. She emphasized that, although exploration is commonly regarded as play, much contained within the exploratory act is serious, concentrated activity which should be distinguished from more playful behaviours. In a 1966 study by Hutt, a completely new toy was designed from which, by moving a lever, children could produce lights or sounds or clock-up counters. The toy provided both novelty as well as complexity (Hutt 1966). One hundred three- to five-years-olds were allowed to play with the toy on six successive occasions and an interesting sequence of behaviour emerged. The child would initially approach and inspect the toy, then investigate it by touching, feeling and manipulating the lever. Once most of the features and properties of the toy were discovered, the child would then proceed to use it 'playfully' and its 'functional fixity' (Bronson 1973) was gone: the child's emphasis had shifted from enquiry to invention. Behaviourally, this transition was most marked: whereas during exploration children were intent and attentive, during the later playful activity, they were relaxed and at ease. The information and knowledge acquired during exploration was then being used and extended in play, indicating that while exploration was *assimilatory*, play was *expressive*.

The main point to be made here is that a distinction between exploration and play may be made on several grounds and, far from being an academic exercise, it becomes imperative to do so when one considers the implications for learning. If children engage prematurely in playful activity with a resource, before they have learned all there is to know about it, they are unlikely to acquire any further information during the play episode, thus curtailing the potential for learning. As we shall see later, the type and timing of adult involvement is critical, being essential in epistemic (exploratory) behaviour but requiring sensitive intervention in ludic (playful) behaviour which often has its own structure, language and rules.

Although the full implications of her work have still to find their way into many classrooms in which teachers purport to support and provide a play-centred curriculum, Hutt showed clearly that exploration is a powerful forerunner to full-blown play. Many teachers and other educators are guilty of hurrying children on to 'production' when the joy, excitement and learning to be gained from exploring the materials first – running one's fingers through the sand, sawdust, lentils, shiny paper – has equal importance. In other words, the process is as important, if not more so at certain stages, than the product. Observation is crucial in order to assess the current level of any play episode and provide for sensitive intervention.

What is the role of play for observing, assessing and recording children's progress?

This is an important question, particularly in the present educational and political climate. The dangers of assessing children's learning and development out of context and in situations and languages with which they are unfamiliar have been highlighted on numerous occasions (Clarke 1988; Tyler 1989; DES 1990). Play provides opportunities for close observation of children in activities in which they have chosen to engage and which are relevant and meaningful to them. Kalvaboer (1977: 121) makes a relevant point in relation to observation:

> Only by taking time to observe children and at times to play with, and alongside, them will adults be able to recognise that play contains crucial information about a child's developmental level, his [sic] organising capacities and his emotional state.

In relation to assessment and record keeping, Alexander *et al.*, (1992: para. 116) remind us:

> Assessment and Record Keeping are not synonymous, though they are frequently treated as such. There is little point in developing an elaborate record-keeping system if the evidence upon which the records are based is inadequate. The precondition for good records is, therefore, good assessment.

The diagnostic value of play cannot be over-emphasized – the example of the child observed in the morning struggling with the simplest of jigsaws, unable to match by shape, colour or by looking at a picture of the completed puzzle, and equally defeated when presented with a 'flash card' in the afternoon, is a salutary one for all adults. If the valuable clues provided by children in their play are ignored, the match between child and activity will not be achieved and children will fail.

A variety of strategies and techniques for observing, recording and assessing children's play must be employed – Vicky Hurst explores these more fully in Chapter 14. As also pointed out by Moyles 1989, these might range from the use of tape recorders, video cameras, photographs, diaries, notebooks and journals to the use of systematic recording systems involving time and event-sampling, target-child methods, structured interviews, record sheets and check lists. The Froebel Blockplay Research Group point out the dangers inherent in employing only one system of recording, suggesting that a simple naming of a child's completed construction is insufficient. The emphasis must be on: 'knowledge of the processes the child used in creating the structures . . . our records need to reflect both processes and products' (Gura 1992: 144).

Bennett and Kell (1989: 29) also found that adults in their study had a tendency to 'limit their assessment to the "products" of children's work, and only rarely did they attempt to observe the processes or strategies deployed by children in reaching their goal'.

What is the role of play in the curriculum?

Moyles' (1989) assertion that play is not *the* curriculum for four- to eight-year-old children and the Rumbold Committee's reiteration of the fact that the National Curriculum is not *the* curriculum for under-fives (DES: para. 64) are important points to bear in mind when addressing this question.

Hall and Abbott (1991) provide a range of case studies of play in which a great deal of attention has been paid to the variety, quality and appropriateness of the provision in each context. The language, culture and experience of the children are given careful consideration, and attention has been paid to the notion of 'extendibility'. A good example of this is the way in which infant- and junior-aged children play with the same provision set up as a 'railway station'. These examples go well beyond the token home corner still to be found in many early years settings and are clearly examples of the kind of 'worthwhile' activities to which Webb (1974) refers.

Pollard and Tann (1987: 5) point to a number of common dilemmas with which teachers in primary schools are constantly faced. These include:

Attempting to integrate elements of the curriculum	>	Dealing systematically with each various discrete area of the curriculum
Trying to build up cooperative and social skills	>	Developing self-reliance and self-confidence in individuals
Maintaining consistent rules and understanding about behaviour and school work	>	Being flexible and responsive to particular situations
Presenting oneself formally to the children	>	Relaxing with the children or having a laugh with them

A useful exercise for educators is to take some examples from this list and to consider how far a structured play area such as an airport, travel agent, café, hospital or building site provides opportunities for 'relaxing and having a laugh with children', 'being flexible and responsive to particular situations', 'building up cooperative and social skills or attempting to integrate various elements of the curriculum'. As a starting point for a staff-development session this provides a wider and more appropriate focus than a consideration of the degree to which, for example, attainment targets have been met.

In working with Year 6 children in a railway station play area devised by infant children, Strahan (1992: 119) claims:

> The older children had recognised a number of important qualities necessary to the setting up and implementation of their structured play area. They identified the importance of 'being able to get on with each other – cooperating and helping', 'not being bossy', 'needing to talk a lot – so that everybody knows how each other feels', 'listening to each other', 'being sensible – thinking before speaking and doing something', 'being well organised'.

She also points out that 'the undoubted success of the activity had much to do with the amount of autonomy the children had been allowed in setting it up' (Strahan 1992: 114). As a teacher in a school where infants and juniors had recently amalgamated, she quickly realized that: 'it was not just teachers who had feelings that "playing" was not the way learning was done at school. The junior children also had fairly definite ideas that, whilst play was a good thing outside the school context, in school it was either "naughty" or "babyish".'

A further dilemma highlighted by Pollard and Tann (1987: 5) is that of 'giving children a degree of control over their use of time, their activities and their work standards' as against 'tightening control over children's use of time, their activities and their work'. Strahan clearly recognized that 'it was important for us as teachers that we not only challenged our own assumptions but challenged those of the children as well' (1991: 114).

Lack of time and opportunity for teachers to help children to develop these qualities in meaningful situations create some of the dilemmas to which Pollard and Tann refer (ibid.). Yet Strahan's is a good example of opportunities being created for eleven-year-olds to recognize their play needs and being able to talk about them with supportive adults in a context in which play is valued and valuable as a learning process. (Neil Kitson also takes up similar points regarding socio-dramatic play in Chapter 7.)

As Alexander *et al.*, (1992: para. 103) emphasize, 'teachers need to be competent in a range of techniques in order to achieve different learning outcomes'. Structured play also provides ideal opportunities for teachers to, 'give precise instructions, to explain ideas clearly, to demonstrate practical activities, to pose different kinds of questions, and, to help pupils understand how well they have done'.

A key question facing primary teachers relates to the ways in which appropriate play experiences fit within the framework and requirements of the National Curriculum. It is important that in curriculum planning processes are given equal consideration alongside content and context. These include:

- collaborating;
- making choices;
- organizing;
- explaining;
- talking and communicating;
- sharing;
- taking responsibility;
- asking and answering;
- recording;
- interpreting, predicting, recalling and reflecting.

These processes were clearly in evidence in an 'airport' set up by four Year 1 and 2 classes, about which Sparrow (1991: 107) writes:

> the airport is an excellent example of a realistic situation and one which, in its basic organisation, demanded co-operation, co-ordination and interdependence . . . It enabled the setting up of problems, searches for solutions, posing of questions and the transfer of skills into the real world, outside school. It was surprisingly easy to establish equivalent but conflicting needs in the airport. In the ticket office, arguments about who should be given the last seat on the aeroplane were rapidly taken on board by children when an elderly person in a wheelchair was brought forward at the same time as a woman with a young baby. Whose need was more pressing?

Further reading of this report shows how the various situations presented in the airport play posed problems demanding discussion, asking questions, providing arguments, analysis and brainstorming for their solution.

In dealing with quite sophisticated conflicts, Sparrow (1991: 108) suggests that 'the children proved themselves to be most adept at diplomatic solutions and ideas, enabling and empowering them to feel directive, involved and determined in using their developing skills . . . their performance was astonishing, the more the ideas and observations were incorporated into the provision, activities and resourcing, the broader their application of skills and concepts became.'

What is clear in this example is that much more was involved than merely providing a set of 'props' and leaving children to get on with it. For the staff in this particular school, play has a high status and central role in the curriculum through the primary school. It is seen as a demanding, intellectual activity, but it has the virtue of allowing staff to understand fully what it is they are doing when they make claims about the learning potential of play in the curriculum. The adults' role is also clearly defined.

What is the role of adults in play?

What are the skills required and what are the 'needs' which must be met in order to ensure quality play? In considering these questions, it is necessary to return to the Rumbold Report (1990) and the Committee's identification of a number of conditions to be fulfilled if the potential value of play is to be realized. These include a concern for:

- sensitive, knowledgeable and informed adult involvement and intervention;
- careful planning and organisation of play settings in order to provide for and extend learning;
- enough time for children to develop their play;
- careful observation of children's activities to facilitate assessment and planning for progression and continuity.

While the Rumbold Report focused specifically upon adults working with the under-fives, these concerns echo those of Manning and Sharp (1977) who, focusing on the early years in general, placed great emphasis on the quality and type of adult involvement (a feature explored by every writer in this book). Despite much evidence to the contrary, teachers and other adults still rarely involve themselves in children's play. It is understandable, particularly in the present climate, that when children are engrossed in their play, teachers take the opportunity to work with children individually, in small groups or to hear readers! But the perceptions children gain about adult views of play and its status within the curriculum are largely derived from the messages they receive *from* adults. King (1978: 18) points to the implicit assumptions about play contained in statements such as: 'Wayne, people are working here; go over there to play,' or: 'That's your playtime voice; we don't want it in the classroom.'

Children very quickly gain the impression that those activities with which adults choose to become involved, or feel forced to involve themselves in (see Angela Anning, Chapter 5), are those which are deemed to be most important. The work/play dichotomy quickly emerges even with the youngest children and the status of play is further reduced by the type of organization where children are allowed to 'choose' once the 'important tasks' have been completed, where play is seen as a reward for work, and where work is done in the morning and play in the afternoon. However welcome adults might be in children's play, it is not always easy for them to become involved.

Involvement and interaction can be extended to all adults (Nigel Hall, Chapter 9, gives further examples). Pauling (1991: 97–98) also offers evidence of the way in which play in a 'travel agent's' was extended by the involvement of several parents from different ethnic backgrounds, who willingly gave up time to sit in the 'travel agency' and answer children's questions. She claims that this type of parental involvement does not rely on well-travelled and highly articulate parents. The only necessary ingredient is a parent who is prepared to become involved and spend some time interacting with a group of children.

For children to accept adults in play, sound relationships based on mutual trust and respect must be developed. The Rumbold Committee consider that 'a child's emerging self-awareness and confidence depend on the quality of early encounters' (DES 1990: 37). Sensitivity in knowing how and when to intervene in play – if at all – is needed and is dependent upon knowledge of children and on the nature of play itself. Manning and Sharp's (1977) distinction between initiation, intervention and participation is a useful one but, as adults know to their cost, ill-timed intervention has resulted in a breakdown in the sequence of activity and a sense of failure and alienation on the part of the adults involved.

Strahan (1992) considered that the way staff felt *they* were learning through children's play and their involvement was one of the most powerful features of the project in which she was engaged. This is shown clearly in the following extract from an interview conducted with her teacher by a ten-year-old:

Child: What do you think you would be learning if you were doing structured play?
Teacher: I am doing structured play.
Child: No – if you were in it.
Teacher: I am in it and I am learning things, because I've not really done structured play before so I'm learning from it as well. I'm learning alongside you really, things that you're learning . . . how to set things up and how you can bring it into school and make people realise it's not play as in when we go outside and have a run round – that it's worthwhile and leads onto other things here in school and that all areas of our school day can be brought into structured play.

A project in which both children and teachers recognize that they are learning is an extremely powerful one for any school.

A successful initiative started by a another school committed to play involves parents in play evenings where staff and parents engage in all the activities in which their children have been involved during the day. By playing themselves, parents are able to share those experiences with their children and to understand the tremendous potential for learning in each activity. Such evenings have proved to be an ideal vehicle for getting away from the 'I only played' syndrome and for parents and children to share 'the excitement and joy of learning!'

Adults aiming to increase both their involvement in play, and the quality of their provision, could usefully focus on the following questions:

1 How far are the children involved in making decisions about the choice of play areas?
2 Who has ownership over the play – adults or children – or is there a shared responsibility?
3 How far and in what ways are equal opportunities provided in terms of culture, race, gender, special educational needs?
4 Is the play supportive of children's learning?
5 What knowledge, skills and concepts are a) required for play to be successful, and b) will be acquired in play?
6 How far does the organization for play provide for independence and autonomy?
7 Are materials and resources appropriate and of the highest possible standard?
8 What roles will adults adopt in this area?
9 Is there an atmosphere of approval and acceptance?
10 How far does planning provide for coherence, progression and continuity?
11 How will learning and development be assessed?

The provision of quality play experiences for children is a demanding task, as Chris Pascal and Tony Bertram highlight in Chapter 13. Alexander *et al.*, (1992: para. 124) raise the notion of 'fitness for purpose' as *the* important criteria in making decisions about the choice of organizational strategy to be employed. They claim that: 'While recognizing that the match between teaching and learning can never be exact, teachers should provide learning tasks which at the same time engage with the pupil's current level of understanding and provide the level of challenge which will move that understanding forward' (para. 137).

I believe that quality play provision allows us to meet this challenge. However, it should be remembered that in teaching to the tomorrow of the child we must not ignore the yesterday. Play also provides opportunities for legitimate regression and for building on firm foundations.

Countless researchers and educationalists have made, and continue to make, the very powerful point that the education of young children is founded on play. My personal belief is that, as educators, we ignore this at our peril.

7 'Please Miss Alexander: will you be the robber?'
Fantasy play: a case for adult intervention

Neil Kitson

Observing the socio-dramatic play of young children can be a most delightful experience. Sharing this fantasy situation can be even more rewarding, both for those adults caring for the children and for the children themselves. Yet this form of adult intervention in dramatic and socio-dramatic play is often limited (Hutt *et al.*, 1989). Many practitioners view children's play as being for children only and feel that fantasy play, even more than other forms of play, allows children to operate without adults almost as a form of therapy. Working on their own, children will frequently repeat the same forms of play, engage in the same role activity, model the same type of behaviour, and resolve similar problems. Effective intervention can channel this learning, helping children to construct new dilemmas and challenges, encouraging and supporting individuals and extending and motivating language performance and competence (see Nigel Hall, Chapter 9).

In this chapter, the case for intervention by adults in children's fantasy play is put forward. Looking first at the development of fantasy play, the evidence supporting the need for adult intervention in such activities is assessed and opportunities for development discussed. Nowhere will it be suggested that children should be deprived of the opportunity to engage in 'free-flow' fantasy play (see Tina Bruce, Chapter 15): rather that play can be extended through direct adult intervention with minimal qualitative changes to the *activity* but with very significant differences to the *learning* potential for children. This intervention has to be sympathetic to the needs of the children and operate within *their* fantasy. The adult's role is to provide a structure within which the children can interact – to challenge, to set up problems to be solved, to encourage children to test out ideas and, perhaps more importantly, to open up personal learning strategies to children.

The nature of fantasy play

Children engage in a wide variety of play activities, as is evidenced throughout the chapters of this book. Elements of fantasy will occur at differing levels within individual children's play and games and at different levels of maturity. In order to discuss the relationship between fantasy and socio-dramatic play it is useful to put it in context and to view it as something separate from other forms of play (Smilansky and Shefatya 1990). *Socio-dramatic play* is, for the most part, concerned with the nature of role and of social interaction, while other types of play involve bodily activity or the use and exploration of objects (see Hutt's model in the Introduction to this book). As Peter Smith discusses more fully in Chapter 1, there are four main types of play: functional play, constructive play, rule-governed play and socio-dramatic play. In socio-dramatic play children demonstrate a growing awareness of their social surroundings, consciously acting out social interactions and, in so doing, experiencing human relationships actively by means of symbolic representation. The significant difference between socio-dramatic play and dramatic play is that in the latter children can pretend on their own. They can act out a situation to the exclusion of others, while the more mature socio-dramatic play, as Smilansky and Shefatya (1990) define it, requires interaction, communication and cooperation. Dramatic play is imitative and draws upon first- or second-hand experiences and uses real or imaginary objects. This play becomes socio-dramatic play if the theme is elaborated in cooperation with at least one other person and the participants interact with each other in both *action* and *speech*.

Smilansky and Shefatya (1990: 22) proposed six elements necessary for fantasy play. These are:

1 Imitative role play: the child undertakes a make-believe role and expresses it in imitative action and/or verbalization.
2 Make-believe with regard to toys: movements or verbal declarations and/or materials or toys that are not replicas of the object itself are substituted for real objects.
3 Verbal make-believe with regard to actions and situations: verbal descriptions or declarations are substituted for actions or situations.
4 Persistence in role play: the child continues within a role or play theme for a period of at least ten minutes.
5 Interaction: at least two players interact within the context of the play episode.
6 Verbal communication: there is some verbal interaction related to the play episode.

The first four of these apply to dramatic play but the last two define only socio-dramatic play. This difference can be illustrated with two examples. In the first Joseph, aged three, put a cape on his shoulders and ran around the nursery saying, 'I'm Batman. I'm flying and getting the baddies.' This behaviour has elements of 1 and 3 present, so it can be defined as dramatic-play. In the second example two girls are playing 'hospital' in the doctor's surgery. They are wearing white coats and are giving each other instructions such as, 'You go and use the phone.' Questions like, 'Can I have the listening thing now?' and statements such as, 'I've got the medicine spoon,' suggest elements of imitative role play are present but they are not *interacting*: merely informing each other what is going on. They are engaging at the very basic level of socio-dramatic play. Contrast these with two children pretending to build a house for a pigeon with make-believe tools, talking as if they are doing the job: this would be an example of higher level socio-dramatic as elements 2, 3, 4, 5 and 6 are present.

The importance of socio-dramatic play

A great many writers have considered the value and function of fantasy play. Although it is a crude distinction, one can look at the research in terms of psychoanalytic theory as exemplified by Freud and of cognitive processing theory as suggested by Piaget, to which can be added the more functionalist views postulated by Bruner. Irrespective of their differing views on the contribution to child development, all stress the importance of fantasy play and advocate its inclusion into the on-going education of individuals (the difficulties of actually researching this area have been discussed in detail in Chapter 1).

Freud saw fantasy as a way to gain access to the psyche. Emphasizing the function of the child's instincts in fantasy play he suggested that through play, children will show their 'inner-selves'. Play becomes like a mirror to the child's subconscious and as such this play can be used as a diagnostic and therapeutic tool. The child constructs a role by projecting on to it an imaginative and emotional component. Acting out roles through fantasy play helps the child by weakening the effect of the emotional pressure and, by so doing, helps the child assimilate the traumatic experience. This process Freud refers to as 'sublimation'.

While one can appreciate the implications behind this theory, as a practitioner working with young children I have found that the situations where children have presented behaviours which could be identified as therapeutic are, thankfully, few. (I would suggest such investigation is better left to those with specific drama- or play-therapy training.)

Piaget examined fantasy play in terms of assimilation and accommodation (see Chapter 1). He set up the theoretical notion of 'schema' (a collection of associated ideas) to which new ideas and new relationships of existing ideas are conjoined through experiences. This process he calls assimilation. He suggests that in fantasy play the fantasy elements within the play can be assimilated into a particular schema. Even though it is fantasy the assimilation process occurs as if it were happening in real life. If children make up a story about going on a journey, they draw upon existing knowledge of journeys (their existing schema) and add to it any new information obtained through the play. If the new information is completely novel and there is no existing schema into which it can be incorporated (or if it actually contradicts the existing schema), the existing schema must be accommodated in order for the new information to 'fit'. As a result, new interconnections will be made. Fantasy play can help the child test out ideas and concepts and by so doing make sense of them mainly through assimilation.

This appears to be far more useful as a way of explaining what occurs in the fantasy play of young children. Through their fantasy play, they create new pretend situations. These can contain within them a wide range of seemingly unconnected elements all drawn from the child's previous experiences. *Fantasy acts as a way of unifying experiences, knowledge and understanding, helping the child to discover the links between the individual components.* Moreover, as children are able to control the fantasy play, they are also able to control its components. Young children engaged in a fantasy about a space journey will selectively combine a wide range of components about 'space' and 'journeys'. They will consider what it is like to go on a journey, how to get ready, how time does not stand still during absence, how good it feels to arrive, and consider aspects of space, such as darkness, distance, the need for oxygen and special clothes.

The manifestation of the fantasy element (the play) develops as the child grows older. According to Piaget, children progress through stages of functional play, through dramatic play and on to socio-dramatic play. Throughout, the child is bringing to the fantasy play existing knowledge, skills and understanding of the world which they then assimilate within existing schema or create new and novel interconnections. If insufficiently valued, this natural facility for developing the children's understanding changes the way in which it is manifested from the processes of accommodation.

Piaget postulates that fantasy play will, over time, change into rule-governed activities. Bruner *et al.*, (1976) on the other hand sees fantasy play as being a precursor for social rules. What we learn through fantasy play then forms the basis of rule-governed behaviour. He illustrates this through simple peek-a-boo games played by young children, showing how these lead to the development of structured interactions with turn-taking. In a professional capacity, I have noticed that the fantasy element developed up until about the age of seven becomes submerged if not sustained and actively encouraged.

These observations are supported by Singer and Singer (1990) who suggest that fantasy play goes underground at around seven-plus years of age, to manifest itself later either as day-dreaming or outward expressions of internal thought such as poetry, art or theatre. What is needed in the early years is the development and extension of fantasy play, the legitimizing of it, so that children themselves can come to understand the value of it: through this activity considerable learning about people's lives, human interactions, the workings of society and the individual's role within it can take place. Erikson (1965) stresses the importance of the life-rehearsal element in fantasy play, suggesting that, through play, children can begin to learn to cope with life and with a range of complex social issues such as failure, loneliness and disappointment. In encouraging children to enact fantasy scenes, he discovered that these scenes were metaphors of the children's lives. Bolton (1979) takes this one stage further by arguing that all socio-dramatic play and drama is a metaphor for the children's lives and that it is the function of the teacher to enable the children to reflect on the significance of their play in order to learn from it.

Imaginative play is fun, but in the midst of the joys of making believe, children may also be preparing for the reality of more effective lives.

Singer and Singer (1990: 152)

To summarize thus far, the value of fantasy play and in particular socio-dramatic play can be seen in its therapeutic, diagnostic and cognitive developmental functions. It helps the child to assimilate information into the existing schema and to begin accommodating new information to prepare for unknown situations. It also places the child's experience of life into a context which can be interpreted through reflection. This is something of a paradox for educators: while cognitive growth is enhanced by fantasy/socio-dramatic play, the very fact of this cognitive development will mean that the child has less need of the fantasy in order to explore simple behaviour patterns and motives through observation of those immediately around them. As Smilansky and Shefatya (1990) suggest, the increasing influence that the child actually has on the world, coupled with the decreased need to test out and explore family roles and the development of reading enabling the child to open up and explore new horizons, means they have less cause to explore these elements through fantasy play! Educators need to move children beyond these immediate horizons so that they can begin to look at the deeper level of 'role' and the greater complexity of life. For this to happen, they need to be challenged.

Socio-dramatic play in action

There is a rationale in both psychodynamic and cognitive developmental theories for the specific benefits to the child engaging in fantasy play. The theoretical advantages of assimilation and role-learning are clear, but how might these be developed in early years context?

The first point to make is that the potential benefits to be gained from fantasy play are very difficult to quantify and we are forced to discuss them in general terms. Singer and Singer (1990) identify three areas where the benefits of fantasy play can be seen:

1 actual spontaneous verbal out-put (around 50 per cent) in socio-dramatic play;
2 a corresponding increase in social interaction;
3 a significant improvement across a range of cognitive skills after 'training' in imaginative play.

Singer and Singer (1990: 151) provide clear evidence to show the increase but are still reluctant to identify more specific factors:

> We cannot avoid the belief that imaginative (fantasy) play serves important purposes in the emergence of the psychologically complex and adaptable person. Individual differences in the frequency and variety of such play seem to be associated not only with richer and more complex language but also with a greater potential for cognitive differentiation, divergent thought, impulse control, self-entertainment, emotional expressiveness and, perhaps, self-awareness.

Smilansky (1968) proposes a range of generalizations relating to the value of socio-dramatic play which, although questioned by Singer (1973), show how socio-dramatic play can influence the creativity, intellectual growth and social skills of the child. These generalized statements do, however, provide a useful basis for what otherwise might be seen as abstract constructs.

Among Smilansky's generalized notions of the benefits of socio-dramatic play are the following points relating to children's potential learning:

1 Creating new combinations out of experiences;
2 Selectivity and intellectual discipline;
3 Discrimination of the central features of a role sequence;
4 Heightened concentration;
5 Enhanced self-awareness and self-control;
6 Self-discipline within the role context (e.g. a child who is playing a special role within a game might inhibit crying because the character in the game would not cry);
7 The acquisition of flexibility and empathy towards others;
8 The development of an intrinsic set of standards;
9 Acquisition of a sense of creativity and capacity to control personal responses;
10 Development of cooperative skills since make-believe games in groups require effective give and take;
11 Awareness of the potential use of the environment for planning and other play situations;
12 Increased sensitivity to alternative role possibilities so that the notion

of father need not be one's own father but may include many kinds of behaviour associated with the broader concept of fathering;

13 Increased capacity for the development of abstract thought by learning first to substitute the image for the overt action and then later a verbal coding for both the action and the image;

14 Heightened capacity for generalisation;

15 A set towards vicarious learning and a greater use of modelling.

(Smilansky in Singer 1973: 224)

It would be wrong to argue that every child engaged in fantasy play will automatically take on these functions: nor will the child *not* engaged in fantasy play fail to have these areas of learning available to them. Rather it is argued that fantasy play provides an opportunity for the child to gain access to opportunities for these identified elements.

Fantasy play and social dimensions

It is important to acknowledge the role that fantasy play has in the development of *morality* (Peters 1981). Children test out their ideas and attitudes in a number of different situations and practise what will happen in real life (both Audrey Curtis, Chapter 2, and Tina Bruce, Chapter 15, take up these points) but within the safety of the enactment. This safety and the feeling of success that can be engendered support the child's learning. The success that results contributes towards building self-confidence and self-esteem. Furthermore, socio-dramatic play aids the development of the social dimension within the child. Such social contact is important to young children and as Blank-Grief (1976) indicates, role play serves to imitate and facilitate the contact: children develop the social skills they will need later in life.

Bruce (1991), Heathcote (1984), Bolton (1979) all show how such role play is based on first-hand experience and how by interacting with it in this way, children are practising what will happen in real life. The child, then working in the 'as if' state, is operating within the confines of the activity 'as if' it were real. Such a strategy allows children to project themselves into activities and situations that cannot be actually reproduced but only represented (Smilansky and Shefatya 1990). There is, however, more than imitation occurring with such activities. Individuals are operating within the reality element. They are working, speaking and acting 'as if' they were those people. It is important that we help children move from the state of simply working out 'what-to-do' to thinking 'as if' they are that person.

Weininger (1988) gives a lovely example of this difference, telling of two boys engaged in fantasy (socio-dramatic) play on the theme of fire-fighters rescuing a cat stuck up a tree. In one the child is getting everything ready, working out what things will be needed, how things should be arranged, and what they might say. This is the lower level 'what if' state. The second child is engaged with the activity and is dealing with the perceived 'reality' (the cat up the tree) 'as if' he were a fireman.

Adult involvement and intervention

So far we have talked in general terms about how young children engage in fantasy play but, to return to the title, one of the most valuable contributions which adults can make to such fantasy play is their own involvement. All too often adults do not take part in socio-dramatic play activities. Those who do tend to restrict their involvement to a very superficial engagement (Hutt *et al.*, 1989). By becoming part of the socio-dramatic play, the adult can capitalize upon the great learning potential offered by this as a way of working. Skilful interaction can stimulate and act as a catalyst (Moyles 1989), help focus the children's attention and set up challenges (Heathcote 1984), all of which enhance and deepen the child's experiences through intervention in fantasy. Adults are able to enhance the benefits of fantasy play and create learning areas appropriate to the needs of the children (Jane Hislam explores several aspects of this in Chapter 3). Adults need to consider Vygotsky's concept of a 'zone of proximal development' (examined more fully by Peter Smith in Chapter 1) in order that the child's greatest achievements are possible, achievements that tomorrow will become their basic level of real action and moral reasoning. What is argued here is that selective interventions on the part of the adults can make the zone of proximal development and the corresponding learning more precise. For as Hutt *et al.*, (1989) indicate, it is not engagement in fantasy play that is significant to the children's development but the active intervention of the adults in that fantasy play. Children need to be encouraged to struggle with ideas, concepts and morality. In such activities failure is unknown since both adults and children are working with fantasy: nothing of the real world has been altered; nothing has changed.

The nature of intervention

There are many ways in which intervention might occur. For example, through the introduction and development of incongruity within the fantasy play we are able to help the children struggle with the elements that do not appear to fit and look for reasons behind the obvious. The children meet a police officer (the teacher in that role) but the police officer is crying (the element of incongruity, as police officers are not supposed to cry). The police officer is frightened of the dark and now has to work at night. The children have to talk, discuss, persuade and draw upon their own experiences of the dark in order to help the police officer. All these skills are engaged in at a level well above what might normally be expected from the children. Yet once they have worked through the problems and functioned at this higher level, such strategies will become part of their everyday behaviour.

Interventions allow for the development of structure within the children's socio-dramatic play. As with most forms of play, socio-dramatic play has a structure and rules but, as Garvey (1976) points out, these are often subsumed as part of the action. At first glance this structure is not apparent, but it is there nevertheless. Social play needs rules that we all understand in order for the interaction to take place. The adult becoming part of the play can facilitate the implementation of the rules as well as act as a behavioural model for the children to copy. Garvey (1976) further points out that in order to play we must understand what is *not* play. Part of this is helping the children differentiate between fantasy and reality. It is useful to identify clearly for the children when socio-dramatic play is taking place. This can be done very effectively by the adult working with the children saying, 'We are going to make up a story,' or that, 'We are going to make up a play.' In this way the children are clear about the expectations of the activity and also have a much clearer idea of when they are, and are not, involved in the fantasy. It is equally important for the adult to make it really clear when the socio-dramatic is over. This is merely the formalization of what children do for themselves. Their play will begin with, 'Let's pretend . . .' and will terminate when either the rules are broken or the children move away from the activity with, 'I'm not playing any more!' (Garvey 1976: 176)

Any episode of socio-dramatic play entails the exercises of shared imagination and the shared development of the theme of that particular episode. Young children are naturally egocentric and find it difficult to share. By selective interventions the able adult can monitor the negotiation of the children's ideas and act as a facilitator. They can help the children remain consistent within their role and so aid the development of the story. One of the great strengths of this way of working is that, through the fiction, a great many learning areas can be explored. Problems can be set up which children can resolve within the story. The adult working within the fiction is able to set the problems and then keep the children on task, so making them confront the challenges. For example, in the children's story they have to get past the Queen who guards the gate and into the castle. By having to persuade the Queen to let them into the castle the children are employing and extending social skills. Their preferred solution may well have been to employ magic but such a solution would have merely avoided the social learning potential generated.

Intervention in socio-dramatic play enables the participating adult to keep the activity going by motivating the children to persist. While some children engage in such play readily, others need to be guided and encouraged to play a full part. The adult can help to re-focus the story in order to bring the group together and generate excitement by introducing tension into the story. These are both essential to the development of socio-dramatic play but difficult for young children to attain for themselves. Working in a nursery school with a group of 18 children, I was asked to make up a drama on the theme of building. The children wanted to make up a story about building a house for the people in a book which had been read to them. After sorting out what had to be done, the work started. It was not long before the children began to lose concentration in the 'building' as there was little to hold their interest. In dramatic terms there was little or no *tension*. It was at this point that intervention was needed. I then pretended to receive a phone call from the boss who was going to come round and check up on our work. We would have to make sure that the house had been put together properly. Immediately the children were drawn back into the fantasy play and found a renewed vigour and purpose, created by the injection of tension and the tension for evaluation. Equally effective could have been completing a given task in a set time (for example, 'We've got to build the hut before night comes,'), meeting a challenge, ('Do you think you could help me put out this fire?'), solving a problem, ('What food should we give the animals now the snow's here?') or posing a dilemma for the children to work out, ('But if we take the curing crystal how will the people who own it feel?') These inputs into socio-dramatic play become the subtle tools of the adult working with children. Within the play, the adult is able to enrich and deepen the play and open up new learning areas for the children. They are able to intervene and structure the learning from within, without significantly reducing the children's ownership, a strategy Neelands (1984) defines as the 'subtle tongue' of the teacher.

It is important to remember that, although the adult can guide and to some extent shape the socio-dramatic play, essentially the play and action must be that of the children. *Their* ideas must be used. The words spoken must be *their* words expressing *their* thoughts. It may perhaps be that the adult simply joins in an existing 'game' with the children without the intention of simply being in the group but rather of moving the children's learning on, placing obstacles in the way of their story so that, by overcoming these obstacles, learning opportunities are created. A development of this is to construct the story with the children. 'What shall we make up a story about today?' Feeding from the children's ideas, both children and adult construct the fantasy. The adult's role is again that of facilitator, stretching and extending the children while maintaining interest and excitement. This adult participation legitimizes the play and encourages the children to see what they are doing as something valuable.

Such adult participation or intervention also allows for the structuring of learning areas for the children through the selection of themes or stimulus areas (Moyles 1989). By setting up post offices and fantasy realms, the children are involved with maths, language, social skills, manipulative skills and so on. If such pretend areas become a garage or a desert island, then a new set of learning potentials are created. By selecting appropriate pretend corners for the children's needs, the adults can then give access to appropriate areas of learning. If they then also interact with the children, they can enrich, deepen and re-focus the socio-dramatic play from within the story, setting up challenges and obstacles to be overcome.

Adults need also to interact with children. Left to themselves, children may operate within the socio-dramatic play at a superficial level. Enriched learning comes about when the adult is working in the story alongside the children (Smilansky and Shefatya 1990).

Summary

Fantasy play is important in the cognitive, social and emotional development of the young child. It progresses from object play to dramatic play and finally to socio-dramatic play. Socio-dramatic play offers great learning potential for those working with young children. Structuring the play enables us to extend and enhance children's learning. Through the socio-dramatic play, educators are able to create a situation and generate motivation which will encourage the children to behave and function at a cognitive level beyond their norm. This is most effective when done through sympathetic intervention by adults and in particular where the adult intervention is interactive. Educators within the socio-dramatic play situation can stimulate, motivate and facilitate the play, encouraging the children to work at a deeper level than they would if left to their own devices. Not only does the adult in role provide the children with a model of behaviour but the role can be altered to bring a galaxy of 'people', problems, challenges and so on, into the play.

Only when educators acknowledge and recognize the importance of their role in children's fantasy play, will they feel able to intervene and begin to develop its true potential.

8 Making play work in the classroom

Peter Heaslip

The publication of the Rumbold Report reflected an increasing concern with the quality of provision for young children – a concern felt by parents and teachers alike. With the introduction of the National Curriculum, the media has been swift to capitalize on this concern and to adopt its own criteria for determining quality. Too often these criteria have been associated with test scores and achievements in core subjects. Parents have been influenced by strong and often hostile media coverage and this has brought considerable pressure on schools to produce 'results'. The quality of a school is now increasingly being evaluated by parents through inappropriate accountability systems. Teachers are reluctantly finding themselves caught up in 'media hype', and many feel that uninformed public pressure is forcing them to reconsider their methods and decision-making in the classroom.

The difficulty is that a learning programme can be assessed in many ways. Lilian Katz (1992) has indicated several approaches to quality assessment, suggesting that educators must accept only a model which is appropriate to the task. Her two main perspectives are:

1 The *top-down* perspective, which takes into account considerations such as the ratio of adults to children, the suitability of staff, the quality and safety of the resources and environment;
2 The *bottom-up* perspective which uses as its basis for assessment, 'What does it feel like to be a child in this environment?'

In this chapter, I shall argue that, when considering the quality of play provision in the classroom, it is essential that staff use a bottom-up model for at least some of their decisions about play provision, and consider the provision from the perspective of the real 'client' – the child!

The 'basics' for young children – what are they?

At a time when there is such a strong move to return to 'basics', educators must ask themselves, 'What are *the basics* for a young child?' To do this we must be clear about our own definition of education. Too often practitioners experience difficulty in stating this, but a clear understanding of educational beliefs will help determine what is 'basic' for young children. Being co-partners with the parents as custodians of the child's education, what are the absolute educational priorities which must be at the forefront of practice for professionals? Experience suggests that most early years practitioners believe that there are at least two basic essentials associated with their educational intentions with young children and these remain paramount. They are: a child's belief in itself, a positive self-image, and a respect for the individuality of each person. These two beliefs are considered fundamental by most early years practitioners and, as such, must be basic. The 'three Rs' are, of course, important in the educational process but they are *not* necessarily basic. When educators are clear about their educational fundamentals, their task is then to ensure that, as far as possible, these fundamentals are achieved. The programme in operation in classrooms should then support basic beliefs.

The learning environment and the place of play

If the bottom-up model is adopted, and the programme is considered from the child's point of view, serious questions must be asked about practices in many early years settings. To what extent is the curriculum on offer promoting a positive self-image in the child? How does the programme enable children to support the esteem of others and allow each child to recognize not only his or her individuality and have it respected and enhanced, but also contribute towards this in others?

When these questions are asked, a *delivery style* in the early years classroom appears to be singularly unsuitable. To provide a learning environment in which children's developmental needs can be met, and in which active learning can take place, play seems the natural and most appropriate learning medium. But too seldom are practitioners able to counter the charge that play is the time-wasting by-product of the lazy adult! Sadly, this is the perception which a large section of the public holds. 'Play is fun, but children can do that at home.' (Whether they now can is in serious doubt, as David Brown argues in Chapter 4.) Children are sent to school to learn!

Perhaps part of the fault lies with the teachers of young children. For too long they have just 'got on' with the task of educating children, busy with the demands of the task and not heeding or facing the criticism of their child-centred, active learning approaches. The time has now come, indeed it may be almost too late, for teachers to tackle the critics head on and become advocates for an early childhood education which puts children and their developmental needs at the very centre of the debate (as Angela Anning forcibly argues in Chapter 5). Professionals must have conviction in their methods, rigour in their approaches and eloquence in the exposition of high quality practice (see Chris Pascal and Tony Bertram, Chapter 13).

Teacher-training institutions have not necessarily given students the strongest support for this demanding role. They, too, have felt the pressures of the National Curriculum, and the emphasis on initial training courses has been on core subjects at the expense of a broad and balanced curriculum. Too few courses have given a strong emphasis to child development or developmentally appropriate practices, and it has often been left to busy practitioners to try to draw from their own practice its relationship to sound theory.

The Plowden Committee (DES 1967: 193) established a sound rationale for thinking about play and its role in children's learning:

> Adults who criticise teachers for allowing children to play are unaware that play is the principal means of learning in early childhood. It is the way through which children reconcile their inner lives with external reality. In play, children gradually develop concepts of causal relationships, the power to discriminate, to make judgements, to analyse and synthesise, to imagine and to formulate. Children become absorbed in their play and the satisfaction of bringing it to a satisfactory conclusion fixes habits of concentration which can be transferred to other learning.

These words are as relevant now as they were in 1967, but restating them is insufficient. Professionals need to be able to justify through their *practices*, how play is the supreme way through which young children learn, and then, just as importantly, be able to articulate this to others – parents, governors and colleagues. This is not a simple task, for the very nature of play itself is complicated, multifaceted and varied in its function (Pelligrini 1987). If, however, we believe that the most important gift we can bestow upon a child is a belief in itself, a positive self-image and a high self-esteem, it then becomes easier not only to see, but also to explain how high quality play can foster this.

Play empowers children with control of the activity in which they are involved. In an educational system which seems progressively to remove control and decision-making from children (and adults!) and replace it with obedience at the best, and subservience at the worst, the children, through play, can pace themselves appropriately, make choices and develop self-confidence. Through play, children can try and try again until they succeed or decide when to elicit help, when to give up, or when to modify plans and intentions without feeling that these attempts have been a failure. Children, through play, are unravelling the world at their own pace, savouring new experiences as they unfold, reconstructing and revising them. Essentially the child is in control. This active exploration, this involvement and the sense of ownership of the activity and experience enables the child to feel sustained and satisfied. Observations of children engrossed in exploratory play show the extent to which their sense of wonder is being sustained. When ownership of the activity is removed from the child, this valued sense of wonder and enquiry often disappears too.

All play, however, is not of equal value. A child in home corner, dressed in a policeman's helmet can, through make-believe play, be contributing change substantially to personal and social development (as Jane Hislam suggests in Chapter 3). Equally the child can be a serious threat to law and order!

The adult's role

Far too often the key importance of the adult in enabling and promoting developmental play has been neglected (as Neil Kitson has suggested in the previous chapter). The adult's role is neither passive nor active. It should be proactive. Margaret Clark (1988: 277), having evaluated the research evidence regarding the education of children under five, states that, although a free-play setting has potential for stimulating learning in young children, if it is to be an effective learning environment, it must be carefully structured, with the adults playing a crucial role in its organization by selective intervention with the children in their play (a point made strongly by all contributors to this book but particularly by Neil Kitson in the previous chapter).

As others in this book have also emphasized, there is scope for adults to consider Vygotsky's (1978) 'zone of proximal development'. However, the busy early years practitioners face a dilemma. The number of children in the class may be too large for optimum interaction with children and the timing and style of intervention is critical. If the intervention is too early or too directed, it destroys the discovery. If it is too late, unnecessary repetition and boredom can result and valuable opportunities for learning and development can be squandered. Pascal and Gamage (1992: 8) describe the interactive teacher as a matchmaker between the child and the materials:

> it means that the teacher must have a solid understanding of both the intellectual demands of the materials and the cognitive abilities of the children. Brierley, talking of intervention at the right time, says that Christian Schiller once wrote of a headmaster who said, 'I always say to teachers, leave the children alone until they need help: but remember that they won't come and tell you when that moment comes. To seize that moment is the art of teaching young children.'

The question which practitioners *must* ask themselves is, 'Will intervention enhance or devalue the child's play?'

So often the practitioner, restricted for time, makes an intervention
which contributes nothing and may even devalue the activity in which
the children are involved. Consider the following scenario:

> Two four-year-olds, Nadia and Jason, have been playing with large
> blocks and have built a tall construction when the teacher inter-
> venes. Almost without thinking the teacher comments, 'That's a
> great building you have there. I wonder if it is taller than you are,
> Nadia.' Nadia, used to this sort of question, immediately stands
> beside the blocks while Jason steps back a pace to await the next
> question. He glances at Nadia and the construction and stoops to
> pick up another block which he places on the top so that the
> heights are now equal. The teacher's voice, high in modulation,
> but low in credibility then asks, 'How can we tell if they are the
> same height?' Jason looks for a stick or ruler to lay across the
> blocks and Nadia's head so that the teacher can see if it is level.
> 'Yes,' the teacher continues, 'you have made them the same height.
> Well done!' And she moves on to intervene in another group
> activity. Meanwhile Nadia and Jason continue with their block-
> play construction of a submarine. They had just been about to
> submerge it when the teacher had asked Nadia to measure her
> height against, what to them, was the conning tower. Who but a
> teacher would ask you to measure your height against the conning
> tower of a submarine as it was about to go under?

The teacher's intervention had neither sustained nor promoted the
activity. It had, in effect, served to devalue the children's play – the
submarine had only been of use as a measuring instrument. A teacher's
intervention in play needs to be based on close observation, as Vicky
Hurst suggests in Chapter 14. If the teacher had taken just a few moments to observe and listen to the children's dialogue as they were
involved in their block play, appropriate supportive language could have
been fed in and the activity could have been enhanced and extended.
The children would have been encouraged to feel that their play was
valued, understood and appreciated by the adult and been motivated to
continue and extend their thinking.

Through their play, children are not only learning how to learn; they
are learning about themselves. It is necessary to have high but realistic
expectations of children, and to be available to provide support when
the child falls short so that failure is seen as a positive learning experience. Practitioners need to have considered carefully how they plan to
assist children to have high expectations but to be realistic when these
cannot be achieved. Parents, too, need to see 'mistakes' in a positive
way (Heaslip *et al.*, 1992: 30). Children of course, thrive on success, but
the play environment should be sufficiently secure that the child feels

encouraged to try without being assured of immediate success. Adult remarks sometimes have a hollow ring to them. Mary Jane Drummond speaks of the, 'That's lovely dear! Put it on the piano,' syndrome. Children know only too well when the complimentary remark is little more than a platitude from a busy adult. Mark Twain once said that he could live for three weeks on a single compliment, but that compliment must not only be *made*, it must be *meant*, and it must be *seen* to be meant! Most early years practitioners harbour uneasy feelings of *deja être* when they hear Joyce Grenfell monologues (Grenfell 1977: 17). There is a familiar ring to what she describes as:

> putting on a special voice that you would not use to talk to people of your own size. Talking to three-to-five-year-olds . . . is still what it always was: bright, bluffingly calm, cheerful, encouraging and occasionally desperate.

Educators need to be aware that sincerity still rings through in their dialogues with children, no matter what the pressures of the moment or the stereotypical role in which they may feel placed.

Children's choices

The practitioner has control over much of the physical resources from which children may choose for their play. Too often children are daunted by the huge differences between what they have experienced at home and what they are faced with at nursery or school. So there must be a range of resources which enable real choice. Children need to make choices, but often they need guidance in their choice-making.

As adults, an occasion when we are often at our most indecisive is when we are confronted with the sweet trolley when we are out for a meal. The wider the range of desserts on offer and the more delightful they are, the more difficult becomes the choice! Too often we try to get others at the table to make the selection first and then follow their choice. Or again make a choice and immediately regret it. How much easier it would be if the decision had to be made from a choice of three desserts, or if we had been suggested recommendations, or had benefited from more experience of such a wide choice!

For children, too, the range of exciting choices open to them is often too great, and it is little wonder that some new entrants will flit from one activity to another, sampling many but not continuing with any. Just as many parents quietly withdraw toys in the home when a child has too many, bringing them out again at a later stage, practitioners often do the same by not making available to the children all the resources at all times. Adults can aid and support by talking through choices with children, perhaps, at times, even making suggestions – it is amazing how much easier it is for many children to make a choice when there is supportive body contact!

If children are to develop their independence they need not only to increase the scope and extent of their decision-making but also to reflect upon their choices. Those who have used a High/Scope or similar reflective programmes know how productive the review procedure can be in making the choices more discriminate.

The choices which children make need to be *real* choices. It is no choice for me if, on a Saturday morning, my spouse asks me, 'Well, do you want to wash the car, mow the lawn, mend the light switch, vacuum the house, or go to the supermarket?' when I have other clear options and intentions in my *own* mind. So often, to encourage children to make anticipated choices, the practitioner uses 'teacher talk', such as, 'Would you like to paint a picture now?' which the child knows really means, 'You *will* paint a picture, and *now*!'

Practitioners need to look at the learning environment from the child's perspective, asking themselves:

• What are the choices available that I would wish for if I was a child in this room?
• What will the choices on offer do to foster a positive self-image?
• Is the range and scope sufficient to cater for the developmental needs of each child in the room?
• Are the choices mundane and occupational, or are they exciting, stimulating, attractive and challenging?
• In what ways can the choices build on the experiences children bring with them, yet extend these experiences to open new horizons?
• Where is the potential for wonder, awe, contemplation, absorption and reflection?

If these questions are satisfactorily answered, real choice for children is likely to exist.

To allow children to make choices, the resources which children are likely to require need to be available to them without lengthy queueing for seeking approval or permission for access (Moyles 1992 and 1993). Variety is needed too. A selection of materials which not only encourage individuality, but allow children to match the resource exactly to the task in mind, should be available.

Children need to be able to make refined choices. If they plan to glue lentils to cardboard, more than one type of adhesive needs to be on offer. Different glues have different properties and the child needs to be able to choose the glue which will be satisfactory for the task. If the wrong choice is made, there should be opportunities for reflection on the choice with a supportive adult or peer.

Regulations can often restrict effective choice-making. In many class-rooms the home corner has a restriction placed on it of the number of children who may use it. From experience, four often seems to be the prescribed number in many settings. If in their make-believe play the children have adopted the roles of mother, father, baby and sister, the restrictions mean that it becomes impossible for grandma and grandpa to visit too. If the space in the home corner is restricted, surely it would be better for children to decide that? 'It's too crowded in here,' says grandad, 'I'm taking the baby out for a walk. Is anyone coming with me?' Deciding for themselves that effective socio-dramatic play is not possible when six children are in the home corner is educationally more purposeful than just obeying a classroom regulation or tradition.

A close examination of areas of the room will show that very often tight rules exist, and these may not necessarily have been determined by reasoned consideration of the teacher or another adult. Children often make their own rules – ones which work to their own personal advantage. The home corner can so easily represent a matriarchal order with a dominant girl determining the rules and expecting others to obey. Other areas of the room can be dominated by other children laying down their own rules in a similar way, not always to the advantage of all, and adult intervention is necessary to ensure equality of opportunity and some social justice.

Gender and cultural differences

The provision of resources which is not culturally biased and which breaks down stereotypes is a major consideration for those responsible for play activities (Jane Hislam explores this in some depth in Chapter 3). The transition from known and familiar objects and materials to those which allow the child to experience the richness of the multicultural society in which we live starts with our youngest children. Often this responsibility falls heavily upon the teacher who has to face up to stereotypical attitudes from some parents.

Entrenched attitudes to race, often based on ignorance and prejudice, are so often passed on to even the youngest children that, in the early years setting, practitioners need to seek resources, both human and physical, which will break down these views. Fantasy and socio-dramatic play, supported by appropriate materials and with a sensitive and positive attitude to anti-racism from the adult, can contribute greatly, especially in regions where children do not have the benefit of experiencing first-hand the richness that each can gain from the other.

There was a time when early years teachers steered clear of what was called 'structured play'. There was a connotation about it which suggested that it removed ownership of the play from the children, with the adult dominating and dictating what the children did. Structuring the play provision, or whatever we choose to call adult intervention, does not mean determining what and how the children will play. Rather it means that the adult has to take on the responsibility of enabling and promoting situations which will allow things to happen – things which are developmentally and socially appropriate not only for the children collectively, but for each child individually. The deployment of staff, the layout of the room, the composition of children in the group, a thorough knowledge of each child – all these must be considerations in creating a learning environment in which development and learning is fostered, rather than the curriculum 'delivered' through a top-down process.

Staff need to be aware of the purpose behind their provision. They need to ask themselves what settings children need which allow socialization, exploration, experimentation, successful interaction, competence with others and which allow children to feel wonder, a growing and increasing confidence in their own ability, to develop a positive self-image and a respect for the individuality of others. Occupational play in which the child is a passive recipient of predetermined activities only leads to the child learning that you get along best if you do not challenge the system.

Young children are exceedingly good guests. There are a few exceptions to this and those who are become notorious, but in general children under seven want more than anything, to please. Girls, I believe, are conditioned earlier than boys, to be good guests. Young children tend to accept with resignation and without resentment or outward protest what is offered, whether it is appropriate for them or not. They very quickly learn that it is easier, and to their ultimate advantage, to become 'teacher-pleasers' than to hold out for what they really need or want and, in their minds of wonder, for what they yearn. This can so easily lead practitioners into believing that the programme on offer is suitable as children will most likely seem 'happy enough'. Only detailed observation of children as individuals and collectively, their situations, and of the adults themselves, will indicate the real matching of the curriculum to the children's needs.

Observing children at play

Part 4 of this book deals specifically with observation and assessment, but it needs restating that to be effective in our knowledge of what the children are doing, to determine the form of intervention which is necessary and to be clear exactly what the adult role should be, directed observation, monitoring, recording and assessment is necessary.

Even after careful observation the teacher can still be unsure about the exact timing and form of intervention. Being aware that exploration is an essential element in play and knowing that, if there is insufficient exploration children fail to grasp and refine concepts, but also having an awareness that continued exploration can lead to purposeless, repetitive occupation or tedious boredom, the adult has to decide when to intervene and in what manner. What is right on one occasion with one child is entirely inappropriate with another child, or even the same child at another time. A child who is insecure or distressed may need a long time in repetitive and apparently purposeless activity with materials such as sand, water or clay. The child may not be able to face the risk of an activity with an end result, or even the companionship of associative play. Another child in a similar situation may find comfort in a simple jigsaw which is completed, turned out and done again many times. It is only the professional's experience and detailed knowledge of children, gained through observation and links with home, that can guide the many difficult decisions about the form support and intervention should take.

There are times when the most appropriate action is to stand back and allow the child to take initiatives. Children need space and time for learning to take place. My experience with children, and particularly as I watched my own children growing up, helped me to realize that I taught them very little (Holt 1991); instead I made provision for them to learn. This often meant being extremely patient and forcing myself to take a back seat in the learning process. It is as well for teachers to reflect that some adults need children more than children need the adults!

While classrooms full of active children involved in their play tend to be lively, busy and often noisy places, there needs to be a place where a child can be quiet. Just as most adults need a time and a place where they can get away from the bustle and noise of the world, children too need a place in which they can escape from the 'busyness' of an early years classroom. Most classes have bean-bags or comfortable chairs – often associated with the book corner. Although these can often allow for a relaxed posture, children are sometimes unable to escape from the busy classroom noise. The quiet times, which may be timetabled during the day, may not meet the needs of individual children, and staff need to look at outdoor as well as indoor provision to try to provide a place of quiet and solace available at times of need.

Conclusion

At a time when the demands of the media for accelerated progression through the three Rs, and with the knowledge that play in many homes is being replaced by television watching, there is a genuine fear that children may be losing their entitlement to childhood (Suransky 1982). The school has an increasing responsibility to ensure that they are not deprived of the opportunities for discovering about themselves and their world, but are given their right to learning in a way which is appropriate to them – through their play.

Recently, I observed in a reception class where I had heard that the quality of play was good. At the end of the day a mother of a four-year-old commented, 'What he has been doing in this class with his teacher is wonderful. He's learnt so much and can do so much. It has made me feel that my child is special – that he is the most important person in the school, but when I talk to other mothers, each of them feels the same!' What a commendation. What better start could a child have to its school education? Using Katz' *bottom-up model*, this was a classroom with quality provision, where play obviously worked – for everyone!

Part 3
Play and the early years curriculum

Plate 10   Children readily undertake literate behaviour if we provide the right materials and opportunities

Plate 11 *The nature of the relationship between materials-based play and three dimensional activities in art and design is important*

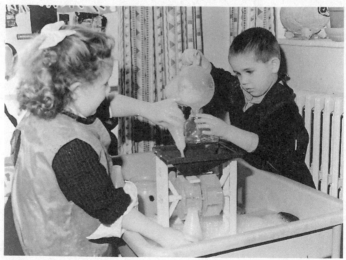

Plate 12 *What is inside those bubbles?*

Play, literacy and the role of the teacher

Nigel Hall

Most teachers of Key Stage 1 children will now be familiar with the notion of play and explicit literacy practices being linked in the classroom. The programmes of study for reading and writing both suggest that part of children's experience of literacy should be embedded in play activities. There is also a recognition of the importance of the print environment in such play. An example from the current Programmes of Study for Reading will suffice:

> Activities should ensure that pupils . . . read in the context of role-play and dramatic play, e.g. *in the home corner, class shop, or other dramatic play setting such as a café, hospital or post office. Such reading might include a menu, a sign on a door, a label on a packet, or a sign above the counter.*
>
> (DES 1990: 29 – my italics)

Such a claim represents a recent innovation. Eight years ago I had never seen a classroom which intentionally, and systematically, incorporated explicit literacy experiences within socio-dramatic play settings. Indeed, I have been informed so many times by people who were trained to work with nursery children that they were told not to have print in their classrooms because it would confuse the children. One wonders how children managed to survive a walk down any British high street?

The arguments for the embedding of literacy and play are fairly clear (for further exposition see Hall, in press). In this chapter, I shall briefly explore how play and English work can have mutual benefits for children and adults in early years contexts and, in particular, in relation to the pretend areas.

Literacy in play

Children need no encouragement to play. Within minutes of being presented with 'props', they are creating detailed and sustained play activities. In these activities they recreate the world they experience outside and inside school: they cook, clean and polish; they plan, travel and explore; they fall ill, are hospitalized and recover; they teach, scold and punish, they fall in love, get married and rear children. (Several writers in this book give ample evidence of this.) There is hardly any area of life that cannot be found in children's play. Educators encourage this by providing support in the form of resources: dressing-up clothes, cups, saucers, beds, cookers, cupboards, tables and many more props. Practitioners encourage experience-related play except, it seems, where literacy is concerned because, until recently, it has been seldom that these play areas could be seen to contain the resource of print. However, in real life all these world-related situations usually have literacy embedded in them somewhere.

Play, based upon real life experiences, offers a number of valuable opportunities for children to experiment explicitly with, and use, literacy in many different, but valid, ways:

It enables children to experience a wide range of different situations within which literacy is appropriately embedded

There are very few episodes in life which have no print associated with them. By providing relevant and associated print within play settings, children are able to experience literacy in meaningful and purposeful ways. Such provision allows children to work with literacy in contextually appropriate settings.

It enables children to have holistic experiences of literacy

Within realistic play settings, literacy is not fragmented by artificial instructional processes. Literacy is used for whatever is appropriate in the play: going shopping, having a meal in a restaurant, going on a train journey, visiting a hospital and so on. The literacy occurs because it is needed in the context of the play, not because instruction demands it.

It enables children to control the ways in which literacy is used and experienced

Within play, it is the children who determine how literacy is used. It is inevitable that they will often use it in ways which are unconventional. However, equally often they will reveal that they have a wide understanding of the different uses of literacy, where certain forms of literacy are appropriate and when they are needed. When the children make the choices, learning becomes a much more powerful activity.

*It enables children to demonstrate what they know rather than
what they can copy*

When literacy is used for real, people switch between the modes of
reading and writing or use them together. We do not set out in advance
to use either reading or writing. It is our perception of the situation
which structures our response. Equally, in literacy-related play it is the
pretend event which determines the nature of the literate response. It
is not because a page in a work-book arbitrarily chooses to focus on
either reading or writing.

It enables children to cooperate in learning about literacy

In play, children interact closely in order to achieve more satisfying play.
When children do this it opens up so many opportunities for cooperative
learning. Children can often be more successful in helping other children learn than can professionals. Children bring to play different experiences and knowledge and in the course of play these are shared.
When one child demonstrates a novel aspect of literacy, it is instantly
available to the others in the play. In this way the meanings of literacy
are negotiated by the members of the group at play.

An example: the literate home corner

Some time ago, I worked with some educators of four-year-old children
to turn their non-literate home corner into a literate home corner. This
area of the classroom already contained a 'toy' cooker, a telephone,
tables and chairs, and several other pieces of equipment associated with
the notion of 'home'. The area also had a desk with paper, envelopes
and writing utensils. Newspapers and letters were pushed through the
door before each session. In addition, diaries, planners, telephone direc-
tories, books, catalogues and other print material were placed in strategic
places.

It was felt important that a wide range of print-related resources were
provided, particularly writing utensils – if the children had any sense of
appropriateness they might fail to display some literacy behaviours if
given only crayons or pencils; after all who writes letters with crayons!

The first comment of the children upon entering the home corner was
'real things!' They then demonstrated clearly that they not only recognized
the items as 'real things' but knew quite a lot about how to use them
appropriately and effectively. When faced with reading matter and
writing utensils, and space and time in which to write and read, the
children moved straight into literate behaviour. They used writing, without any hesitation, in a whole range of ways – they simply 'set to' and
wrote. The children also incorporated the reading items into their play.
Sometimes the items were absorbed within other play and sometimes
the reading items provoked certain types of play. On occasions the children

seemed to be exploring the materials in very personal, non-play ways. In one event a young boy was told by one of the girls, involved in some family play, to read the newspaper. There then followed a five minute solo engagement (the girl had gone away) in which the boy manipulated and manoeuvred the paper until he had sorted it round to the correct orientation and then he sat and gave it the most intense scrutiny. It seems that he was not only exploring the orientation of the newspaper but exploring the role of being a newspaper reader (something children show us over and over again in their play as Tina Bruce emphasized in Chapter 15).

If commitment can be measured, even crudely, by the number of engagements, their variety, intensity and duration, then these three- and four-year-old children were very committed to the idea of using, and enjoying using, print, and were committed to the creation of meaning-laden marks.

Within a single morning session the children created a restaurant and a French café (and used various accents to compliment the play). The children later created a bank and ended up with a session at McDonalds. These play sessions involved different children at different times. Within these play sessions the children involved showed menus, took orders, read packets and wrote on memo boards. The use of any of these literate behaviours was not as a single event but as an incorporated part of the more general context of the play. Thus the print-related behaviour was always used appropriately within the context of the play situation being generated.

There were many events associated with letter writing. This was often accompanied by the reading of letters or acting out postperson roles. They were often delivered within the classroom. In one event the child wrote a letter which he said was to tell people about work. The boy put the letter in an envelope, took it to someone else, opened it and said, 'It tells you to go to work and that you must put a tie on.' These children still had many things to learn about print but it was nevertheless clear that they had some knowledge of a range of its purposes.

These children, when given the appropriate resources, wrote constantly. They filled several hundred sheets of paper, envelopes, and pages in diaries, books and cards. They also wrote on calendars, memo pads in the air, on notice boards and on telephone pads.

The children almost always used the correct terminology. They used 'draw' when they wanted to draw a picture, and 'write' when they wanted to write messages of any kind (and by message is meant any intended meaning-conveying marks). There did not appear to be any confusion between the two activities. It is probably the case that when children have access to an appropriate context, their use of the terminology is invariably correct.

The children displayed a very wide range of mark-making intended as writing. It was clear that the experience of the children in using print was quite varied. For some children the merest of lines or squiggles was sufficient to count as writing, whereas for others, there were intricate mixes of learned elements and invented elements. The children in this class were exploring the use of written language to establish ownership and identity, to build relationships, to remember or recall events, to request information, to record information, to fantasize or pretend, and to declare. They were not waiting for formal schooling to use literacy but they had been waiting for the opportunity to display their use of it.

In the play situation, these young children were offered a chance to use literacy in valid, purposeful and appropriate ways in a realistic setting: they were able to cooperate with each other, they were able to demonstrate a wide range of understandings about literacy and were given the chance to control the ways in which they used their knowledge and skills. In return, the adults were offered the chance to see, in detail, what the children knew about the 'what', 'why', 'when', 'where', and 'how' of literacy.

Teacher intervention and literary play

In the above example the teacher seems invisible. The intervention of the teacher was restricted to setting up the print-rich environment. On the whole this is how socio-dramatic play seems be organized in classrooms. The environment is set up by the teacher or in conjunction with the children. The children then play in that environment, doing whatever they wish to do. There appears to be a reluctance on the part of teachers in Britain to do more than keep an eye on the 'behaviour' of the children during play (as Peter Heaslip points outs in Chapter 8). The prevailing orthodoxy appears to suggest that teachers should stay away from play: it belongs to the children.

It is certainly the case that play can provide some of childhood's most intense experiences, and that children's self-initiated play can be a wonderful vehicle for exploring many different aspects of a child's world. However, there is a tendency to forget that most of the scenarios played out by children are not created out of nothing. It is life, and the experiences it provides, which offer children the material they transform and own in their play. Prior to schooling, these experiences are usually provided both deliberately and incidentally by caregivers. Once in school, it is practitioners who need to continue to provide experiences which extend children's understanding of the world; indeed that is to a large extent the function of schooling. Children continue to have experiences *outside* school, but these are now supplemented by substantial experience *within* school.

At any level, socio-dramatic play occurs in classrooms because of adult intervention (see Neil Kitson's exploration of this in Chapter 7). At one level, adults simply provide space, time and basic resources. In pretend areas children have the greatest freedom to create their own narratives. Another level of intervention is to structure and guide the resources so that there is often a particular direction to the play. This direction (or structure) does not have to be towards literacy for overt use of literacy to occur.

In one school (see Strahan 1992) several classes were involved in setting up a play railway station. The choice of a station for a socio-dramatic play area was that of the teachers. It was to be in a space that could be shared by a number of classes. Seven classes, with children aged from three to seven, were taken to visit a major train-station complex. The purpose was to give the children a general 'flavour' of the station, specific information about certain aspects of station life, and provide an opportunity to travel on a train.

After the visit the children held conferences and discussions, as well as looking at photographs and books. They identified the elements needed in their station. Among them were signs for newsagents, public phones, a post office and the trains. They decided they needed tickets and time-tables. On their own, or with help, the children made clocks, directional signs, timetables, posters, telephone kiosks, and provided newspapers, magazines, tickets and writing utensils. Literacy was not the aim of the play. Despite all this literacy-related activity the point of the area was to play trains; that is what the children did. But, of course, in playing at trains they used the signs, tickets and materials in ways which showed they had some understanding of the context of use and how to use the items.

The observational notes made by one of the teachers captures the flavour of the children's literacy behaviours and demonstrates some of the ways in which literacy-related play occurred:

> I was drawn into the play only once by a child phoning me from the station to ask me to look at the timetable in the travel centre.

> While this conversation was taking place three other children were in the ticket office. No teacher was present. They counted money accurately, used the timetable to tell each other the times of trains and sorted out boxes of tickets into those for 'Manchester' stations and those for 'going to other places'.

> With every class there was evidence of children using print for information and also of children wanting and using writing materials both on the train and in the station.

> A child was standing in the ticket collector's kiosk. She was using paper and a pen found at the post office to conduct a survey of how many times she clipped people's tickets. She began by writing names down every time they came through but then decided by herself that it would be easier to put a tick besides the name after the first occasion (see Figure 9.1).

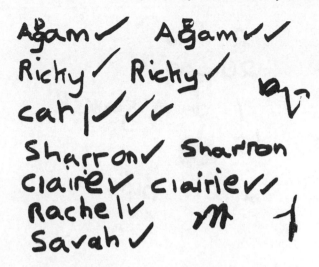

Figure 9.1

In both the examples so far the intervention was mainly concerned with establishing the area and general direction. However, quite positive things can emerge when adults intervene sensitively as participants in the play.

A student teacher, Lisa Quinn, set up a play café in her Year 2 classroom. Her notes record an interesting incident:

> One skill which I introduced by becoming directly involved in the children's role-playing was 'short-hand'. This happened when I took the role of waitress. While in role, I observed that Stacey, who was in the role of receptionist, was writing in long-hand the take-out orders that people phoned through. Noticing how long it took her to write down a take-away order, I showed her an order that I had written in short-hand. I had used a mixture of simple pictures and initial letters of words. I asked her if she could work out what I meant by such things as 'sn soup', 'cup t' and 'tof a' (snake soup, a cup of tea and a toffee apple). She said that this was easy and was able to decode my 'short-hand' very quickly. 'Perhaps you might like to have a go at using your own short-hand when taking orders over the phone,' I suggested. Next time I took an order from Stacey she had used her own short-hand (see Figure 9.2).

Before long the idea of short-hand was incorporated into the role play. Those who knew how to do it were soon instructing others during the course of the play. The following example was typical:

P: What would you like to eat?
D: I would like two cups of tea . . . and soup. Yes, two onion soups.

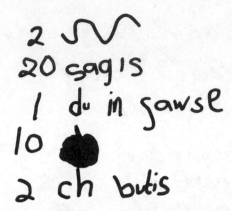

Figure 9.2

P: Let me see that a minute. (tries to grab the menu)
D: Paul, I'm reading it. You get another.
P: I need that one 'cause I need 'onion soups' so I can write it down . . . let me see.
D: Don't . . . you're not meant to do it like that. Miss said we can do it quick writing 'cause we can need to do it quick.
P: I can't do it quick. Let me see it Darren, I . . .
D: You can because Miss . . .
P: I can't see it. I'm gonna tell!
D: Paul, look. Let me do it . . . Pretend I'm not the customer now and then I can show you . . . give me the pencil and . . .
P: Hurry up, Darren, or else we're going to shut.
D: Look, this is dead quick, right. Pretend me and him (a soft toy) wants two packets of crisps. You can do it like this (writes 2 p cr). '2p' that means it says 'packets', 'cause it's 'p'. 'cr' that . . .
P: That means 'cr' for crisps. 2pcr. Let me have a go. Let's pretend you need . . . you got . . . you need two toffee apples. (writes it down)
D: And two toffee bananas.
P: And two . . . do you want two or do you want one?
D: Two.
P: Two 'tof a' . . . do you want anything else? Yes? Or no?
D: Erm . . . No. (See Figure 9.3)

Thus some powerful lessons about the manipulation and flexibility of written language were taking place within the play and the knowledge gained could then be incorporated in future play in the café.

A further level of intervention occurred in a reception class. In this class (where about half the children were four at the beginning of the year), there were well-developed, sensitively planned and rich play

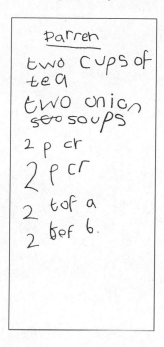

Figure 9.3

experiences as part of the children's curriculum. One such activity was the establishment of an hotel. Through discussion and sharing experiences, the children explored their understandings of what an hotel was and how hotels worked. They contributed to the building of the area (which was just outside the classroom) and made decisions about resources. The class teacher decided that, while the children were free to play how-so-ever they wished while in the actual play area, she would make links from other classroom activities to the play area. Many of these involved literacy. It was a relatively simple matter to draw up a list of a whole range of literate activities that occurred in and around hotels. The teacher was then in a position to decide which ones could most appropriately feature in the children's experience.

In fact, a whole range of activities were undertaken. For instance, before children could play in the area they had to apply for a job in the hotel. The class discussed what jobs would be available and talked about what an application might involve. Apart from the literary knowledge that was being gained, the children were all deepening their understanding of who worked in hotels and what work those people did. The children then wrote their applications. At the age of five they were independently creating persuasive texts (see Figure 9.4).

Around the same time the children created advertisements for the hotel, wrote brochures, devised rules of behaviour for guests, sent post-

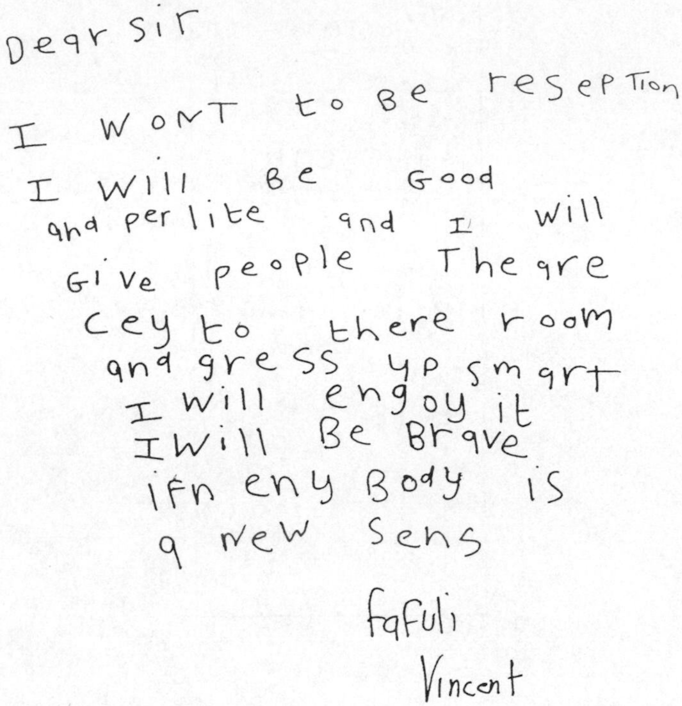

Dear sir

I wont to Be resepTion
I will Be Good
and perlite and I will
Give people Theqre
cey to there room
and gress yp smart
I will engoy it
Iwill Be Brave
ifn eny Body is
q new sens

fafuli
Vincent

Figure 9.4

Translation:

Dear Sir,
I want to be a receptionist. I will be good and polite and I will give
people their keys to their room and dress up smart. I will enjoy it. I will
be brave if anybody is a nuisance.
Faithfully
Vincent

cards (for real), made maps, developed menus, wrote descriptions of
facilities and engaged in many other print-related experiences. All these
were carried out in the classroom, not in the play area. When the
children went out to the area, the kinds of play they engaged in became
much richer as a consequence of the other activities. The play had more
depth, greater variety, and was sustained for longer periods of time.

The literacy-related activities were introduced one at a time as the
play continued. One of the most successful came later on when the area
was very well-established. The teacher introduced the notion of guests
finding something wrong with the hotel. It was necessary to write a
letter of complaint. The children had, of course, never written complaints. Nevertheless, the class discussed the kinds of things that might
go wrong and talked about how you would write about these to the

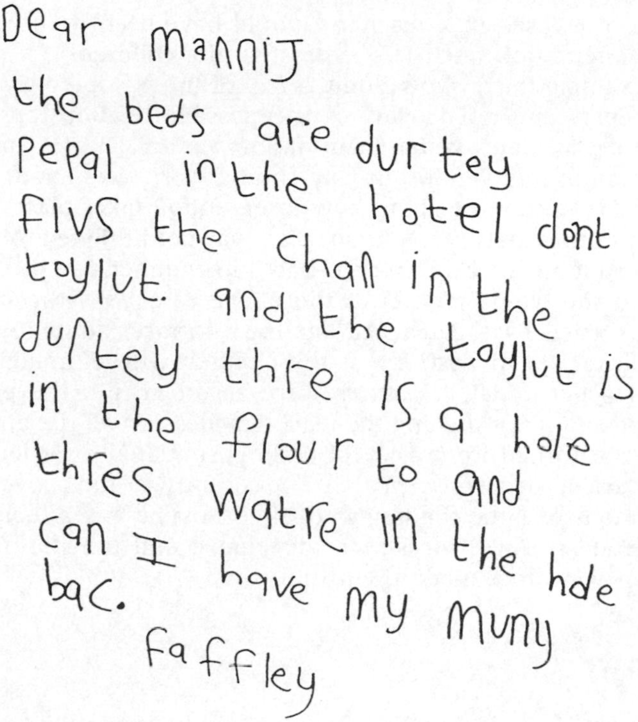

Dear mannij
the beds are durtey
pepal in the hotel dont
fivs the chan in the
toylut. and the toylut is
durtey thre is a hole
in the flour to and
thres watre in the hde
bac. can I have my muny
faffley

Figure 9.5

Translation:

Dear Manager,
The beds are dirty. The people in the hotel don't flush the chain in the toilet and the toilet is dirty. There is a hole in the floor too and there's water in the hole. Can I have my money back?
Faffley

owner. The results were spectacular. Once again the children demonstrated that at a very young age they could begin to handle some very complicated text types (see Figure 9.5). Needless to say the activity of making complaints also featured in subsequent play in the hotel area.

At the end of the six weeks of hotel play, the children in this class had not only had a wonderful time playing in the hotel, but had been introduced to an extremely wide range of forms of text, all of which had been undertaken independently (although after discussion) by the children. Their texts were not copied. The texts represent their own unaided efforts both in terms of meaning and spelling. The play and the English work had become mutually beneficial. The play gave purpose and relevance to the more 'academic' work, and the 'academic' work in turn gave substance to the play. Thus, play gave meaning to work which, in the hands of less sensitive teachers, would have been decontextualized and consequently of much less interest to the children.

These examples have shown only a few of the possible ways of intervening in play and only a few of the possible relationships between literacy and play (for a wider examination see Hall 1991). Those sensitive about adult intervention in play should worry less about intervention as an idea and more about how intervention takes place. In all the above cases of teacher intervention, play was not inhibited: on the contrary it became richer. The children had a new dimension of experience to bring to the play. In none of the above cases was the play taken over and owned by the teacher: on the contrary, adult involvement was significant but modest. It was the children who ultimately decided whether teacher-initiated features were absorbed into the play: there were no penalties for ditching the teacher's ideas. In all the above cases, play was not turned from a joyful children-initiated experience into a mournful teacher-led experience. On the contrary, as the above examples clearly demonstrate, the children were almost exuberant in their adoption of teacher ideas. These ideas were developed and transformed by the children in ways that made them their own.

Conclusion

For the children involved in the above examples, literacy did not have to be forced down their throats. It was not made a decontextualized experience but neither was it pushed into the play in ways that destroyed the fun, and the transformational possibilities. The intervention was sensitive, appropriate and relevant.

Clearly, play can have a powerful and useful position in the primary curriculum and can be linked into a number of curriculum areas (see the following chapters in this section of the book), not just literacy (Hall and Abbott 1992). Recent political attempts to denigrate the role of play represent a gross failure to see the extraordinarily rich potential of play (as Angela Anning so clearly demonstrates in Chapter 5). However, teachers must recognize that, if play is really to offer children extended experiences, then some careful planning and some clever teaching is needed.

10 | Experiential learning in play and art

Roy Prentice

a certain degree of choice, lack of constraint from conventional ways of handling objects, materials and ideas, is inherent in the concept of play. This is its main connection with art and other forms of invention.

(Millar 1968: 21)

Early years practitioners frequently express their enthusiastic commitment to two activities in the education of young children: play and art. Artists and designers very often use such phrases as playing with materials, playing around and toying with ideas, to most accurately describe vital stages in their working procedures. It is the purpose of this chapter to:

- consider more closely the nature and quality of the relationship between the processes and procedures of art and certain aspects of play;
- help practitioners create the conditions through which young children can be initiated into art as a way of knowing through a structured approach to play.

We are reminded by Storr (1989: 69) that:

People who realize their creative potential are constantly bridging the gap between inner and outer. They invest the external world with meaning because they disown neither the world's objectivity nor their own subjectivity. This interaction between inner and outer worlds is easily seen when we observe children at play. Children make use of real objects in the external world, but invest these objects with meanings which derive from the world of their own imagination.

The growth point in art activity is located in the reciprocal relationship which develops between an artist's intentions and the chosen medium of expression. A lifeline is formed between ideas and feelings which inhabit a private, internal world, and a chosen medium which exists in the public, external world. Starting a piece of work can be simultaneously exhilarating and unnerving: feelings are likely to oscillate between confidence and timidity. As an artist reaches out to, literally, make a personal mark on the external world, there is a lot of giving out of self, in an effort to inject life into a piece of work. As the energy generated from within an emergent work of art gains momentum, the artist is compelled to absorb it and make decisions about the nature of future interactions.

It is through a reciprocal relationship between an artist and work-in-progress that ideas and feelings flow, change and assume a concrete form which could not have been predetermined. A practising painter, Ben Shahn (1967: 49) describes this condition as follows:

> From the moment at which a painter begins to strike figures of colour upon a surface he must become acutely sensitive to the feel, the texture, the light, the relationships which arise before him. At one point he will mold the material according to an intention. At another he may yield intention – perhaps his whole concept – to emerging forms, to new implications within the painted surface. Idea itself, ideas, many ideas move back and forth across his mind as a constant traffic . . . Thus idea rises to the surface, grows, changes as a painting grows and develops.

Shahn goes on to state that 'painting is both creative and responsive', requiring an artist to function as 'two people not one', being both 'the imaginer and the producer', as well as 'the critic'. Central to creative behaviour is an ability to evaluate from within the activity that comes into being through the activity. As Reid (1969: 81) points out:

> in the making of any art there tends to be rhythmic alternation between the activity of making and enjoying critically and contemplatively what has been done.

The quality of the interplay that evolves between an artist's physical shaping of the chosen medium and a critical response to the form that emerges is analogous to conversational exchange. A fruitful conversation is defined by Britton (1972: 239) as one in which 'the participants profit from their own talking . . . from what others contribute, and above all from the interaction'. Every conversation evolves at its own irregular pace with periods of animated exchange interspersed with passages of silence. In order that such conversational exchange can flourish between artist and work, an artist has to come to terms with the opposing forces of stability and change. Within us all there exists a powerful tug-of-war between a desire to satisfy curiosity, explore the unknown and a need to adhere to that which is familiar, comfortable and safe. For an artist the challenge of the new, the magnetism of the unfamiliar, is stronger than the need to reinforce the status quo. Creative behaviour requires a tolerance of ambiguity and a capacity to cope with a degree of uncertainty in order that situations remain open for sufficiently long periods of time to encourage explorations of alternative ideas, ways of working and materials. Risks have to be taken if artists are to learn from the activities in which they engage and through which their ideas develop a separate existence. An artist's willingness to alter or destroy a part or the whole of something created in order to pursue the potential it offers is at times a painful but necessary part of the creative process.

Some fundamental aspects of play are also identified in the creative process through which artists respond to experience. In order to exploit the educational potential of some of these connections between art and play, it seems more appropriate to view play as an attitude and process (Moyles 1989) rather than an activity. By so doing, the focus shifts away from play as a specific category of behaviour towards the nature and quality of an individual's engagements with ideas, feelings and materials (similar to the notion of free-flow play, argued by Tina Bruce, Chapter 15). Such a position also reflects the views of Dewey (1958), who regards playfulness as an attitude of mind, and Lieberman (1977: 5) who asserts that 'playfulness survives play and becomes a personality trait of the individual', thus enabling connections to be made between play, imagination and creativity (Vandenberg 1986). Perhaps the sculptor Richard Long was thinking along these lines when, in a television interview (Channel Four: June 1991) he declared that: 'Artists continue to do things as grown-ups they did as children, whereas other people give up.' Sadly, those 'grown-ups' who 'give up' are denied the full realization of their potential for creative thought and action. Too often, with increasing age, learning through direct experience is replaced by second-hand information and received facts (as Angela Anning forcibly argues in Chapter 4). The evidence gained through sense impressions is mistrusted in favour of predetermined outcomes. Prescribed procedures and preconceived ideas squash the spirit of spontaneous exploration fuelled by curiosity: thus imaginative possibilities dwindle.

Central to play and art is the 'degree of choice' to which Millar (1968) refers; and through which both areas of experience promote the development of self-determined behaviour. Exposure to unlimited choice can be unproductive, resulting in not knowing where to start or a series of personally unsatisfying, superficial encounters with too many ideas and materials in rapid succession (Peter Heaslip also takes up this point in Chapter 8). Play, like art, provides opportunities for imaginative leaps to occur, encouraging inventive ways of handling ideas and materials beyond the constraints of convention. Familiar objects can be placed in unfamiliar settings as a result of which they are perceived in different ways: a device exploited by the surrealists to disturb and amuse. Individual objects combined and recombined in new arrangements relinquish their utilitarian functions, assume new identities, reveal new possibilities. Handled in such a playful way, objects cease to be context-bound, and we can change their colour, texture, scale and function. Objects can stand for anything we choose; they become visual metaphors invested with personal meanings which suit our present purpose (Singer and Singer 1990).

Through engagement with a wide range of two- and three-dimensional materials, play provides powerful opportunities for individuals to get to grips with the qualities and properties of the external world. As Gentle (1985: 59) points out, 'A child's play shapes what the material can offer as much as the material predicts what the child can experience.' An echo of the kind of conversational exchange already referred to in art is witnessed in play as idea has an impact on material at one moment, and, at the next, material has an impact on idea. Ideas come to the surface, change, become submerged and re-emerge over a period of time. This requires sustained involvement in the process and the confidence to take risks. As well as making something, the maker is also making critical judgements about what has been made in order to determine what happens next.

The relationship between play and art and design education in enriching early years practice

In many early years settings sensitive educators develop creative environments and climates which maximize the potential of play as a starting point for learning in art. Regrettably such practice is uneven. As Gentle (1985: 59) reveals:

> Play is potentially one of the greatest ways of learning but it can so easily remain formless and lack development or personal satisfaction and challenge, subsiding into vague therapy or time-filling.

Unfortunately, in some people's minds, play has become synonymous with notions of totally free expression and 'popular' approaches to child art which advocate a non-interventionist role for the adult.

If educators are to engage children in sustained play which is personally satisfying and challenging, they require a structure within which experiences can be planned, provided and extended (see also Lesley Abbott, Chapter 6). The degree of ease or difficulty with which connections can be made and developed between ideas, feelings, objects perceived, media and procedures is significantly influenced by the 'setting' within which these elements co-exist.

A classroom is a working space which should be designed with care in order that it can operate as a coherent resource (Moyles 1992). The layout, visual, tactile and spatial richness of a room encourage and support certain behaviours while discouraging and being unsupportive of others.

The appropriateness of the organization of the working space for specific activities, the nature and amount of mobility and interpersonal interaction it permits, and the manner in which materials and tools are made available, all operate as controls over what children do, and the directions in which their involvements can continue. The ways in which children perceive, think, talk about, and are motivated to use materials in their immediate surroundings, are influenced by the manner in which adults make them accessible and the values with which they are invested. A clear set of guiding principles needs to be established as part of a whole-school policy and on the basis of which materials are selected, arranged and made available to children. Familiar things placed in unfamiliar contexts and unfamiliar things placed in familiar contexts provide powerful triggers for the release of creative energy.

Alternative ways of introducing children to an activity need to be considered as part of the planning process. Preparation based on a consideration of replies to questions such as the following, establishes flexible ground-plans for explorations by adults and children:

- Should a given situation be 'presented' by the adult or 'discovered' by the children from a range of possibilities?
- When an activity incorporates both approaches, how and when is the change from one to the other to occur and how is fragmentation to be avoided?
- Is the initial input to be a group or individual experience and, if the former, at what point are individuals encouraged to extend their individual paths of discovery?
- On what basis are decisions about the scale of work, the combinations of media and the duration of an activity made by adults or children?

It is likely that inadequate preparation will reduce a practitioner's self-confidence and encourage an instructional approach.

When adults' perceptions of children's creative efforts are clouded by their own aesthetic preferences or a narrow view of art, it is difficult for them to extend children's creative responses. By heightening their own perceptions of children's creative responses in art as in play, it is likely that practitioners will develop a more caring attitude towards the objects of attention. When things are cared for, it usually follows that their qualities are even more sharply perceived.

An adult's acceptance of children's creative responses is communicated through a wide range of verbal and non-verbal messages. The gestures made, the degree of sensitivity with which tools and materials are selected and used, convey to children information about the values and expectations. Sometimes conflicting messages are transmitted. A private utterance of acceptance of a particular response is unlikely to have credibility if the responses to be granted public approval, by being displayed in the classroom, reflect different criteria. Most educators declare, verbally, that they encourage children to be creative but, in practice, there is sometimes an absence of those conditions which maximize opportunities for creative behaviour. Verbal encouragement of risk-taking, a flexible use of ideas, materials, space and time, must be accompanied by practitioner's personal behaviour which embodies these qualities and classroom organization which allows such behaviour to flourish. Carefully formulated non-judgemental comments about children's creative responses, the warmth of a supportive smile, the introduction of an appropriate medium or tool at a crucial moment, provide children with confirmation that they are able to create something external to themselves. Through this they can share ideas and feelings with interested adults, by whom they are valued. Through their rich use of language, teachers particularly are able to illuminate the qualities of children's art and reveal certain aspects through which future developments can be made possible. Attitudes are modified as a result of looking at, and discussing, individual responses to works of art. Participants become increasingly flexible in their attitudes and tolerant of alternative points of view. Discussions should be based on specific, focused observations of the work of children and a wide range of mature artists. Stereotyped phrases such as 'interesting texture' should be avoided in favour of vivid vocabulary: analogy, metaphor and simile provide more potent means through which precise responses to visual things can be achieved. As Bruner (1976: 63) reaffirms:

> Metaphor joins dissimilar experiences by finding the image or the symbol that unites them at some deeper emotional level of meaning. Its effect depends upon its capacity for getting past the literal mode of connecting.

Learning through sensory experience is equally highly valued by early years practitioners and artists, craftspeople and designers. Gentle (1985: 63) argues that 'the main purpose of the teacher's work with young children is to extend and enrich their sensory experience'. It is important not to lose sight of the fact that children bring to early years settings an unevenness of sensory experience which parallels that of language skills (Nigel Hall, Chapter 9). Thus the enrichment and extension of play requires educators to have a sharp perception of individual differences and an ability to match expectations to individual competency levels (Vicky Hurst, Chapter 14).

In order to 'ground' in actual practice some of the issues raised so far, I shall now consider ways of initiating children into art as a way of knowing, with reference to three-dimensional and two-dimensional processes and procedures.

Art as a way of knowing

Three dimensional experiences
Young children develop an intelligence of feeling through direct bodily contact with diverse surfaces and through manipulating a range of

substances and objects. Playing with sand, water and clay helps to develop a sense of weight, balance, softness, warmth, coolness and moistness; as well as angular and curved, large and small forms and movements. This is captured by Barrett (1977: 41) in a description of a child's involvement in and increasing control over a piece of clay:

> The hand holding the clay has a sensate experience of its wetness and coolness; by moving the hand the clay is found to be plastic and malleable, i.e. it retains and records the movement of the hand over the clay. The fingers and eyes are conscious of this change of shape and the manipulator becomes aware of the forms created, the potential for change and the creation of new forms. These forms engender ideas, impulses and feelings which, in turn, create needs and possibilities for further manipulation and consideration of alternative forms to develop the concept.

Constructional toys provide an extended range of possibilities through which children are able to develop increasing control over interlocking components and moving parts as they acquire, refine and apply a range of skills which include: grasping, sliding, rotating, slotting, pulling, pushing, winding and stacking. A systematic approach to three-dimensional work exists in a minority of primary schools. In early years settings what is commonly called 'junk modelling' – the random sticking together of found materials, mainly commercial packaging – provides further access to resistant materials. Using scrap materials and objects can form the basis of fruitful work in art and design. However, such activities frequently lack challenge and rigour, and fail to identify technical skills and concepts. It is essential that materials are carefully selected for their intrinsic qualities and properties, and arranged and presented to children in such a way that they learn to make informed choices.

Technology in the National Curriculum provides a refreshingly new context within which inventive three dimensional activities have a major role to play. At present the most common approach to three-dimensional work in art and design in primary schools reinforces a skills-based rationale, which reflects narrow, craft-based traditions. In this approach, materials and processes have become associated with particular prescribed outcomes. With the advent of Technology as a school subject, there now exists an exciting opportunity for teachers of young children to help define it, the values it embodies, its content and the directions in which it could develop. A re-examination of the nature of the relationship between materials-based play and three-dimensional activities in art and design should be an important part of this process. Three-dimensional work with plastic and resistant materials should provide progressively complex opportunities for children to control tools, investigate materials and extend their understanding of spatial relationships, texture and form.

Resistant materials

Constructions from:	paper, card, boxes, wire, straws, tubes, wood, plastic, textiles, yarns, threads
Skills involved:	cutting, joining, folding, bending, tearing, interlocking, shaping, measuring, estimating

Plastic materials

Modelling with:	dough, plasticine, clay
Skills involved:	manipulating, squeezing, rolling, pinching

The landscape artist, Richard Long, makes sculpture which is fundamentally ephemeral, constructed from pieces of slate and rocks, for example, in their natural environments. His approach, it is suggested by Mitchell (1991: 96):

> can be traced to the many tactile and kinaesthetic experiences felt and enjoyed by young children. What child hasn't enjoyed seeing the trace of their own footsteps in freshly fallen snow, or the path made in a wheat field just before harvesting in the months of summer? Equally the print of wet, bare feet on pavement, path or rock, made during play in a paddling pool or river, offer pleasure and fascination. Children run in circles, follow the painted games markings on the school playground for their own pleasure: they observe with interest, the effects of a changing pattern of water on a wall, created by a jump in a nearby puddle or similarly, the cascade of water down rocks at the seaside.

Early learning through tactile experiences provides the starting point from which an increasingly complex range of skills and concepts can be developed, through a gradual introduction to three-dimensional art activities of quality. Children should have opportunities to:

- look at, collect, handle, talk about, a wide range of objects which have different functions, which come from diverse cultures and which were made at different times in different ways;
- gain an understanding of similar and contrasting shapes and structures, rough and smooth textures, angular and curved forms, drawn, painted and printed surface decoration, through their own making, and through an introduction to the work of adult artists and designers;
- make things on both large and small scales;
- work individually and collaboratively;
- become familiar with plastic and resistant materials, a range of shaping and cutting tools and processes, including new technologies;
- participate in experimental ways of working e.g. group constructions of an ephemeral nature, perhaps out of doors, on an environmental scale, through which ecological issues could be raised together with an involvement of the performing arts.

Two-dimensional experiences

Children make marks on surfaces with whatever media are to hand: jam, toothpaste, crayons, or a stick trailed through wet sand. The ways in which children communicate and express their ideas and feelings, graphically, are influenced by the qualities of the drawing materials to which they have access, and over which they gain control. It is vital for a teacher to be aware of the relationship between the original experience and the medium through which a response is to be made. Gentle (1985: 172) suggests four categories into which mark-making materials can be placed in order to accentuate their qualities:

• soft and smudgy;
• waxy and greasy;
• wet and runny;
• hard and linear.

In addition to providing a simple organizational structure for graphic media, it also encourages a creative way of thinking and talking about the range and qualities of the marks they are capable of producing when fully exploited.

While it is common to find painting materials in most early years settings, successive HMI reports refer to much of what children do with them in school as rather 'lacklustre'. Too often children produce paintings in a vacuum: they fail to provide a powerful, non-verbal, means of responding to experience and they seem uninformed by the work of other artists. Sometimes motivation is low because paint and brushes are of poor quality and they are presented in an uninviting manner. Early paint exploration is purely physical and tactile; with increasing age, children need to gain control over a wider repertoire of practical skills and demonstrate their fluent use of colour, shape, pattern, texture: some basic elements of a visual vocabulary.

Children should be introduced to different ways of applying paint to a surface, using, for example, fingers, hand, palette knife, sponge or sticks. A consideration of substances which can be added to paint, to alter its consistency and texture, such as sand, sawdust, PVA glue or water, alerts children to a wider range of 'painterly' possibilities and extends their capacity to make informed aesthetic judgements.

From an early age children should be encouraged to mix paint using the following basic palette, from which all secondary and tertiary colours can be achieved:

• white
• chrome yellow
• lemon yellow
• vermilion red
• crimson red
• cobalt blue
• prussian blue.

Offering a limited range of colours encourages children to be inventive, and to make personal decisions about colours to be mixed. Dialogue with an adult is vital when children are engaged in this activity. They need to be encouraged to 'test out' colours on scraps of paper, make informed guesses, estimate, consider the reasons why a colour changes as it dries, and when it is placed next to another colour. Throughout such practical involvements children need to be exposed to, and develop, a critical language through which they are able to discuss and increase their knowledge and understanding of the work of other painters.

A thumb print reaffirms the uniqueness of each individual. Prints made with fingers and hands are a personal record and lead young children on to make random records of assorted objects and surfaces. Printmaking is immediate. Printed images can be repeated and confidence is boosted as random arrangements become organized patterns. Through printmaking children are able to explore the qualities of surfaces by recording their textures. Colours and shapes interact and can be superimposed to create more complex images that reveal movement and changes of scale. Printmaking is a means of recording a surface using a medium and a press. From humble beginnings, increasingly challenging and rigorous experiences can be planned within the following framework:

Surface
ready made – finger, hand, foot, sole of shoe, woodgrain, coin, grills, mesh
constructed from – card, string, wool, sand, fabric

Medium
water-based printing ink, plasticine, clay, sand

Press
human – hand, foot
mechanical – roller, printing press

The importance of experiential learning is emphasized by Salmon (1988: 48):

> As most nursery school teachers would readily acknowledge, inquiry is the impetus to understanding. We construct our world in the interrogations we make of it, the questions we put to it . . . it seems that we can develop our understanding only through our own inquiries, we cannot undertake new ventures within the terms of another's initiative.

Conclusion

Through play and art young children have rich opportunities to interrogate the world in a variety of ways. They need to learn how to formulate appropriate questions to assist this process. The brief reference already made to art activities outlines the kind of approach and structure through which children's learning in art can be supported and extended. Attention is drawn to the interrelationship between making art and understanding the work of other artists along with the central role of language.

Art can be taught, and taught well, by early years teachers who have a special responsibility: to initiate young children through play into art as a way of knowing and doing. The need to establish an entitlement curriculum in art, to be achieved through a structured approach to art activities, is stressed by the members of the Art Working Group (DES 1991b: 9):

> Young pre-school children learn to speak naturally and their acqui-sition of speech and writing is aided by the teaching of the formal skills of literacy. Similarly, in art there is a visual language, a system of marks, symbols and conventions with a syntax of its own, which must be learned systematically if skill, knowledge and understanding are to grow and mature in a coherent way. Pupils need to be helped to acquire this visual language in the same detailed way in which they are helped to read and write. The visual vocabulary contains specific elements including line, colour, tone, texture and form with which pupils need to become familiar. But visual lan-guage only conveys meaning when formal elements and technical skills are used with understanding to communicate ideas, feelings and experiences.

11 Bulbs, buzzers and batteries – play and science

Jeni Riley and Jane Savage

In a west London reception class, David, four years old, is blowing bubbles in a water tray. He has a short piece of hose pipe and the water contains washing up liquid and is dyed blue.

Half an hour later David is still gently blowing. The bubbles have completely covered the surface of the water in the tray. He stops from time to time and gazes intently at the changing, glistening pattern.

For another fifteen minutes he continues to blow, the bubbles rise still higher. As a teacher goes by she stops and looks with David for several moments at the shimmering mass.

David: Can you see if you look carefully the sides of the bubbles are all flat, 'cos they're squashed against each other.
Teacher: Mmm – and what do you think is *inside* the bubbles?

The early years classroom that naturally employs an enquiry-based explorative mode of teaching and learning has great potential for science. In a book that is focusing on play and its attributes there is little need to restate this. However, when considering the acquisition of scientific understanding, it is useful to examine Hutt's Taxonomy of children's play (see Figure 1.2, Introduction) in relation to more recent work on learning in and through science (Driver 1983).

Hutt's work, as already discussed in the Introduction, draws on Piagetian principles and distinguishes between epistemic and ludic aspects of play. Through epistemic behaviour the child acquires information, knowledge and skills. Ludic behaviour allows children to make the understandings their own. The distinction is similar to Piaget's accommodation and assimilation (discussed in some detail by Peter Smith in Chapter 1), through which the children's intellectual task is to adjust to the acquisition of new understandings in such a way that they can make use of the information. Play, we believe, is a valuable vehicle for such cognitive activity. Science is the perfect subject area to engage the child's purposeful interest: this is the focus of this chapter.

Learning, play and science

The research of Driver (1983) provides a further and complementary framework of learning which can be acquired through the epistemic behaviours of problem-solving, exploration and the productive use of materials and acquisition of skills.

This 'constructivist area' of science research is identified with the following principles;

1 The current thoughts of the learner are important and are related to previous knowledge, attitudes and goals. Play provides many opportunities for adults to observe the actions that indicate the nature of the child's thinking, for example, while constructing and testing bridges made of building blocks.

2 Individuals construct their own meanings through social processes and interaction with the physical environment. For instance, working and playing with their peers making cheese straws, children are able to develop through collaboration and experimentation.

3 The construction of meaning is a continuous and active process. Learners are continually involved in generating, checking and restructuring ideas and hypotheses. Activities exploring the floating, loading and sinking properties of a variety of materials are valuable. The use of objects of different sizes, shapes, colour, weight and density challenge children's logical thoughts of deduction based on the evidence before them.

4 Learning involves conceptual change; concepts may have to be radically reorganized. Children consolidate the concepts of hot and cold through the preparation of drinks, and by experiencing the contrasting sensations through handling materials in many contexts.

5 Meanings, once constructed, can be accepted or rejected. They do not always lead to a change in belief. A group of nursery children firmly believed the model animals that could swim in real life, would also float when placed in the water tray. The safe, unthreatening situation for this work allowed acceptance or rejection of the scientific proof.

6 Learners have the final responsibility for their own learning. They need to be involved in setting their own goals and controlling their own learning. Learning through play is not passive but purposive (as Tina Bruce explores in Chapter 15). Also, the meaningful activities need to be generated from children's own ideas and suggestions.

7 Some constructed meanings are shared. Children often have similar ideas about specific content areas. Discussion provides the crucial insight into the level of understanding that has occurred, and the organizational methods of the early years classroom facilitate interaction of this type (Peter Heaslip discusses further aspects of this in Chapter 8).

8 Science teaching is not only concerned with transmitting knowledge but is also about organizing situations in the classroom and designing tasks which provide opportunities for science learning.

9 There is a parallel between the way children and scientists develop concepts in science. Both are concerned with the checking and modifying of ideas. Neither children nor adults are able to enhance the developing understanding without engagement with first-hand and intriguing experiences. David and the bubbles in the opening scenario is an example of sustained involvement with an activity.

10 There may be multiple explanations for events which may not match the generalizations the teacher had in mind. Science is complex and teachers need to realize that the outcomes of practical work are often ambiguous and varied (Driver 1983; Scott 1987).

These findings appear to support the best of all early years teaching and learning.

Children, play and science

It is necessary to establish what an individual child knows and thinks about a particular issue. The adult needs to discover *why* the child thinks in a particular way, to value the idea even if it represents a partial model of current scientific thinking. The adult is then in a position to provide carefully conceived learning activities which will help the child to challenge, develop and reflect on her views so that the thinking becomes more sophisticated, more generally applicable and hence more useful as a tool to help understand the world about them (Driver 1983). The issue of subject expertise is important here. Teachers themselves may have to go through the learning process in order to be able to provide opportunities with the potential required.

The early years context clearly provides both the opportunity and appropriate pedagogy for working in this facilitative and learner-centred way. Play is also of particular benefit in allowing children to experience uncertainty in a non-threatening arena, if the materials and ideas provided by the teacher build on previous, as well as new, experiences. An example of an activity that has this potential is modelling with found materials. A sequence of materials and adhesives might be introduced such as a card of varying thickness, with both matt and smooth, shiny surfaces. Different joining mechanisms, starting with wallpaper paste to more sophisticated polymer-based adhesives, butterfly clips and string, might then be supplied. The problems are solved by addressing the particular design issue posed by the different materials provided. In this way, many play activities provide the vehicle for children to continue to establish and extend scientific process skills and conceptual understanding. The role of the teacher is to make explicit the developing scientific rationale and allow trial-and-error opportunities. As children encounter new materials, they are encouraged to explore properties and inter-relationships, and more varied and complex materials can be gradually introduced to refine and extend understanding.

Less confident children can also try ideas out and repeat familiar activities, both alone and with peers, secure in the knowledge that they are not always going to be asked to write, draw or discuss it! Open-ended problem-solving through practical activities often leads to multiple 'answers' and 'solutions'. This can be threatening and uncertain for the child who is lacking in confidence, and who needs to achieve the security of the 'right answer'. It takes peer and adult support to encourage divergent thinking.

Play provides the opportunity for the adult to observe which children are drawn to particular materials and activities (as Vicky Hurst discusses in Chapter 14). Children of all abilities and ages are more willing to share and discuss a self-chosen, self-structured activity when given the time to explore an area of interest. It is at this stage of education that children must be allowed the time to become involved for long periods with their own investigations. Play activities enable children to start with what they already know, look for structures between ideas and explore and give status to their intuitive and imaginative ideas.

> The most important single factor influencing learning is what the learner already knows; ascertain this and teach him accordingly.
>
> (Ausubel *et al.*, 1978: 163)

Children, science and real-life experiences

Other research has clearly indicated the need to relate scientific activities to the real-life experiences of the children (Hayes 1982; Harlen 1985). The value of recognizing and broadening the young child's egocentric view of the world have been most fully exploited by early years teachers and educators. This now needs to be extended throughout the primary age phase in a much more systematic way. Real-life experiences need not only to be integrated into topic or English and Mathematics work (as shown by Nigel Hall and Rose Griffiths in Chapters 9 and 12) respectively but the scientific real-life experiences of children should be more firmly based in science activities and play situations. Activities such as play with construction materials, cooking, creative opportunities with a wide range of resistant and non-resistant materials (see Roy Prentice's discussion in the previous chapter), skills with which the children come into contact through peers and their families, all need to be actively encouraged and structured. Historically, primary practitioners are not so strong on the abilities to recognize and extend the science concepts and process skills in order to construct science concepts. These skills are observing, predicting, hypothesizing, planning, investigating and fair testing, explaining, interpreting, raising questions, recording and communicating, measuring and critically reflecting (Galton and Harlen 1990), within activities and making them explicit to both teachers and children. The powerful notion that we are all learners and that we learn best through play and work, can enable us to become 'experts' in something in which we are particularly interested, and this gives an important perspective in the role of play. A two-way sharing with parents and carers about the varied nature of the experiences provided for the children through their interest is of great benefit.

Presenting challenges in science through play

The work of Children's Learning in Science (CLIS) and Science Processes and Concept Exploration (SPACE) projects can be of particular help in directing and structuring practical activities; organizing collections of objects on an interest table or something similar can help children both to challenge their existing ideas and then to extend them through exploration. For example, a sequence of objects on a science display with the purpose of introducing and extending ideas and the associated manipulative skills about electricity could be provided as follows:

Stage 1: Bulbs of various sizes and magnifiers
Questions for discussion or activity:
- What are different parts of the bulb made of?
- What do they look like?
- What is the same in all the bulbs?
- What is different?

Stage 2: One bulb, one battery, one wire
Question:
- Can you light up the bulb?

Stage 3: One bulb, two wires, one battery
Questions:
- Can you light up the bulb?
- What happens if you change things around so they are joined in a different order?

Stage 4: Bulbs, wires, batteries
Questions:
- How many bulbs can you light up from one battery?
- Are they all the same brightness?

- What happens if you add more bulbs, more batteries, more wires?
- How many different arrangements can you make that light up bulbs?

Stage 5: Bulbs, buzzers, wires, batteries
Questions:
- What difference does it make if you make a buzzer buzz rather than a bulb light up?
- What is happening?

Stage 6: Bulbs, buzzers, motors, wires, batteries, paper clips, switches
Question:
- What can you find out about these?

Stage 7: Bulbs, buzzers, motors, wires of many colours, batteries of various sizes, switches, conductors and insulators, etc.
Questions:
- Can you switch things on and off?
- What does a switch do?
- What does a motor do?
- What could you use it to do?
- Do the wires make a difference?
- Why do some things make it work and others don't?

The children are free to use the materials as they wish, but the teacher is clearly sequencing and structuring their experiences. Resources themselves powerfully dictate the experience. The knowledge and understanding of the teacher will influence the conceptual framework behind the sequence that is planned. The CLIS and SPACE research, although mainly undertaken with older children, can provide the evidence of patterns that have emerged in categories of intuitive thought through developed teaching sequences which promote conceptual change (Driver 1983). This is true of learners of all ages and stages.

Science in the early and primary school years consists of both process and content: a way of working and a body of knowledge. It is also characterized by children exploring and finding out things for themselves and reflecting on their understandings and actions (Harlen and Jelly 1989). If children chose an activity and discuss it with their peers, in the course of their conversation the opportunities to play can become a powerful learning opportunity. This conversation between reception-aged children playing with bulbs, batteries and wires is a good example:

'Hold the wire here and pretend it's working.'
'Let's try it with a red wire . . . a short wire . . . no, a red, short wire. Well, it doesn't matter. It doesn't work.'
'Well . . . try a long wire then!'

This does not preclude the same materials and experiences being used in a more structured way, with or without teacher intervention and presence. Every practitioner knows the value of multi-level activities in a busy primary classroom!

Developing positive attitudes to science

An additional and critically important component of science is the consideration of the development of scientific attitudes. This has importance to learning in all areas and needs to be built into play activities as well as providing a foundation for a culture for learning and sharing within a school and classroom. Scientific attitudes include curiosity, respect for evidence, critical reflection, flexibility and sensitivity to living things and the environment (Harlen 1985). The main science conceptual areas are those concerned with: sight and light, hot, cold and temperature changes, hearing and producing sound, movement and forces, breathing and air, ourselves and other animals, soil and growing plants, how things behave in water, sky, seasons and weather, simple electric circuits and materials and their uses (Harlen 1985). These topics provide the majority of the curriculum through the early years and can usefully, with the previously mentioned attitudes, provide a framework for scientific play activities. A shop conversion of the home corner or pretend area provides such a focus. A garden centre might promote the planting of bulbs, seeds, corms and plants; it would provide science work that is real and meaningful and also involve the children in close observation and the measurement of growing things.

Progression, continuity and differentiation

Progression and continuity are important issues. Individual children's ability levels, the balance and breadth of play experiences offered within one class during the course of the academic year, need to be planned. Play activities could be broadly structured as an on-going and integral part of the science opportunities that are on offer to the children in the same way that topics are planned, throughout the school. One example could be based on observation. Are the children being encouraged to use all their senses and to what level? How are the children encouraged to discuss their observations for a variety of audiences in different ways? The value of discussion in eliciting children's responses and helping them to make sense of them cannot be over-emphasized. Can the children try out ideas and new vocabulary in a secure, self-chosen environment before it becomes part of the formal learning classroom experiences? The confusions which can occur from the differences in the everyday and the scientific use of language can best be trialled and explained in small groups when the situation occurs (Osborne and Freyberg 1985).

Recent work which has concentrated on how to assess children's learning in science (Galton and Harlen 1990) has also highlighted children's lack of understanding in extending and checking observations using scientific and measuring equipment. Young children need to have open access to equipment such as measuring instruments, mirrors, lenses and magnifiers and be encouraged to use them in appropriate ways to help extend, verify and quantify observations. These resources should be easily accessible, and used in a variety of situations and contexts, so that the children will learn how to use them appropriately and accurately.

Lack of subject knowledge continues to be the greatest handicap in the provision of formulating scientific play experiences. Despite science being the first subject of the National Curriculum to be introduced and the focus of widespread inservice education for primary teachers, many practitioners still do not feel confident in teaching all science content areas. This has led to some areas being partially ignored. Introducing materials for exploratory play, for example those concerned with electricity and magnetism, can be a less threatening entry route for both teachers and children. Activities based on the children's initial explorations and questions are both easier to build on and focus directly on the child's present levels of understanding and questioning. For example, the three- and four-year-olds in the earlier scenario also thought that the red plastic coated wires they had been given made a bulb brighter than the black wires. This was despite the evidence of their observations. They were subsequently given a wider range of plastic coated coloured wires. Through experimentation and exploration it became obvious that the colour of the plastic coating on the wire made no functional difference. The teacher was able to structure future activities at an appropriate level and had valuable evidence of the patterns of logical thought the children were developing. Children and adults do not always believe concrete evidence. Play allows conflicting information in a variety of contexts to be presented in a non-threatening, self-guided manner.

Issues concerned with science and gender can also be explored through play. By making the science explicit in all activities, including play, children can recognize the science content in their everyday activities, interests and ways of working. Play activities based on the children's real lives, such as shopping, cooking, building and constructing, are especially fruitful for the teacher to note who chooses what and how the children are operating. The implementation of alternative ways of working can raise awareness and widen the range of experiences while ensuring equality of opportunity (as Jane Hislam has suggested in Chapter 3). One strategy which can be used is to have occasional single-sex groups working with constructional toys or engaged in balancing activities in the home corner, as well as allowing free choice during other times. Individual differences in the ways the children participate in activities in terms of their interaction with each other, the content matter involved and what is actually achieved, has become clearer. The links between planning, teaching and assessing the type of activity provided, monitoring who was involved and the individual behaviour and responses of children are important here. Teachers need to take account of the range of processes and content areas involved in science, and individual children's interests. They need to recognize the potential for science in the everyday, real-life experiences of the children as well as creating specific opportunities to further develop scientific skills, processes, attitudes, knowledge and understanding. If the teacher is not actively engaged in a teaching situation, observing children at play is both a revealing and realistic option. Similarly, playing with children can be a powerful diagnostic learning and teaching tool. Joining a game of rolling cars down a ramp provides the opportunity to increase gradients and debate the relative merits of the different vehicles.

Conclusion

Children need to be introduced to opportunities for science play in a systematic, structured manner both at eleven and three or four years of age. The powerful nature of this method of learning, when introducing new content and skills as well as extending other opportunities, needs to be built into teachers' planning and assessment, as are more formal teaching activities. The National Curriculum for Science states that:

> Pupils should develop the intellectual and practical skills which will allow them to explore and investigate the world of science and develop a fuller understanding of scientific phenomena, the nature of the theories explaining these, and the procedures of scientific investigation. This should take place through activities that require a progressively more systematic and quantified approach which develops and draws upon an increasing knowledge and understanding of science. The activities should encourage the ability to plan and carry out investigations in which children:
> (i)   ask questions, predict and hypothesize;
> (ii) observe, measure and manipulate variables;
> (iii) interpret their results and evaluate scientific evidence.

We believe strongly that carefully planned and challenging play activities can provide this powerful and appropriate learning experience for science, not merely in the early years classrooms but throughout the primary school.

12 | Mathematics and play

Rose Griffiths

To many people, mathematics and play seem to be mutually exclusive activities. One friend of mine, who teaches in an infant school, was adamant that: 'If I enjoy doing something, then I know it can't be maths. I was never any good at maths when I was at school, I hated it.' Like others, this friend had assumed that it was her *own* lack of ability which caused her difficulties with the subject. She had never considered the possibility that her feelings of inadequacy may have stemmed from the *methods* which were used to teach her.

Many people use the way *they* were taught as the basis of the way in which they then teach. When we show children how to tie shoelaces, reminiscences of our own childhoods return: since my mother showed me how to tie bows as a child in an effective way, it is reasonable for me to repeat it for my children. I am also able to think of other ways of teaching this skill with a child who needs a different approach because I understand what I am doing.

But what about other people who have been taught in ways which has left them confused, miserable and lacking in enthusiasm? Should they use the methods by which they were taught, if they become teachers themselves? It obviously makes little sense to do so, yet it is difficult for teachers in that position to generate other useful strategies simply because they will almost certainly lack confidence in their own abilities. So a vicious cycle is perpetuated.

There are, unfortunately, many ways of teaching mathematics badly. The Cockcroft Committee (1982), set up in response to concern about the standards of mathematics teaching in England and Wales, considered that many teachers used too narrow a range of both mathematical content and teaching styles. The Committee also echoed the concern of many employers and teachers that children (and adults), when faced with real-life, practical problems, often have difficulty in making effective use of the mathematical skills they actually possess. The Cockcroft Committee (DES 1982: 84) point out:

> emphasis on arithmetical skills does not of itself lead to ability to make use of these skills in practical situations. It is only within a broadly based curriculum that the ability to apply mathematics is enabled to develop.

Fortunately, there are many ways of teaching maths well. Children do not all learn in the same way and teaching is most likely to be successful when teachers are able to use a variety of methods and processes. The benefits of using play as a significant part of that repertoire are considerable: learning mathematics successfully through play is the focus of this chapter. First, I shall explore some of the advantages of learning maths through play and second, offer a range of suggestions for successful play activities which promote the development of mathematical skills and understanding.

The advantages of learning mathematics through play

There are, I believe, five key factors which it is worth exploring further: purpose, context, control and responsibility, time and practical activity.

Purpose
All of us learn better when there is a clear purpose to what we are doing. When children (or adults) play, a clear and significant purpose is enjoyment: there may be other purposes too, but fun is often sufficient to encourage us to concentrate and persist on a task for long enough for learning to occur.

Context
One of the things which makes maths a difficult subject to learn is the fact that some elements of mathematics are very abstract. Paradoxically, this abstraction is also what makes maths such a powerful tool – the use of symbols and mathematical models to represent real problems helps in the finding of solutions to them. Ways need to be found of helping children to see the links between concrete and abstract ideas. This can often be done using a starting point which makes human and practical sense to children in a context provided by play (Hughes 1986).

Control and responsibility
Many adults find it much easier to encourage children to make their own decisions when they are playing than when they are in a more formal learning situation. Allowing, and positively promoting, children to take control and ownership of their own activity is a very important

aspect of teaching mathematics. It is difficult to become more skilled at problem-solving, investigating or discussion if the teacher is always telling children what to do and how to do it. Adults need to strike a balance between providing structure or direction and expecting children to take responsibility for themselves. Children who are used to organizing themselves in play and learning activities are more likely to become confident and creative mathematicians than those who are continually 'spoon-fed'.

Time

Time for mathematical play, like other forms, provides children with a welcome and valuable opportunity to repeat things and gain mastery over actions and ideas, to raise questions, to discuss things with their peers and to clarify ideas, free from pressure to progress too quickly to the next mathematical concept. This is especially important with those aspects of maths which are hierarchical, where understanding each new idea depends on having understood its precedents. Everyone needs time for new ideas to be assimilated.

Practical activity

Play ensures the emphasis rests on practical activity, not written outcomes. For children to increase their mathematical understanding, it is important that their written recording should serve a purpose which is useful to each child and is linked to activity and discussion. *Written recording for its own sake will not help children with mathematical skills and understanding.* As Hughes (1986: 170) asserts:

> If they cannot tell how many bricks result from adding five bricks to nine, then there is no advantage to be gained by writing down the problem as '9 + 5 = ': this gets them no nearer the answer.

All the foregoing points are useful in thinking about planning for children's mathematical activity but particularly for those who do not feel very confident with maths themselves. Liz, a teacher of Year 1 children expressed her own anxieties:

> I want to let the children learn through play, but I worry that there's not enough maths in what they are doing, so I ought to be doing something more formal.

This raises two important issues:

1 Adults may not always recognize the mathematics in an activity, particularly a play-based experience, and may need time to analyse it carefully, preferably with a supportive colleague. For example, a teacher who was concerned about the mathematical value of playing with a railway layout was reassured when she realized that children were, among other things: gaining practical experience of comparing and measuring distances, using straight, curved and parallel lines, discussing position and movement, using diagrams and building in three dimensions.

2 The activity may not actually provide much opportunity for particular mathematical learning and it may need replanning to make the maths more explicit. For example, a teacher who had hoped that playing in a pretend shop would lead to children sorting, categorizing and counting soon realized that this was not actually happening. Although the shop was full of 'goods', there were generally only one or two of each item – unlike a real corner shop, where, for example, there would be at least 10 or 20 tubs of margarine. The teacher increased the amount of sorting and counting the children could do by providing a larger number of a smaller range of items, and also discussed with the children how the shopkeeper might keep some things in the stock room (a large cardboard box!) but would always try to keep the shelves looking full.

Playing *with* children obviously provides educators with time to discuss children's own ideas and, in addition, gives opportunities to share information and to teach them in a more direct way (Peter Smith takes up such points in his chapter). Some mathematical facts are rules or agreements which people in the past have established, such as:

• we call a shape with exactly three straight sides a triangle;
• this is how we write a figure five: 5;
• when we count things, we count each thing once; we don't miss any out or count any twice.

Children might eventually realize that these things are true by observing other people, but it is more straightforward and less frustrating for learners to be *given* this kind of information as and when they need it or want it (a point taken up by many other contributors to this book in relation to Bruner's 'scaffolding' principle).

Some mathematical facts, however, are ones which children need to work out for themselves, if they are to gain understanding and are to be convinced by them. For example:

• when we count a group of things and we do not take any away or add on any more, then there will still be the same number there when we recount; or
• 3 add 5 makes 8 or 5 lots of 3 make 15.

Frequent use may lead a child to knowing these facts off-by-heart, but, if children forget, they should be able to work each fact out again from scratch through understanding the processes. Play can provide the variety, repetition, motivation and persistence needed to eventually establish both understanding and fluency in an enjoyable way. Open-ended mathematical games provide a play context for learning skills and encourage interaction with both peers and adults.

Successful provision of mathematical learning through play

Play can give children the confidence to tackle quite complex ideas. The role of the teacher is to suggest new possibilities, to give information, to support children's ideas and to encourage discussion. The rest of this chapter will focus upon examples of play-based activities, planned to be enjoyable and mathematically useful. They are grouped under two main headings: *play and counting* and *play and shape and space*.

Play and counting

Learning to count groups of objects accurately takes a surprisingly long time for young children. Yet counting skill underpins children's understanding of arithmetic: if, for example, a child cannot count ten objects consistently then it makes no sense to do formal written arithmetic with numbers up to ten of the sort presented in many infant maths schemes. If children are to be good at arithmetic and be able to see number patterns, teachers must first help them to enhance and improve their counting skills. It is vital to provide short but frequent periods of counting practice in a way which fosters children's own abilities to organize and check results for themselves.

This group of activities all concentrate on number and algebra. Children find the play materials and games described much more attractive to play with than more abstract counting equipment such as cubes and counters. The problems devised make sense to children because they are set in an understandable context.

Helicopters

Children like making things to play with. Using a piece of paper folded in half lengthways, and cut across from one long side to the middle fold, to make flaps (see Figure 12.1) Shaun, (six years old), decided to draw helicopters. Other children drew teddies, dogs, fish, cars and babies, among other things. Shaun played with his strip by himself, with friends of the same age and with younger children in the class, then took it home to play with his younger sister. They enjoyed taking it in turns to turn down the flaps and ask each other, 'How many helicopters can you see?' Sometimes they counted to get the answer; sometimes they did sums: 'Two there, and one there, that's three.' Children who made a longer strip could work with larger numbers. Whichever number they had chosen, they became familiar with the combinations of numbers which made that total very quickly.

Teddies' teatime

The home corner was set up as the bears' house, and a variety of food was made for the teddies to eat in a reasonable quantity, so that there was enough to count when a group of children played together. Cookie shapes were cut from vanilla and chocolate coloured playdough and baked at a low temperature until they were hard enough to play with: jam tarts were made in the same way, with a small-sized cutter and 'jam' painted on after they had been baked, using red, green or yellow

Figure 12.1

acrylic paint. Corrugated card made sandwiches and crackers, and a variety of beads and bricks were used to represent fruit and other food.

Some children needed no prompting at all to count as part of their play; others only started to do so after watching and listening to the adult or other children. Each child operated at a different mathematical level. For example, Kerry mostly used none, one or two: 'What do you want, Blue Bear? Two cakes?' Anna set herself much more complicated tasks: 'I don't know about these jam tarts, if I can give them all five each or if there's not enough.'

Sitting with children who are playing and talking often gives us the chance to review their achievements and think about what they might benefit from doing next, in a way which is more accurate than more formal methods of assessment.

Monsters in the Bath

Monsters were drawn by the adult on a piece of A5 card, then photocopied to make four cards showing Monsters having a bath (see Figure 12.2). Monsters love playing with sponges, and these were made by cutting two sponge kitchen cloths (one blue, one orange) into small pieces. Children played with the cards and sponges in a variety of ways. Some children wanted time to play on their own to start with, without any suggestions from an adult or peers. Others wanted an idea to get them started.

Figure 12.2

Most often, a start would be made by choosing a number which the child needed to practise counting. Suppose it was six. Just for the first go, the adult would count six sponges on to one card to show what was wanted. Then the child would give the other Monsters six sponges each, too. The most popular way of playing was in a pair, when each child had four Monster in the Bath cards and they rolled a dice or picked a card from a pile of number cards to choose which number to count. When they had given their own Monsters their sponges, they would count each other's to check. In the course of one turn of the game, each child, therefore, had counted the practice number eight times.

Children could also make up sums for each other: 'Monster had four blue sponges and five orange ones. How many did she have altogether?' or 'Monster used to have ten sponges but she's lost two. How many has she got now?'

Some children liked using the little sponges to wash Monster's face or to polish the bath taps, and some sponges turned up in the bath in the dolls' house! Children liked drawing or painting pictures of Monster, and some wrote titles for their pictures, or wrote on a number to say how many sponges there were. They wanted to represent the maths they had done on paper, and they did so in ways which made sense to them, which only gradually moved closer to using numerals and other symbols. The parallels with the ideas of 'emergent writing' (Whitehead 1990) seem strong here. Emergent mathematics is usefully covered in Atkinson (1992).

Children's skills with mental arithmetic are very important and playing games and using play-based materials help them to develop mental images to use when they are calculating. Using a calculator alongside their game, to check or reassure themselves, is also useful. It provides them with a real reason for needing to know the number symbols +, − and =.

Figure 12.3

Monsters in the Bath was just one of a group of similar counting games which were used, including Spiders on Webs and Ladybirds in Gardens (see Griffiths 1988).

Dogs and Bones
Children who have used counting games like Monsters sometimes come up with ideas of games which they can make themselves (see Figure 12.3). 'Dogs and Bones' was Kelly's idea. She drew and cut out one dog, which she had help in fixing to another piece of card so that it would stand up. Her friend Jo (aged five years – a year younger than Kelly) drew the other dog, and both children cut 'bones' from little pieces of card.

At first the children used the dogs in the same ways as Monsters. Then they invented a simple new game: they took it in turns to throw a dice on behalf of each dog, and gave the dog that number of bones, so that each dog gradually accumulated more and more bones. Every now and then they counted to see how many bones each dog had got altogether. When they ran out of bones they made some more, and only stopped playing when each dog had such a large pile that they were finding it difficult to count them.

It was easy to extend this with a bit of thought. After watching a children's television programme where two puppets were sharing five apples between them – One for you and one for me; one for you and one for me. Oh, there's one left over! What shall we do? – a three-year-old shrieked excitedly at the television, 'Cut it up! Cut it up!' The puppet, unfortunately, was not aware of this possibility, and said, 'We'll have to put it back in the bowl.'

Why were the writer and producer of this programme apparently so frightened to introduce halves as an obvious solution to a real problem? We should not have such low expectations of children when presenting ideas in a context which makes sense to them. Fractions may be difficult to deal with when the expectation is one of calculating with them using pencil and paper, but this does not mean we should, or can afford to, ignore them at earlier stages.

So I talked with Kelly and Jo about sharing bones fairly between their two dogs. It was agreed that, if we had four altogether, each dog should have two bones. But what if we have five bones: how could the dogs share the extra bone? Kelly thought the dogs should just take it in turns, and have a lick each, but Jo said they wouldn't like that because they might want to crunch it up. He thought we could try hitting it on a rock, or sawing it up with an electric saw, or possibly running it over with a steam roller. Then Kelly produced scissors and snipped it in half!

The children were told that a half is written like this – $\frac{1}{2}$ – and were given a blank dice with the numbers $\frac{1}{2}$, 1, $1\frac{1}{2}$, 2, $2\frac{1}{2}$, 3 on each face. I showed them that, when counting up how many bones each dog had, it is possible to fit two halves together and count it as one bone. They played their Dogs and Bones game again, with adult prompting at first on how to say the numbers. They had no difficulty in counting out the right quantity, with the aid of the scissors if appropriate. After a few sessions of playing on their own, they were happy to work out in their heads the answers to questions such as: 'If your dog had one and a half bones, and you gave him two more bones, how many bones would he have altogether?'

Board games

Have you ever played snakes and ladders and found yourself wishing that someone would hurry up and win so that you could all go and do something else? If so, you will recognize at least one of the difficulties of games. Different games appeal to different people but all games can be frustrating. Perhaps it would be possible to reduce the frustration of snakes and ladders by having fewer snakes and more ladders.

In theory, many board games should encourage children to count, match and follow rules. In reality, children often play these games without gaining much in terms of mathematical experience. For example, when children play in a group, those who most need counting practice frequently have their pieces moved for them by more experienced players, or are told where to move to. If the main purpose of the game is to become the 'winner', there can even be good logical reasons for counting badly! Games where children compete against each other are often less likely to encourage them to explain things to each other and to discuss what they are doing, than cooperative games with a common purpose.

Making up a board game for oneself can involve a considerable amount of maths but the whole process can seem too daunting for children whose skills at measuring and drawing are still at an early stage. A preliminary stage of providing the children with a teacher-made blank playing board and some component play pieces can, however, produce some very interesting ideas. Playing boards made by drawing grids with a permanent pen on pieces of plastic table-covering are a good start. The most popular board I have made was a rectangle of four squares by eight squares, where each square measured 10cm. (One of the advantages of making games is that they can be made to a large scale.) The simplest way of using this board was for 'race games'. For example, four plastic animals, toy people or cars were lined up, and one or two children took turns to throw a dice and move the pieces to see which one would get to the end first.

Variations are plentiful. Using the same board, one group of children made 'ghosts' from cotton wool and had ghost races. Taking up the idea, a second group invented a new version where toy people raced, each with a ghost just behind them. For each turn, a dice was thrown twice – once for the person, once for the ghost – and the person had to try to get to the end before being caught by the ghost. The children experimented with different rules to give the toy people a reasonable chance of escaping! After a great deal of discussion, they decided that giving them one extra throw of the dice to start was best. Numbers were made for the board by writing them on separate 3cm squares of plastic material which children could fasten on to the main board for themselves, using blu-tack. Sorting the numbers into order and deciding where to put them is quite challenging for many children.

These numbers, along with cardboard cut-out snakes and ladders (made by glueing lolly sticks together) were used to make our own snakes and ladders game. Before playing, agreement had to be reached as to where to fasten the snakes and the ladders: it was possible to have only ladders, but the children decided it was more fun to have at least one snake!

Designing a board game uses many aspects of mathematics, not just number. Measurement, shape and ideas about probability are also important. The final section also looks at a range of mathematical ideas but concentrates on shape and space.

Play and shape and space

Play and counting

Many activities which children enjoy use shape, pattern, movement and position. Building, threading, sewing, printing, dancing and climbing are just a few examples. Children learn more when they have problems to solve (Fisher 1990; Tina Bruce's chapter) than when they are just asked to name shapes or describe what someone else has done. As I emphasized

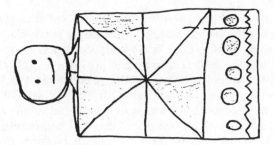

Figure 12.4

early on in this chapter, children need to use and apply their growing mathematical knowledge.

Towers for tortoises

Katie sometimes made small piles or lines of wooden bricks, but she never seemed to be very confident or enthusiastic about building. The turning point came after she had spent some time talking about how (especially at only four years of age) it is possible to see much more standing on a chair. At that time, the family had two wooden pull-along tortoises which we decided must sometimes get fed up, because they could only see people's ankles. Katie decided to build them a tower, to give them a different view. Katie's building now had a definite purpose, and she returned to the problem several times over the next few days. At first she did not want anyone else to copy her or help her, but then she relented and enjoyed working with others, getting ideas from them in return. For example, she started to think about ways of making bridges so that the tortoises could get from one tower to another. She learned by trial and improvement, becoming quicker, more skilful and more imaginative with her constructions. In quite a short space of time, Katie's new confidence in her skills with wooden bricks encouraged her to be more adventurous and thoughtful with other construction toys.

Sleeping bags

Talking with a group of five-and six-year-olds, I discovered that they had all, at some time, slept in sleeping bags. They were very keen to take up the suggestion that they could make little pipe-cleaner people and sleeping bags for them (see Figure 12.4). First the people were made, then the important things about sleeping bags were discussed before finally making them. Sleeping bags are cosiest if a person can stretch out and still have their shoulders covered, but it should not be so big that the person disappears completely inside it. Most sleeping bags have a pattern on them, and most are rectangular. The children had paper, coloured pencils, scissors and sticky tape. Cutting out a rectangle proved to be more difficult than most of them had thought it would be. Trying to judge how big to make the rectangle so that it would be the right size for their person once it was folded over was challenging, too, and called for a great deal of trial and improvement. (One child decided that changing the sleeping bag to fit the person was much too hard, so she cut her person's legs shorter instead!) The children were reminded not to fasten their sleeping bags together with sticky tape until they had decorated them. They used a variety of designs, sometimes like ones the children had seen themselves. Some drew on pictures (dogs, fairies or racing cars); others did spots, stripes or geometric patterns. Some of the children made tents from folded card, or chalets from small boxes, but many preferred to make another little person for the sleeping bag, the second time much more expertly than the first. They enjoyed playing with the things they had made, and they had developed their knowledge of shape, size and pattern.

Gymnastics

Sometimes children's spontaneous play from dinnertimes or playtimes gives them ideas they want to pursue when they come back into the classroom. So it was with Emma and her friend who had been playing 'gymnastics' after lunch. Emma (seven years of age) wanted to count up how many different positions she had tried. She tried describing them and counting at the same time, but lost track after just two or three, and said impatiently, 'Oh, give me some paper, I'll write them down and count them.'

Representing something from real life (i.e. in three dimensions) on to paper (in two dimensions) can be quite difficult to do, but Emma managed very well. Before she did each new drawing, she checked to make sure she had not already drawn herself like that before. She numbered her drawings as she went along, and was very pleased to find 15 positions altogether. (There may be doubts about the twelfth item in Figure 12.5 – see what you think!) Emma's concentration was remarkable – except if you realized how much she really wanted to know the answer to her own question.

Physical activity is an important part of learning about shape and space and there is usually no good reason to want to record what you do with paper and pencil. Just as with number work, children's written work in shape and space is most likely to be successful if the children can see a purpose in it for themselves. It should build upon practical activity and play, and never become an end in itself.

Conclusion

Maths and play are very useful partners. If we want children to become successful mathematicians, we need to demonstrate to them that maths

Figure 12.5

is enjoyable and useful, and that it can be a sociable and cooperative activity, as well as a quiet and individual one. We must be careful, too, to remember that play is not just a way of introducing simple ideas. Children will often set themselves much more difficult challenges if we give them control of their learning than if it is left to adults.

Plate 13   If we want children to become successful mathematicians, we need to demonstrate to them that maths is enjoyable and useful

Part 4
Assessing and evaluating play

Plate 14   *The child is at the centre of the evaluative process*

Plate 15   Observation, including participant observation, is central to early childhood educational processes

Plate 16   Through our childhood play we are partners with our future

13 | Evaluating and improving the quality of play

Christine Pascal and Tony Bertram

Providing young children with opportunities for quality play experiences is a challenge which all early childhood educators must address. There is strong evidence that high quality early childhood education, which embraces play as a central vehicle for learning, can have a significant and long-term effect on children's educational and social development (Beruetta-Clement *et al.*, 1984; Osborn and Milbank 1987). Unfortunately, research has also shown that the quality of play provision in many early childhood settings leaves a lot to be desired and recent legislation may be threatening this provision even further (DES 1990; Pascal 1990a). Clearly, the quality of play needs to be reviewed and improved if all children are to experience the vision of the 'excellence of play' outlined by the contributors to this book.

The importance of establishing procedures for evaluating and improving the quality of play provision in all early childhood settings was highlighted in the Rumbold Committee of Inquiry (DES 1990):

> We believe that it is vital that for all adults with responsibility for young children to recognise that for them play is a great deal more than recreation. (para. 91)

> We consider that regular monitoring and evaluation . . . is essential to the achievement of high standards. (para. 134)

It is important that all early childhood educators regularly ask themselves two critical questions:

- What is the quality of the play I am providing?
- How can I improve it?

These questions set in motion a cycle of evaluation and potential improvement. They demand commitment to a process of critical reflection and lead to action aimed at enhancing practice. This process of reflection and action lies at the heart of early childhood professionalism and should be applied to all aspects of the work of an early childhood educator. It seems absolutely appropriate, therefore, that play should be prioritized for scrutiny in this way.

All educators need to know what is happening in their professional settings, what is effective and what might be developed further. The evaluation and improvement process described in this chapter will help early childhood educators to identify needs, priorities and, most importantly, what appropriate action they might take to improve the quality of their play provision. Our work in a wide variety of early childhood settings has demonstrated that many practitioners are looking for a framework to support them in this process. We believe the Model for Evaluating and Improving Play contained within this chapter provides one such framework.

Some conceptual considerations

'Quality' is a much over-used word that is in danger of losing meaning in the political rhetoric and invective of our times. Philosophers, from the time of Plato and Aristotle, have engaged in debate about definitions of quality or excellence. Attempts to identify key elements in any definition of quality, be this related to play or any other aspect of educational or social life, have proved to be problematic and contentious. The difficulty lies in the concept of quality itself. As early philosophers pointed out, quality is a subjective and qualitative notion. When Plato discusses the concept of beauty, for example, he argues that it can only be understood after exposure to a succession of objects that display its characteristics. It is only understood when reflecting on the quality of those experiences. As Pirsig (1974: 85) also points out, 'Quality is neither mind nor matter, but a third entity independent of the two . . . even though Quality cannot be defined, you know what it is.' Attempting to give play quality fixed dimensions, to be objectively identified and measured, is perhaps a spurious and mistaken exercise.

We would argue therefore that because quality evaluation is essentially a value-based enterprise, it is best achieved through the active involvement of participants in the process. The subjectivity of the definition is thus acknowledged and celebrated as being central to the debate about quality. Quality is defined by the shared reflections and agreement of experienced practitioners. It is validated by the 'lived experience' held up for the scrutiny of peers (Whitehead 1989). We are very committed to this notion of a 'democratic' approach to developing quality. It aims

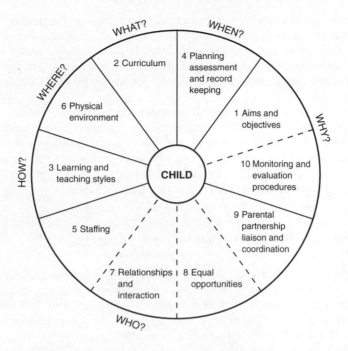

Figure 13.1 Pascal/Bertram quality evaluation framework

N.B: • the child is at the centre of the evaluative process;
     • there is an emphasis on people and relationships;
     • all dimensions are viewed as interrelating and are not discrete (Pascal and Bertram 1991).

to make provision responsive, to ensure that it is fit for its agreed purpose and, crucially, it empowers those who provide it (Pfeffer and Coote 1991). The process of review and implementation thus becomes part of the definition. Paradoxically, then, this definition of quality is not static or finite but dynamic, and varies with time and place. We make no attempt to give a fixed definition of the quality of play or to measure it quantitatively or objectively. Rather, our aim is to capture the quality of play as it is reflected in practice and to encourage practitioners to explore how the individuals in each setting, including parents and children, perceive and experience the quality of play.

Our Model for Evaluating and Improving Play is based on a theoretical framework of quality evaluation in early childhood education which has been developed by the Worcester team (see Figure 13.1). It has drawn extensively on the views of practitioners, parents and children in a range of settings and on an informed understanding of research about how young children learn. There is, therefore, an emphasis on the importance of the social context of learning and, in particular, an emphasis on the importance of the staff in establishing this context. This reflects our belief that learning only takes place when young children have positive relationships with those with whom they are interacting – a significant point made over and over again by the contributors to this book.

Within this framework, ten dimensions or aspects of quality may be identified. These dimensions represent the factors highlighted by the many early childhood educators we have worked with over the last three years as significantly affecting the *quality* of their provision. They are not intended to be an exhaustive list but we believe they provide a broad overview of the quality of play in any setting.

Ten dimensions of play quality

Although the ten dimensions are presented individually to facilitate ease of analysis, we must emphasize that in practice they are interrelated. They are also not presented in a hierarchical order. We believe *all* the dimensions are important and that all must be addressed to achieve quality. The significance attached to each dimension will vary according to the setting in which they are being applied and the perceptions of those involved in the evaluation process.

1   Aims and objectives
This dimension refers to the written and spoken statements of policy within a setting in which the aims and objectives of the play provision are made explicit. It also focuses on issues such as how the policy statements on play are formed, who is involved in their formation and how they are communicated to involved parties. The extent to which these aims are initiated, shared, communicated and understood by all the involved parties also needs to be considered.

2   Curriculum
This dimension is concerned with the range and balance of play activities provided and the learning opportunities they present for young children. The curriculum is interpreted very broadly to embrace children's all round cognitive and social development. It includes a consideration of the extent to which the play activities provide learning opportunities in language and literacy, mathematics, science, technology, physical, human and social, moral and spiritual, aesthetic and creative areas of experience. It may also include reference to the National Curriculum core and foundation subjects where this is appropriate (see Angela Anning's discussion in Chapter 5). When considering issues of

continuity and progression through play, the extent of differentiation within the play to cater for individual needs is also addressed.

3 Learning and teaching strategies
This dimension is concerned with how the play is organized and structured to encourage learning and discovery. The extent of children's independence and autonomy and the rules which govern behaviour and participation in play are considered. Who is participating in the play and what roles are being adopted by adults and children are key issues (Lesley Abbott also emphasizes this point in Chapter 6). The competences being displayed by the children in their play are also highlighted here.

4 Planning, assessment and record keeping
This dimension looks at how play is planned, and issues such as who is involved in the planning process and how far the planning builds upon the previous assessment of play activity. The assessment of children at play is considered and the efficacy of the methods of recording play activity and experience are noted (see also Vicky Hurst's examination of these issues in the following chapter). Access to and the sharing of records, and the use to which they are put, falls within the considerations of this dimension.

5 Staffing
This dimension focuses on the opportunities for the involvement of staff in children's play activity. Issues of staff deployment, ratios, management policy and attitude towards play are relevant. Opportunities for staff development and training, which focuses on play, are noted.

6 Physical environment
This dimension looks at the context in which the play occurs. The use of space, both inside and out, to create an environment for play is considered. The availability, condition and appropriateness of the play equipment are documented (points also discussed by Peter Heaslip in Chapter 8).

7 Relationships and interactions
This dimension looks at how the children and adults interact in their play. How far and in what ways relationships are expressed and developed in the play activities is considered. The social rules and codes of conduct which operate are seen as significant. The opportunities for self-initiated play and the degree of staff intervention would fall within this dimension. The involvement of the children, and their interactions in the play activities, is highlighted as a means of reflecting on the quality of the educational experience they provide. (Chapters in Parts 1 and 2 emphasize many of these points in their different ways.)

8   Equal opportunities

This dimension refers to the way in which the play reflects and celebrates cultural and physical diversity and challenges stereotypes. The play equipment and the play activities are scrutinized with regard to issues of race, gender, disability and social class.

9   Parental partnership and liaison

This dimension focuses on the nature of the partnership with parents and the ways in which they, and other members of the local community, are involved in the play activities. The extent to which the play reflects the children's home and community environment is explored. Links between the setting and other play providers are also noted.

10   Monitoring and evaluation

This dimension looks at the procedures by which the quality and effectiveness of the play policy and provision are monitored and evaluated. Who is involved in these processes, and how the results of this process are acted upon, are considered.

These *ten dimensions* form the basis for the Evaluation Phase of the Model and have been translated into a schedule of evaluative questions (see Figure 13.2).

Implementing the model

Practitioners who wish to evaluate and improve the quality of play in their setting need to bear in mind that this process will not be achieved overnight and without effort. Effective and long-term improvement takes time and commitment. We estimate that the whole cycle of evaluation and improvement embodied in the Model will take at least nine months to implement. This timescale may need to be extended if the setting is unaccustomed to this kind of self-evaluation and development process, or if the proposed improvements are fundamental and involve considerable resourcing in both material and human terms. Less fundamental improvements may be achieved in a shorter time scale. Time is a precious commodity in the present climate but the benefits of such a commitment to improvement are wide-ranging and necessary, if the issue of play quality is to be addressed.

The Model for Evaluating and Improving Play has four key stages which practitioners need to consider:

Stage 1: Evaluation
Stage 2: Action-planning
Stage 3: Implementation
Stage 4: Reflection.

Figure 13.2 Schedule for evaluating the quality of play

1 Aims and objectives
Is there a policy on play?
How did the policy arise?
Who does it apply to?
What are the expressed aims and objectives of play?
What is the rationale for the play provision?
How is the policy communicated?
How far is the play policy shared between educators, parents and children?

2 Curriculum
What play activities are available?
What kind of play do these activities facilitate?
What curriculum experiences do they offer?
How broad and balanced are these experiences?
Is there continuity and progression in children's play?
How far does the play cater for individuals?

3 Teaching and learning strategies
How is the play structured or directed to encourage learning?
How is the play organized and managed?
What rules operate and who sets these?
Who is participating in the play?
How are the children using the play activity?
What competencies are the children displaying?
What is the role of the adult in the play?

4 Planning, assessment and record keeping
How are the play activities planned?
Who is involved in the planning?
Are the children assessed in their play and how is this managed?
How is this assessment recorded?
What use is made of these play records?

5 Staffing
Which staff are involved in the children's play?
How is the staff involvement managed?
What staff development opportunities are offered which focus on play?

6 Physical environment
How much space is available for play activities inside and outside?
How is this space organized and utilized?
What facilities and equipment are available?
How developmentally appropriate are they?
What condition are they in?
How are they organized and utilized?

7 Relationships and interactions
What kind of interactions are occurring in the play?
Who initiates the interaction?

What relationships are observable in the play activity?
What relationships does the play encourage?
How much involvement is there?
What codes of conduct operate?

8 Equal opportunities
In what ways do the play activities reflect cultural and physical diversity?
How far and in what ways does the play challenge stereotypes?
Do the play equipment and facilities reflect an awareness of equal opportun-
ities' issues?

9 Parental partnership and liaison
How are parents involved in the play?
In what ways do parents, and other adults in the community, contribute to the
play activities?
Does the play reflect the children's home and community environment?
What liaison is there between the setting and other play providers in the
community?

10 Monitoring and evaluation
How is the quality of play within the setting monitored and evaluated?
How often is this done?
Who is involved in the process?
How is this evaluation acted upon?

Stage 1: Evaluation
In this first phase, practitioners work together with colleagues, parents
and children to *document* and *evaluate* the quality of their play provision.
The evaluation questions detailed in the Schedule for Evaluating the
Quality of Play (Figure 13.2) provide the framework for this phase.
Evidence is gathered by the practitioner to answer the questions relating
to each of the ten dimensions. Methods which have proved helpful in
providing evidence to answer the questions include:

Documentary analysis
Documentary analysis in which the published policy statements of a
setting are critically analysed to determine the stated philosophy on play
and the settings, aims and objectives regarding its play provision.

Observation
Systematic and focused observation of children at play, play activities,
the use of play space and equipment and the role of adults in play
provide a wealth of evidence to facilitate the evaluation process. Video,
audio-taped and still photographic data can be helpful. A journal or
logbook kept by the practitioner over a period of time in which personal
observations and perceptions may be noted is also valuable. (Vicky Hurst
takes these points up in detail in the next chapter.)

Interviews
Interviews of colleagues, parents and children about their play experience, their perceptions of the play opportunities provided and their
attitudes towards play allow for a wider perspective in the evaluation
process.

The evidence collected about each of the ten dimensions is collated by
the practitioner into a detailed case study which should capture the
quality of play within the setting. This case study is then discussed by
the participants and carefully evaluated. The perceptions and views of all
participants are given status and acknowledgement. Contradictions,
agreements, common themes and issues are identified.

This stage should take approximately eight weeks in total.

Stage 2: Action-planning
From this evaluation, the practitioner identifies priorities for action and,
equally importantly, the resources and expertise required to achieve
these. Discussion with managers and other resource holders is essential
during this phase and the practitioner *must* be prepared to promote and
explain carefully what is required and why. It is also vital to explore as
many sources of support as possible. Creative and radical approaches to
finding the required resources may be needed and the practitioner should
not be afraid to try these.

Communicating clearly to all those who will be involved in the action
to improve play, what is to happen, and how they can help, is a critical
part of this phase of the improvement process. Making people feel involved, and giving them some ownership and investment in the improvement process, will ensure their support and also share the burden
of any changes which are required. Children, parents, members of the
local community and colleagues all have something to contribute and
should be offered the opportunity to do so. It is necessary to organize
meetings which provide real opportunities for dialogue and sharing.

At the end of this stage a structured and realistic Action Plan for the
improvement of play should emerge which has clearly defined objectives to be achieved within an identified time scale (generally six months).

This stage should take approximately two weeks.

Stage 3: Implementation
In the third stage the Action Plan is implemented. This will entail a
programme of individual and/or institutional development which relates
closely to the agreed priorities. Throughout this stage, progress through
the Action Plan will be monitored and the practitioner is encouraged to
gather evidence and reflect upon the effect of the action on the quality
of the play in the setting. Again, regular and systematic observation of
children and adults at play is critically important to enable any judgement to be made about the effectiveness of the improvement process.

This stage should take approximately six months, but this may be considerably shorter or longer, depending on the extent of the changes proposed.

Stage 4: Reflection

In this final stage the practitioner is encouraged to reflect upon the evaluation and improvement process, and to review the impact of their Action Plan in the light of experience. It is particularly important to look carefully at the effect of the action upon the quality of the children's play and to scrutinize the evidence of this. This should then lead them into a further cycle of evaluation and improvement.

This stage should take approximately two weeks.

Strategies for success

(a) Be open and honest about your intentions: share what you are doing with all who might be affected. Try and involve them as far as possible and keep them fully informed throughout the Evaluation and Improvement process.

(b) Do not rush through the process. Change takes time and it is important that those involved don't feel over-pressurized, as resentment will creep in and the development will suffer.

(c) Make sure your Action Plan has a clear purpose and focus and that this is clearly explained to all who are affected by it. Uncertainty and fear about what you might be doing will engender resistance.

(d) Be realistic in what you aim to achieve – it is better to progress step by step. Small victories will fuel larger developments and give participants a sense of achievement. Try and break down your larger scale intentions into prioritized, short-term goals.

(e) Be prepared to set aside time and energy for the process. Success will not be achieved if this process comes bottom of your list of priorities. If you are not wholly committed to improving the quality of play in your setting it is unlikely that others will be motivated to do so.

(f) Be systematic and organized as you progress through the stages. Data-gathering needs equipment, time and organization. Notification of meetings need to be given in advance and the venue and format given careful consideration if they are to be productive.

(g) Be prepared to act as an advocate for what you believe in. Convincing others of the rationale for your action is critically important, particularly in the competition over resources. You must be prepared to promote the importance of excellent play in your setting and be absolutely clear about what you need to achieve this. Putting play on the agenda of all decision-makers and resource-holders is the key to success.

Conclusion

In discussions with colleagues who have used the Model, we have been made aware that the Model offers a useful framework for school and staff development. One reception teacher volunteered the following comments:

> The Model acted as a prompt, reminding me of areas I have not concentrated on lately. It made me think deeply about the nature of play, particularly in the context in which I work. I already had some internalized notion of a definition/concept of play and completing the questionnaire brought me to various understandings . . . it is of paramount importance to understand the play going on in my classroom if it is to be extended appropriately for the benefit of the child's learning . . . continuity must be considered both within and without the classroom. This means working with parents and with colleagues. Writing this critique has helped me sort this out.

Many teachers felt their policies, aims and values were communicated easily to others simply because they were implicit in their practice. Another colleague highlighted this in her response:

> Between members of staff, there is an implied understanding but it needs to be developed into a coherent and generally agreed policy. It is obvious that aims and objectives vary between individuals although all would adhere to the assumption of a child-centred curriculum. Policy at present is communicated through classroom practice which is why ambiguities are apparent. Our recent chat sessions for Reception parents and for Governors allowed us to share our philosophy on play. It was suggested that similar sharings should take place with different year groups.

In writing down and sharing views about play, practitioners had to confront the fact that not everybody shared the same vision and many were mistaken about other colleagues' rationale. This gave rise initially to some difficulties and required tact, compromise and negotiation. It also required a re-examination of one's own beliefs and the confidence to hold them up for scrutiny. Sometimes this meant abandoning or altering long-cherished beliefs. This process became part of the professional development of individuals, making them more articulate about what was central to their view of play and more positive about its value:

> Through doing the evaluation schedule, I was able to reflect upon the provision of play in my Nursery. On the whole I was pleased with my findings. I am not smug or self-satisfied because I know that there are areas that need attention. Equal opportunities, for example, needs more of a positive approach. However, we are heading towards certain goals and ideals – not in a hurricane approach, more like a gentle steady progression. Things I wanted to do 12 months ago are now coming to fruition and without a revolution.

Their knowledge and articulacy was enhanced by the process and often a 'commonality of belief' emerged (Bruce 1987). There has been much recent evidence to suggest that there is a gap between the rhetoric and the reality of play in school settings and we need to question why this is so (Pascal 1990b). The Plan helped many practitioners to confront this and to address the reasons for the compromise of their principles.

> I found the whole process a valuable and salutary exercise. I think everyone should confront such probing. It encouraged you to think of how you actually evaluate your practice, how you implement your philosophy and communicate this to others – staff, parents and governors. It highlighted areas where improvement of technique and classroom management are necessary because they have become sloppy or are not actually up and running. It encouraged critical reflection. Do I practise what I preach? Are my values being compromised? Why? How? Do I do this or is this what I would like to achieve? I feel the questions could be used to access any part of the curriculum whatever the emphasis. I'll use them again to evaluate my own practice and I think they could be used as part of inservice work with our own staff or with teachers from other schools in our Early Years Support Group.

The process of reflecting, justifying, and rehearsing strengthened the professional understanding of these educators. This honing of their beliefs not only improved the quality of their practice but, just as importantly, it gave them the tools to become more confident, more knowledgeable and more articulate in their advocacy of the importance and excellence of play in the early years of education.

Authors' note

We should like to acknowledge the help and critical support of many of our friends, students and colleagues who work with young children. In particular, we shoud like to thank Ros Bunting, Alison Foster and Anne Ramsden for their comments on the Evaluation Schedule.

14 Observing play in early childhood

Victoria Hurst

Observation is central to early childhood educational processes. It gives the factual information upon which the other processes, including monitoring and assessing the progress of individual children, depend. Planning the whole curriculum for children under the age of eight requires information which only observation can give, and practice cannot be evaluated without it.

Observation is a high-level professional process, requiring a well-founded understanding of early childhood education and the development of classroom expertise. Observation of play is both demanding and rewarding for practitioners: it challenges them to learn from what they observe of children's spontaneous behaviour. This requires a high degree of insight, knowledge, and competence in order to link the professional's knowledge of the children with the range of knowledge and understanding of the world which young people are required by society to acquire. It also enables practitioners to evaluate the effectiveness of what they have planned by comparing what they intended to achieve with the actual effect of their work on children's quality of learning.

In this chapter, I shall examine three main aspects of observing play:

1 observation in educational settings at the present time, the current scene and its background;
2 how observation is – and can be – used as a tool for teaching and learning;
3 recording the evidence of observations.

My aim is to show that learning from observation is an active process. If staff believe in play and in what they can learn from observation of it, they must incorporate this belief into their daily practice (a point emphasized by Chris Pascal and Tony Bertram in the previous chapter). There is, however, a need to be aware of the complex interplay of influences which work against our best intentions. In order to examine the way in which these forces help to form attitudes to professional responsibilities, staff need to know about the philosophical and economic influences which affect their attitudes to various aspects of their work and attitudes and actions relating, in particular, to the observation of play.

Within this chapter, I recount some of the messages received about the difficulties and conflicts practitioners say they encounter in their professional lives. It is very important that their concerns are aired. When their dilemmas are taken seriously, it is possible to help practitioners to meet their responsibilities and professional tasks more effectively. These insights about professional experiences in turn need to be related to what is known about how young children develop understanding and knowledge about the world and the skills – social, linguistic, physical and cognitive – with which they do this. From this discussion, it should be possible to make recommendations about the place of observation in early childhood education and professional practices.

Observation in the 1990s

Professionals and pedagogic principles
Early years practitioners of all kinds hold views about the principles that underlie their work. These often take the form of such statements as 'young children learn through play'. In varied settings, and with differing training and conditions, educators at all levels recognize that children have much to gain from play. However, practitioners themselves do not always find it easy to be clear about the implications for their work (Bruce 1992). This has led to a devaluing of play: practitioners have often used children's free-play opportunities as an occasion for them to get on with something else. If, however, play is seen as an opportunity for children and adults to explore the links between children's thinking and the pedagogic concerns of the adult, it becomes a natural part of the educational process – Peter Heaslip stresses this and related points in Chapter 8.

All the connections between play and young children's development have not as yet been marked out (see Peter Smith's analysis in Chapter 1), but recent studies (such as Gura 1992) are establishing that, by observing play, practitioners can improve their sensitivity to children's cognitive engagement with different ways of exploring, understanding and representing different aspects of the world. This gives present-day meaning to the tradition, established by Susan Isaacs, of seeing play as a source of information for educators (1933: 425–6).

There is no doubt that much useful information can be gathered through noting everyday interactions in children's play (participant observation) and through structured observations for special purposes. Yet, although observation is clearly the tool needed for teacher assessment at all age phases within the National Curriculum, just as it is in preschool education, observation as a teaching tool is not yet widely acknowledged in early childhood education generally. Observation of play, in particular, is the most crucial aspect of all.

Educators in conflict

Observation has always been a demanding professional undertaking and it is the first pedagogic process to suffer when practitioners are under pressure because of inadequate resources of staffing, accommodation, outdoor space and equipment.

In the last few years much has changed in nursery and infant education, and in the voluntary and social service sectors of provision for children under five years of age. The view that the early years of education are about inculcating the basics of the subject curriculum, (perhaps only the core subjects at that), has run counter to the idea that we learn how to teach young children from knowing them as persons and understanding their needs and ways of thinking. Perceptions of the professional task have altered in consequence, and it has been tempting to think, for instance, that a curriculum for the early years can be defined in terms very similar to the 'basics' of an impoverished subject-based infant curriculum – as Angela Anning forcibly argues in Chapter 5.

It is striking how often adults who state that they value play in early childhood actually show by what they do – or rather by what they do not do – that they do not really believe what they assert. Although they are apparently committed to it, other factors seem to get in the way. Nearly every discussion of observation throws up issues that cast light on the conflicts and problems that staff are experiencing in their work. In the hectic and pressurized climate of today, it is easy to lose the sense of a professional standpoint, with a consequent loss of hope and self-esteem as well. We have to face the fact that, whatever practitioners say about their professional commitment to observation, they are subject to pressures which subvert their intentions.

Influences on educators' use of observation

An informal collection of recent comments from educators about observation will give some idea of what accommodations are being made to the conflicts they face:

> My job is to get them ready for 'big school' – they don't do that sort of thing [play] there.

> I can't afford the time [for observation]. I must keep up with the National Curriculum or they'll get behind.

We're here to teach them, not to observe them.

I wouldn't like the parents/the Head to see me not working.

As can be seen, there appears to be uncertainty about what education in the early years should be about (see Tina Bruce's discussion in the final chapter). Is it about preparation for the learning that is to come later? For some people this is the accepted view: teaching is seen as a form of instruction alone, with the demands of later age-phases dominating. Assessment is also, more often than not, seen as testing. Practitioners are discouraged from observing in order to find out how children are progressing in anything other than the 'testable' areas. The curriculum becomes dominated by the need to be sure that, for instance, a set pattern can be copied, with the consequence that the child's own patterning is marginalized. Another aspect of this approach is the idea that observation is for children who have, or are, problems: 'We'll do it if there seems to be something wrong.'

Some educators would like to observe the children but find that taking in more children at a younger age precludes observation. The pressure of numbers, the ethos of the school, the way the classroom is organised: all take precedence over the need to accommodate observation:

I can't talk and write and observe at the same time.

There are too many of them to observe individuals.

They can have 'choosing time' [for play] when they've finished their work. That's when I hear readers, so I can't observe them.

Other people seem to avoid observation on principle, finding different ways to explain the position:

Of course, we do it all the time anyway, but we haven't got time to write it down.

The experienced staff can keep it all in their heads.

Good teachers know their children naturally.

The impression here is that the person speaking is relying on an almost mystical professionalism, which gives knowledge without effort and without the need to produce evidence. There is reason to think that this is a defensive position. It is understandable that practitioners should be aware of observation as a rather double-edged process. Observing children gives practitioners insight into the effect that their provision has on the quality of children's learning and provides evidence for professional evaluation. The result may well be necessary changes in practice and in professional development, both of which may be threatening at first, particularly at the present time when professional self-confidence is at a low ebb.

Each of these comments, in different ways, relates to constraints on the use of observation as a professional tool. As observation is the only source of hard data for continuous monitoring and assessment of children, for curriculum development and for self-evaluation, practitioners must be encouraged to resist these pressures. Observation can make their professional task easier and it is to this that I now turn.

Observation as a tool for teaching and learning

Since questions about procedure are secondary to questions about the purposes which observation serves, it is helpful to establish first what observation is for. Different purposes usually require somewhat different approaches: general information-gathering about the group of children, for example, will be different from seeking specific information about a particular child. What we want to find out and how we use the tool of observation must be closely connected in our minds and in practice. Decisions about procedure must be made on the basis of knowledge about young children and how they learn.

Research into development in early childhood
Early childhood has been the subject of a striking body of research in recent years. Writers such as Schaffer (1971 and 1974), Trevarthen (1974 and 1982) and Dunn (1988) have shown that very young children have, from infancy, a strong orientation towards social relationships and towards the interpretation of the behaviour of those closest to them. These studies demonstrate young children's drive towards personal relationships and towards making sense of the world around them.

This, in turn, has illuminated the overall picture of what early years education should be about. Children need to be seen as highly competent learners who, because of their youth and lack of experience of the world, require provision for learning which is very carefully planned to meet their individual and collective needs. Child-development research has been accompanied by a corresponding evolution of thinking in the area of curriculum studies which has had, and continues to have, a powerful influence on our perceptions of what is appropriate for young children. The idea of the developmentally appropriate curriculum incorporates what is known about young children's ways of learning into a framework for practitioners. This is radically different from the subject-based approaches which, not surprisingly, depict the youngest children as the least successful learners. As described by Blenkin and Kelly (1981, 1983 and 1988) the curriculum for young children in any educational setting should have regard both to the understandings and capabilities of young children and to the quality of the context for learning provided by those with the responsibility for their education (Blenkin and Whitehead 1988). The key to the very high quality standards that both teachers and children are capable of is the teacher's knowledge and understanding of the child.

All of this has implications for the way in which observation is used if children are to be provided with a good quality education. Observations need to provide evidence of children's meaning-making about the world, which mostly occurs where they are free to interpret what they do in their own way, particularly in 'free play' situations (Tina Bruce covers this more fully in the final chapter).

Imaginative play and children's understandings about the world

Some writers may question whether there is as much to be learned about children's understanding of the world from imaginative 'free play' as from play provision guided by the adult. The play situations that adults create do enrich children's understanding, and educators will often get valuable insights into children's thinking from observing them as they explore the possibilities offered by, say, a garden centre created after a visit (Neil Kitson and Nigel Hall both explore these aspects in Chapters 7 and 9 respectively). Play that is totally directed by children can give even more insights because children have already established some shared understandings with the adults, and are using play to further their own purposes. Play that is originated by children within the educational framework gives children the freedom and security they need to be able to express themselves imaginatively. It gives educators the opportunity for high quality observations.

Consider the following example from a teacher's diary:

In the classroom the dolls' house was placed on a table, with warm soapy water in bowls and small scrubbing brushes. Two children, Andrew and Pippa, came and helped scrub the little house; Earl watched, as he often did since entering the class a few weeks ago. Andrew and Pippa talked about cleaning in their homes, and about what they liked doing. Earl was silent. Later on in the playground he was seen with a group of boys on bicycles. He had the carpentry box with him, and was offering tools to the others. They took them, not sure what he intended, until with a grin he turned to the gate and began to 'mend' it. They joined him, and continued for some time. An adult went over to keep a distant eye on things. Later on, the adult set up a similar 'real-life' carpentry activity in which Earl took the lead. Some days later he organized a game of building with big blocks to make low walls, at first for children to walk along. He was meticulous about using the blocks in the right way to get them level and steady. The walls eventually went all round the block area. Subsequently, with some other children, he set up a picnic within the walls, with a rug, and was insistent that the adult who had provided the carpentry activity came and shared the picnic.

The activities provided by adults can often be used by children in this tangential way. From the children's own play the adults get insight into what children are focusing on, and how they feel.

Further observations on Earl revealed:

> Earl is still feeling shy and a bit unsettled. He finds it hard to join in with activities where talking is a feature. (English is not his mother tongue.) He prefers activities that are more doing than talking, but is full of initiative and creativity when he can organize his own play. He is able to organize children and has ideas that they were interested in. When he found that the rug would not fit inside the block enclosure, he carefully moved the walls back until the space was big enough. He was nearly right about the rug's size – this might be because he remembered using it the other day.

Understanding children as people is the starting-point for deciding how to teach them. This observation contained information about Earl as a mathematician and as a creator of stories and dramatic play, together with insights into a boy who derives a sense of personal value from helping with carpentry jobs at home.

What is necessary for observation of play?

Once the place of observation in education is understood and accepted, the next step is to consider the relationship between children and practitioners. Observation is almost impossible if adults are constantly having to intervene to prevent harm, and children are unlikely to play imaginatively for any length of time in unsafe or uncomfortable surroundings. The gradual establishment between children and practitioner, and then between children and children, of some unwritten rules and understandings about mutual respect and understanding is a necessity.

Sound relationships have a great deal to do with the adult's knowledge of the children, and the classroom context for learning provision. It also has a great deal to do with the children's understanding of the adults and about what they are intended to learn.

The context for observation

Blenkin and Whitehead (1988) define three kinds of essential professional expertise:

- understanding children and their development in an educational context (p. 60);
- professional competence rooted in a theoretical understanding of educational issues (p. 60);
- the knowledge-content that is to be shared with the children (p. 57).

Observing children is a process that depends for its effectiveness on professional expertise in all three areas.

Developing the curriculum from observation

Matching provision with children's growing knowledge and understanding of the world requires data drawn from children's talk, explorations and play. From the observation of Earl's building and his picnic, it was possible to note some vital information about his capacity for mathematical thinking, his social expertise, and his imaginative capacity. Ideas were gleaned for future provision which would build on his strengths and help him to feel more confident about using English in the classroom. This is one of the main reasons for asserting that observation should be the dynamic source of curriculum development in the early years – it is virtually impossible to make appropriate educational provision without such data. In addition, professionals are rightly required to justify what they do with young children and must give evidence (through the monitoring and assessment of children) that they are extending and developing learning in a balanced and rigorous way.

The demands on practitioners are very complex: relating the general curriculum to individual learners is a sophisticated operation requiring both sound curriculum knowledge and a sensitive understanding of young children. Much can be ascertained through play that could not be discerned in any other way about the learning strategies different children use. Having gained from observation much needed knowledge and understanding of individual children, it is also possible to build classroom provision from this learning. For example, does a child spend much time playing with sand? If so, then may be that is how adults can extend the mathematics and science for that child. Is a particular friendship the high point of a child's time at school? If so, then the pair of friends may be encouraged to build on their enjoyment of shared, collaborative play.

The observations made of children provide vital information about teaching and learning. I now move on to explore the ways in which observations can show whether these efforts have been successful.

Recording the evidence of observations

Throughout the early years, educators want accurate information about how children are progressing in their knowledge, understanding and skills. In monitoring children's development, practitioners fulfil their responsibilities in two ways. They gain information about:

1 the progress of individual children;
2 how well their educational planning and provision is contributing to the quality of all the children's learning.

Making relevant statements

The following observation of a top infant class could give the opportunity to meet both of these requirements. The account, which has been abbreviated and summarized in places, is an example of the normal participant observation referred to early in this chapter:

The children had helped to set up an office in the classroom after a donation of a typewriter. Appropriate clothes and equipment were available. Now five children were involved in sorting out the things they particularly wanted to play with and generally 'making the place their own'. The adult approached within earshot and, after sitting quietly nearby for a while, was invited to 'come in the office'. The following took place:

Adult:	Whose office is it? Is it yours?
Child 1:	It's ours – we're gonna send you a letter.
Adult:	Oh, dear, what have I done?
Child 1:	(in joking voice, perhaps in case the adult did not engage with the play story) You left your car on the line and now you've got a ticket.
Adult:	Oh no, and I haven't got any money.
Child 1 and Child 2:	(instantly fascinated) Haven't you really? Not any at all?
Adult:	Well, only a bit and I need to buy food and pay my rent. And I want to go to the pictures and see *Beauty and the Beast*.

The children discussed this and agreed it was a great film, and that they would help the adult with finances. They wrote out the parking ticket, discussed the cost, and settled down to talk through how much money would be needed for food and rent. The amounts of money cited were negligible but the processes of listing, attempting to add several numbers together, and presenting a total were carried out without prompting. The adult suggested maybe it might be better to go to the cinema next week and watch TV instead this week. The children kindly said they would put on a show for the adult to make up for missing the film, and began to make plans.

The activeness and articulacy of the first two children, the quietness and discretion with which other children pursued their own aims of costing up the adult's accounts and the forms for parking tickets and receipts which were made, were all noted on the one observation form. The form for this first stage of information-gathering needs to be as plain as possible, but with spaces for essential information (see Figure 14.1).

It is important that this format should be minimally structured so that it gives an accurate picture of what really happened. Analysis of this first stage should take place on a separate form, where the practitioner can identify some of the thinking and imagination as well as the social and emotional evidence. It is important to have a format that requires the practitioner to give consideration to these elements, rather than one that goes straight for the curriculum content.

Figure 14.1　Observation format

Date _____

Time (including duration) _____ Place _____

Children's names _____

Ages _____

Actions

_____

_____

_____

Conversation

_____

_____

_____

Play themes

_____

_____

_____

In the scenario above, there is evidence of much more than just the beginnings of writing, reading and number work. These children are confronting powerful issues in their lives and responding with creativity, ingenuity, insight and emotional maturity. The record of these under-standings and the personal responses of the children is a challenge to the practitioner: is what is being offered seen as adequate for these young thinkers who show such qualities? The form to record this reflective analysis also needs to be as little structured as possible (see Figure 14.2), since no practitioner can forecast what children will demonstrate, or how wide and deep their concerns may be.

If there is a lot of interesting material, adults might like to have a third form for general analysis of the observation (see Figure 14.3, page 184). This form can be used to record what has been seen of the shared understandings among the children of the uses of mathematical think-ing, their awareness of literacy in the world around them, the confident reproduction of administrative strategies, and the capacity to assume, at

Figure 14.2   Classroom play analysis

Date of observation being analysed _____

Children involved _____

Staff responsible for the present analysis _____

Evidence seen of children's ideas about

_____

_____

_____

Evidence seen of social and emotional development

_____

_____

_____

Evidence of play and imaginative interests in

_____

_____

_____

_____

a moment's notice, the dramatic roles available. These are all also relevant to the practitioner's self-evaluation.

It is the classroom context of personal relationships, agreed aims, and general ethos which is the most influential in guiding and supporting young children's learning. The invisible network of attitudes which convey educational and personal values and principles in classrooms determine much of the values, principles and attitudes with which children also come to their education. If these are not in sympathy with what the practitioner is trying to do, every step is uphill. So, what did the evidence reveal about this particular classroom? The information showed that, in general, children were seizing hold of the strategies offered to them for learning, including the use of reference books to see how to spell 'Beauty' and (imaginatively) a telephone directory to see where the film was being shown. Ideas about sharing out money for household purposes and about estimating cost were being explored, although as yet, of course, the sums used were small. The adult could be reassured that at least this group of children were making good use of the provision for learning, and that they were able to relate it to real-life issues. This information would also be useful to their next teacher, for, if children did not display this quality of

Figure 14.3   Classroom play analysis – literacy, mathematical thinking (other curriculum)

Date of observation being analysed _____

Children involved _____

Staff responsible for the present analysis _____

Evidence seen of children's ideas and understandings about _____

_____

_____

_____

_____

_____

learning in the following class, questions would present themselves about how well such achievements were being followed on and extended.

In the evidence noted in relation to each child, the forms, receipts, accounts and all the relevant material should be kept or photocopied – some in draft form as evidence of the level of activity, and some as evidence of formal finished activities like the parking ticket, the programme for the show and the seating tickets. Some particular aspects of individual learning should also be noted. These include:

• strategies for listing, adding and interpretation of accounts;
• awareness of the comparative sizes of amounts;
• composition of official letters and informal notes;
• capacity to read and reproduce 'official' English;
• capacity to interpret official phrases such as 'without delay';
• the quality of spelling and handwriting.

Information relevant to the National Curriculum Attainment Targets would emerge from all of this, in ways which have been analysed by the Early Years Curriculum Group (1989). Apart from the ATs, these forms, and the entire approach, are as suitable for under-fives in a variety of settings as for the statutory-age children across the primary school. My observations of children playing and exploring in museum education settings have produced material which can easily be recorded and analysed using this structure (Hurst 1991: 52–3).

When and how often should we observe?
Practitioners should give themselves time to absorb the results of observations and to communicate the information to parents and colleagues,

as well as to receive information from them. Decisions need to be made about how often new information on children and their use of the learning environment is needed. Time needs to be set aside for this. Given that individual records will be regularly reviewed, some people might find it a useful structure to build in a specific time to observe different aspects of the learning environment regularly. Others may prefer a particular moment of the day when there is a relaxation of pressure and it becomes possible to review who is doing what, where and how satisfactorily. This regular structure of observation should continue throughout the year, with targeted observation used when necessary as in the cases given below.

Targeted observation
There are many kinds of further knowledge that practitioners may want in the aftermath of reflective analysis of play observations. They may want to know more about:

- the children;
- the classroom;
- an area of learning (such as the use of books);
- an area of provision (such as the use of the outdoor learning environment).

Because targeted observation is, by definition, about specific enquiry, it makes sense to structure it more closely than would be sensible for normal information-gathering purposes (see Figure 14.4). Educators may well wish to use particular strategies in order to elicit answers to particular questions (see Sylva *et al.*, 1980). These involve:

- deciding in advance that observation of a child will take place in a structured fashion;
- observing at preordained intervals (say, two minutes in every twenty);
- keeping a continuous observation going in a particular place for a period of time, noting particular kinds of behaviour as it occurs.

The strategy to be used depends on what concern(s) caused the enquiry. In each case, the strategy can be applied to individuals or to groups, whether the focus is primarily on a particular child, a place or an event. It is certainly necessary to think how the strategy chosen relates to the intended enquiry, and whether the information provided will contribute to a better understanding of the issue in question.

Observing outdoor play
Increasing weight is being placed upon the outdoor learning environment, and nursery staff in particular are frequently concerned to know how they can improve the learning experiences presented there. Which children go outside? What do they do there? The youngest children in the reception class frequently show considerable resistance to going outside at break; observing their experiences in the playground may

Figure 14.4   Targeted observation form

Time/place/event to be monitored _____ e.g. playground

Focus of enquiry _____ e.g. under-fives activities

Date _____

Time (inc. duration)	Place	Children's names	Ages	Activities
10.15–10.35	Playground	Child A etc	4.2 years	_____
_____	_____	_____	_____	_____ etc.

Children's talk, comments, etc.

_____

_____

_____

_____

This observation form could then be analysed using a form similar to the others shown above.

make the reasons clear and impel the school to make better provision for them. As David Brown explores in Chapter 4, the same type of enquiry is profitable right across the primary school and may yield many surprises.

Positive diagnostic approaches through observation

What practitioners learn from observation of play leads them to go with the force of children's development – and not against it. Development is often very uneven, with fine motor skills lagging behind during the early years. The capacity for oral expression greatly outstrips writing competency even in children who are adept with pencils. Some highly creative and original people, even as adults, have poor fine and gross motor skills: Doctor Johnson, for example, was notoriously clumsy, messy and ill-organized physically. Concentration on what children find difficult ties them down to their lowest level of operation, while it is their strengths which draw them on to further learning. Play shows us where these strengths lie and how we can best support them. This learning enables early years practitioners to meet responsibilities to the children, the parents and colleagues with whom they work by developing professional understanding and insight. What is learned from the initial and follow-up observations and the reflective analyses arising from them teaches educators about their own strengths and weaknesses and protects them against the dangers of their own stereotypes and blind spots. As Margaret Lally suggests, 'In placing the needs of children at the centre of the curriculum, teachers must regularly confront their own assumptions and prejudices' (1991: 152).

Sharing information from observations

The accuracy of evidence obtained through observation makes an invaluable contribution to practitioners' talks with parents and other adults. Parents, governors and staff frequently approach the educational partnership with different understandings of what is involved. If practitioners can give parents evidence of their children's achievements based on observation, there is something tangible for discussion and mutual understanding. Tizard *et al.*, (1988) point out how little some nursery teachers know of the efforts of parents to help their children at home. Discussion of concrete examples of play activities can help link home and school in ways which may be less open to the undervaluing of either.

Observation and appropriate expectations of children

This kind of assessment differs from that which takes place at the end of a Key Stage. Instead it monitors the child's growing powers of understanding, knowledge and competence continuously, and includes all the particular interests and experiences which parents and practitioners need to know about if they are to motivate children and make the most of educational opportunities. It has been noted by Tizard and Hughes (1984) and by Wells (1987) that school expectations of children can be very much lower than is appropriate, often because classroom provision and teachers' strategies do not take account of individual children's home experiences. Observation of play works to put this right in two ways:

1 The evidence is likely to be characteristic of the child and more reliable than other kinds.
2 In play children are able to control the scenario, the setting, the strategies and the collaborative relationships involved.

Play can make children feel at home, confident and relaxed enough to talk, think, organize, negotiate, adapt and create at their most confident levels. Assessment of play is likely to be recognizably of the parent's own child and may help parents to understand more of what their children have already achieved.

Conclusion – making the case for play

There should be no doubt that practitioners need verification from observations to convince parents, governors and colleagues that their judgements of children are sufficiently accurate and that their proposed teaching strategies are justifiable. In these monetary times, practitioners wishing to justify their claims for funds to buy resources for play, or to maintain the value of organizing the classroom with play in mind, will have to be able to assert that the play opportunities provided *will* benefit children.

Early years educators are the people who help children to build the bridges of understanding between their individual experiences and the more formal understandings about the world upon which later education rests. As experts in the early stages of this process, early years practitioners can, using evidence of learning drawn from observation, contribute to the development of sound educational policies and practices at both local and national level.

15 | Play, the universe and everything!

Tina Bruce

When I was a child I played schools. Sometimes the school reflected my experiences of school and sometimes it began to be under my control. It began to be as my ideal school. Erikson (1963) argues that through our childhood play we are partners with our future. Perhaps there is sense in saying that we should give sitting babies a box of objects and that, depending on what they select, their future will be divulged! Through observing and becoming part of a child's play, as Vicky Hurst has discussed in the previous chapter, we discover an individual child's temperament, and 'tune in' to what makes that child tick.

This final chapter is about this 'tuning in' to the processes of children's play and the need for committed adults to justify and defend the right for us all to free-flow play.

And so to free-flow play!

Tom, at two years, spent an afternoon cracking a bowl of nuts with two types of nut cracker: a corkscrew model and a pincer model. He was involved in forces, holes, broken parts. By three years, he was making paper aeroplanes. He was completely fascinated when shown by an older child that he could cut bits out of the wing to make flaps which speed up and slow down flight, and vary the direction of the aeroplane. He wallowed in this, as he had wallowed in playing with the bowl of nuts. He returned to it again and again, 'playing' aeroplanes. He loved to throw sticks during his play at walls, into bushes, into water. He, in Europe, is doing what a group of children aged two years, four years, and seven years are doing on the bank of the River Nile on the African

Continent. They are making boats which will sail in particular directions and float with particular cargoes. He is playing with forces, crashes, splashes, just as they are when they are throwing sticks and large stones into the Nile around the boats that they have made. This kind of free-flow play is happening all over the world (of which Audrey Curtis also gives personal evidence in Chapter 2).

Hannah, fourteen years, is choreographing a solo dance for her GCSE course. This is the culmination of the dance-play she has maintained from the age of ten months, when she began the 'knees-bend' swaying to music indulged in by children in every society. At six years old she danced with her friend Ming, who is four years old, for hours on end, using dressing-up clothes, music on a tape-recorder, homemade instruments, playing at dancing, using everything she knew. It was very ballet-influenced, but then she lives in Europe. In Cairo a different mixed age group comprising three boys, twelve years, fifteen years and fifteen years free-flow play-dance on a patch of park between two busy roads. When they arrive, they bring a ghetto blaster and play Arabic music. They all do their own thing, but, gradually, one echoes what the other does. They all do one-step together, and then go off to play-dance alone, but together. Over the period of an hour, they coordinate more and more until they are dancing together. It is influenced by Arabic folk-dance styles. Yet if Hannah and they should meet, they could all play-dance together without too much difficulty, as long as they remain sensitive to what is difficult for each other. In free-flow play, one of the features is that the players are sensitive to each other's personal agendas as well as a feeling of group sensitivity emerging.

At a conference in England where musicians from different parts of the world came together, Nigel Kennedy spoke of the way they found they could improvise and literally 'play' music together which was of a high standard and respected the different cultural backgrounds they came from. They found they could allow one style of music to emerge and subside, letting another form become dominant at different points as they played. This kind of free-flow playing respects individuals and encourages group sensitivity. It is about functioning, as we have seen in the examples so far, at a high level, and leads to quality in the way that individuals interact with the sciences (Jeni Riley and Jane Savage, Chapter 11) and the arts (Roy Prentice, Chapter 10).

Chris, aged seven years, comes to stay for a week on a cabin cruiser boat holiday on the River Thames with William, eleven years, and Ayo, thirteen years. It is his first experience of boat life. Here is another mixed age group, again untypical of those found in formal schools. The older children teach him to work a lock, tie a knot, move safely on to land, light a barbeque, put up a tent, strip a stick, make an arrow, make a bow from willow, fish, swab the deck and sweep the stairs. He sees the older children settle to an hour's homework each day, and spends that time choosing to sketch, play, read and try lighting his own barbeque.

He also plays, wallows in using the bow and arrow and celebrates his skill in firing. He delights in it and talks to himself. Characteristically, if Ayo had played this at seven years, she would have 'become' Boudicca or someone like her.

Chris is like William at this age: he loves to 'play' scientifically. His imagined world is to do with alternative hypotheses for what will happen to the arrow when he does this, that or the other. Adults are around, but he can take the responsibility and is proud of himself. He senses he is playing at an advanced level. He is in control. Adults do not need to control him. When he needs help, he asks, or an adult notices and comes to offer help. He is told or read a story each evening, and loves King Arthur particularly. There is no competition with other seven-year-olds. He is the only one. He goes at his own speed and sets himself high standards, encouraged by the admiration of others.

The principles of early education

The question arises: is this ideal, or is this what schools ought to be like for children at least until the age of eight years? Chris helps with chores which are essential to living in a boat. Not all of them are pleasant or exciting, but he does them willingly, dutifully and is proud of his contribution. He is involved in a little formal learning relating to shopping (number and money) and literacy (stories, reading and writing). He plays for nearly half of his day, alone and with William and Ayo. He socializes a great deal, doing chores and in games with a ball with William. He is with adults who are able to give him attention when he seeks or needs it, or just to be around them watching as they work. He is encouraged to use what is essential and universal to being a human, his possibility to relate to others, and to act symbolically in a number of ways. He can represent experiences through number, language and free-flow play. He is also encouraged to be himself, to develop his free-flow play according to his own temperament. As T. Berry Brazelton (1969: 281) points out, young children 'show a resistance to being pushed into habits that are not sympathetic to their style, a resistance backed up by all the strength inherent in any well-organized personality, infant or adult'.

Great educators have always been aware of the delicate balance that exists between what is standard to being human, and the unique way in which every human is standard. For example, Froebel in the nineteenth century was constantly aware that there are certain aspects which human beings have in common, which bind them together as a species across the world. He considered free-flow play to be an important one of these, seeing every child as a unique individual who needs sensitive and appropriate help in order to develop and learn optimally.

In Bruce (1987) I extrapolated ten principles from the literature and philosophy of the heritage left by great pioneer educators such as Froebel, Steiner and Montessori. These are:

1 Childhood is seen as valid in itself, as part of life and not simply as preparation for adulthood. Thus education is seen similarly as something of the present and not just preparation and training for later.
2 The whole child is considered to be important. Health, physical and mental, is emphasized, as well as the importance of feelings and thinking and spiritual aspects.
3 Learning is not compartmentalized, for everything links.
4 Intrinsic motivation, resulting in child-initiated self-directed activity is valued.
5 Self-discipline is emphasized. (4 and 5 lead to autonomy.)
6 There are specially receptive periods of learning at different stages of development.
7 What children can do (rather than what they cannot do) is the starting point in the child's education.
8 There is an inner structure in the child which includes the imagination and which emerges especially under favourable conditions.
9 The people (both adults and children) with whom the child interacts are of central importance.
10 The child's education is seen as an interaction between the child and the environment the child is in – including, in particular, other people and knowledge itself.

While there is in the United Kingdom, a considerable agreement about the principles which guide early childhood education (Sylva *et al.*, 1992), there is also considerable variation in the way in which these are interpreted by those working with young children and their families. There are those who choose to package them into an identifiable method (Montessori, High/Scope) and those who instead emphasize the importance of quality training, embedded in sound general principles, as the best long-term strategy to encourage reflective quality practice (see Chris Pascal and Tony Bertram, Chapter 13).

These principles help us to explore what human beings have in common wherever they live. It is not possible for anyone to step outside their culture, society or upbringing, but looking at commonalities between human beings is useful. We know that humans have the potential to function symbolically (Athey 1990). They do this in several ways, for example through language (Whitehead 1990), through representation (Matthews 1988) and through play (Bruce 1991; Moyles 1989).

In a previous book (Bruce 1991), I focused upon commonalities in relation to children's play, and the contribution of free-flow play to the learning process was explored. This involves looking at the triangle which makes up a quality curriculum (child, context and content):

• the *child*: this involves the process of free-flow play as part of the child's development;

- the *context*: this involves people, culture and environment and access to play;
- the *content*: what the child knows, wants to know and is expected to learn, and the role of play in facilitating this.

Because there is widespread confusion about what play is, 'free-flow play' was adopted as a term because it expressed a view of play supported by twelve features, extrapolated from the literature:

Feature 1 It is an active process without a product.

Feature 2 It is intrinsically motivated.

Feature 3 It exerts no external pressure to conform to rules, pressures, goals, tasks or definite direction.

Feature 4 It is about possible, alternative worlds, which involve 'supposing' and 'as if' (Atkin 1985–8), which lift players to their highest levels of functioning. This involves being imaginative, creative, original and innovative.

Feature 5 It is about participants wallowing in ideas, feelings and relationships. It involves reflecting on, and becoming aware of, what we know – or metacognition.

Feature 6 It actively uses previous first-hand experiences, including struggle, manipulation, exploration, discovery and practice.

Feature 7 It is sustained, and when in full flow, helps us to function in advance of what we can actually do in our real lives.

Feature 8 During free-flow play, we use the technical prowess, mastery and competence we have previously developed, and so can be in control.

Feature 9 It can be initiated by a child or an adult, but if by an adult he/she must pay particular attention to 3, 5 and 11 above.

Feature 10 It can be solitary.

Feature 11 It can be in partnerships or groups, adults and/or children who will be sensitive to each other.

Feature 12 It is an integrating mechanism, which brings together everything we learn, know, feel and understand.

These twelve features can be summed up through the equation 'Free-flow play = Wallow in past experiences + Technical prowess, competence, mastery and control acquired'.

Commonalities and differences in free-flow play across cultures

Commonalities are necessarily the starting point when we look at areas we wish to study in relation to human beings, such as free-flow play. It is also important to look at differences in the way children play in different parts of the world, if we are to respond to, and value, the uniqueness of each human being. Free-flow play is found among children in all parts of the world, as well as in ancient civilizations. It is part of being a human. It is not, however, treated in the same way throughout the world. In different cultures it is encouraged, discouraged, constrained, or valued in a variety of ways which have a great impact on the way the child has access to free-flow playing (Bruce 1991; Curtis, Chapter 2). There is a tendency among some to see free-flow play as a privilege enjoyed mainly by middle-class children in Europe and North America, and yet the reality is that this is unlikely to be so. It is 'misguided to characterize the middle class as historical pinnacles of indulgent concern for children's needs' (Konner 1991: 196).

As we shall see, it may even be that those in the 'fast lane' of complex industrialized societies are in danger of losing, or at least damaging and seriously eroding, aspects of traditional childhood which are in fact central to being truly successful human adults. 'More haste, less speed' is the dilemma. In complex industrialized life, there is so much that children need to know, that we seem to be slipping into a view that is likely to be erroneous about the way children should be educated. Introducing formal school earlier and earlier, directly teaching and transmitting the culture to children through highly pre-structured experiences, in a predominantly 'tell and write' mode, may not produce the kind of adult who can survive the future nearly so well as the adaptive intelligence, imagination and creativity required of children brought up to actively experience and learn in real-life situations, with opportunity and access to free-flow play. It is not a question of those in complex industrialized societies trying to return to a romantically perceived view of the hunting and gathering or agricultural community where children play all day. It is much more a question of not discarding what is central to humanity by throwing the baby out with the bath water in an attempt to keep a place in the 'fast lane'. Those who study children free-flow playing do not see romance, but a highly effective mechanism giving access to symbolic functioning of a high level vital to the future of humanity as a group as well as to individuals (see Athey 1990; Bartholomew and Bruce 1993; Whalley 1993), a point also well-emphasized in preceding chapters.

Children's play is sometimes used, taken over by adults, as a way of gaining access to guiding and structuring children's learning so that they are, it is argued, adequately prepared for adult life, and yet helped to learn in ways that are appropriate to childhood (see Peter Smith's examination of these issues in Chapter 1). This 'preparation for life' view of play is supported by modern theorists such as Bruner, and has gained great influence in Western Europe and North America.

It is interesting to examine figures produced by Whiting and Whiting's 'Six Cultures Project' (Konner 1991). Five agricultural societies in Kenya, Mexico, the Philippines, Japan and India were studied together with a town called 'Orchardtown' in Pennsylvania, New England, USA. The children in Orchardtown were involved in household and garden chores for two per cent of their time. They freely played for 30 per cent of the time. They were engaged in casual social interactions, watching adults, chatting and so on, for about 52 per cent of their time. Formal school-type learning took up 16 per cent of the time. From these figures, we could perhaps argue that these urban children are playing for a healthy and appropriate part of their day. However, there is more to this as we shall see later.

There is a strongly held view in Europe and North America that a high level of child labour is an infringement and abuse of children's rights, with an undertone that this is cruel and oppressive. There is an equally strongly held view that formal schooling is a sign of an advanced society, which is investing in its future through formally transmitting the culture to its young. This view was typically expressed by Angela Rumbold when opening the world OMEP Conference in 1989, when she spoke with pride of the large proportion of four-year-olds in the UK who were in school. This reflects a philosophy that, 'If you get them in early, you get them on in life.' The United Kingdom is probably top of the league in putting four-year-olds into early formal schooling (Moss 1990). This is not the same as offering nursery education, as we shall see. The picture we have of the formal schooling which 80 per cent of four-year-olds are receiving (e.g. Pascal 1990b; Bennett and Kell 1989) is one where there is little free-flow play, and plenty of teacher-led tasks, not necessarily in a context familiar to the child.

We know from Donaldson's (1978) studies that children perform better on tasks which are embedded, which make what she calls 'human sense' to them. When the tasks are in the context of their own everyday lives, when they have purpose and function, children achieve better results. Their self-esteem is higher. They are more confident. They take pride in what they do. They want to make a good contribution. Free-flow play, she suggests, means the child actually creates the context, and so it has the greatest meaning for the child (Peter Heaslip also argues these points strongly in Chapter 8).

Konner (1991: 309) suggests that we have seen a massive switch in developed industrial societies so that children are now in compulsory schooling in contrast to performing compulsory chores or labour. Using figures from the Six Cultures Project he shows that in agricultural societies, children tend to work at chores for their parents for 17 per cent of the time, in fields or in the home. They play for 44 per cent of their time. They are involved in casual social interactions, chatting, watching adults and so on for 34 per cent of their time, and in formal learning for only 5 per cent of the time.

When we speak of child labour being an abuse of children's rights, we need to be clear what we are talking about. Putting children to work in coal mines and factories with the growth of industrialization is not the same as children helping in the home or on the family farm. Konner argues (1991: 309) that, 'Despite their hardships, chores give children skills they are proud of all their lives, and can bring parents and children closer together.'

In hunting and gathering societies, such as the Kung, children learn through watching, socializing, playing and slowly doing, with virtually no formal teaching. In agricultural societies children are required to do more of the essential chores which arise through living in one place rather than moving on, as well as reflecting on what children learn through play. Pretty Shield (in Niethammer 1977: 27), a member of the Crow tribe, remembering her childhood at the turn of the century, describes the 'chores' element in her education:

> Indian girls were gently led into the art of motherhood, and their introduction to other womanly tasks was gradual, too, at least for the littlest girls. They accompanied their mothers and big sisters while they gathered wild foods, weeded gardens, and went for water and wood. As the girls grew older more was expected of them. A Fox woman, living in the area of what is now Wisconsin and Illinois, told how she was encouraged when she was about nine to plant a few things and to hoe the weeds. Then she was taught to cook what she had raised, and was lavishly praised for her efforts.

Pretty Shield also remembers the importance of free-flow play during her childhood (1977: 25):

> Learning the role of women by playing was the pervading method of education for young girls, and mothers often took pains to see that their daughters had accurate miniatures of real household equipment to use in playing house. In some of the Plains tribes such as the Cheyenne, Omaha, Arapaho and Crow, daughters of the more well-to-do families even had their own skin tents as play-houses, and when time came to pack up camp to follow the buffalo, the girls got their own household – tipe, toys and clothes – packed and ready to move.

(In Chapter 3, Jane Hislam further discusses gender identity in education in Western culture.)

Children in both hunting and gathering societies and agricultural societies learn through watching, playing, socializing and slowly doing according to an apprenticeship model (Audrey Curtis has already given examples in Chapter 2). Children do not have to tell or write what they learn. They have to show their learning by doing (for example, weaving in the context of everyday life). In their play, they reflect on these active experiences and wallow in them, demonstrating the technical prowess they have been struggling to master. Play is about wallowing in what has been experienced, and dealing with mastering and controlling what has been experienced. It is about the application of what is known, using skill and competence that has been developed. We can see this clearly in Pretty Shield's memory of her childhood as well as in more modern times.

In both hunting and gathering societies and agricultural societies, children have the possibility to play, to become proficient and to take pride in doing purposeful, functional and meaningful chores which they understand contribute to their families' life as they socialize with those in their community. Only a fraction of their time is used in very formal direct learning. This applies throughout childhood, with increasing responsibility being encouraged during middle childhood at approximately nine to twelve years of age. Industrial societies have either replaced household chores with child labour in factories and mines or with formal schooling. Konner argues (1992: 310) that school 'attempts to turn children into a workforce with skills that society needs. In these senses, it exploits children just as much as work does.'

Conclusion

We are seeing an erosion of adults valuing children's free-flow play in complex industrial societies. Children are attending formal school for longer hours at younger and younger ages, and this is cutting across the possibility to free-flow play. (Perhaps, as David Brown suggests in Chapter 4, the playground is the only place left for children's own culture, including free-flow play.) In some countries such as Denmark, children attend schools based upon the philosophy of early childhood education expressed in the ten principles at the beginning of this chapter until they are seven years old. Until industrialization, children were not given formal education until eight or nine years of age. It is interesting to note that in Denmark there is virtually no adult illiteracy, but there is a real partnership between parents and educators with great emphasis on free-flow play.

Returning to the beginning of the chapter, it would *not* seem to be the case that children in industrialized society are privileged: their opportunities for free-flow play, rather than being increased, are being fast eroded. As T. Berry Brazelton writes (1969: 281):

> When he must learn via mechanisms that are not yet ready, he will spend energies which may be expensively drained from more important areas of his total development. Perhaps we have an example of this in many of our adolescents, who have been forced intellectually, but drained emotionally, and who cannot cope with the increased demands of our sophisticated society.

This is not to say that young children do not benefit from school; but it does mean that early childhood education needs to be based on an appropriate quality curriculum. This has been stressed by report after report during the last fifteen years, but with little action (TES 1992). Young children benefit from good quality early childhood education until they are at least seven years old. The kind of curriculum which encourages learning in context and free-flow play is not a romantic view of education. It is a survival view.

Societies which neglect their infrastructures are societies which are likely to crumble. Free-flow play is part of the infrastructure of any civilization. Short cuts through childhood which erode free-flow play do not lead to a good future. Societies which indulge in taking short cuts and which lack vision for the future are short-lived. Children in every part of the world need opportunities to free-flow play.

As a Sioux tribesman said, 'We must take control of our destiny, and try to recreate what we have almost lost.'

Afterword

Janet R. Moyles

Plate 17 *It is practitioners who are in the position daily of seeing how much value there is in children's play and how it can be channelled into a very powerful learning tool*

There you have it: the arguments for the excellence of play. Beginning as we did with some scepticism in relation to researchers' abilities to prove the value of play in children's learning and development, we have moved forward convincingly, I believe, to end with the concept of full free-flowing play – and covered a whole world of play in between!

Although many of the contributors' views are clearly compatible with each other, differences in emphasis and difficulties of definition remain and there is always a need to agree to differ on constructs of play because of the formidable prospect of 'proving' anything so potentially and actually ephemeral. As Vandenberg (1986: 19–20) asserts:

> The aspiration for a precise definition of play is an admirable impulse which will lead to further refinements in our conceptualization of the term . . . the belief that airtight definitions are ultimately possible may lead us to be impatient with imprecise definitions and cause us to throw the playful baby out with the bathwater . . . what is needed are efforts aimed at linking the abstract definition with its concrete manifestations, and an analysis of how the perturbating factors influence the specific form of play.

This is exactly what all of us, the writers of this book, are advocating and offering as the way forward. It is practitioners who are in the position daily of seeing how much value there is in children's play and how it can be channelled into a very powerful learning tool. Basic skills learning in play is very different from the kind of 'basics' to which we are espoused daily to return: a view of moving 'forward to fundamentals' (Keliher 1986: 42) is far more consonant with this approach. Children *will* play despite adult approval or otherwise. Perhaps it is better to approve of it, and strive to understand it, when children are young than to allow the harsher elements of play to surface later in vandalism and anti-social activities (Sutton-Smith and Kelly-Byrne 1984). A curriculum which sanctions and utilizes play is more likely, as several writers have argued, to provide well-balanced citizens of the future as well as happier children in the present.

Perhaps like McAuley and Jackson (1992: 20) educators need to be encouraged to give prominence to 'perspectives' rather than 'theories' and encourage a greater respect for 'loosish structures in which spontaneity and freshness can flourish' and where 'respect for children means that one must intervene when it is justified to do so'. All the writers in this book are firmly committed to adult involvement and interaction in children's play, both as models and providers, as a way forward towards ensuring quality provision, greater understanding and, above all, justifiable commitment. Whether we consider this involvement to be structuring the play, directing, enhancing, initiating, sustaining or promoting the play has been a matter of terminology: at the end of the day, the crucial features are children and adults learning together through play for the benefit of both.

We can be certain if we observe children's play that much is happening. But is it learning? Do children *need* play (Woodhead 1987)? The contributors to this book and many practitioners affirm these beliefs. Even if proof remains elusive and both childhood and play are social constructs which we can do without in our present society (Suransky 1982; Postman 1983), can we not give children just a little time in the first few years of their lives to indulge in the excellence of play?

What about the children – what is play to them? The final 'afterword' is left to a five-year-old:

Child: When I play with my friends we have lots of fun . . . do lots of things . . . think about stuff . . . and . . . well . . .
Adult: Do you think you learn anything?
Child: Heaps and heaps – not like about sums and books and things . . . um . . . like . . . like . . . well . . . like *real* things!

References

Alexander, R., Rose, J. and Woodhead, C. (1992) *Curriculum Organisation and Classroom Practice in Primary Schools*. London: HMSO.

Ashton, E. (1978) 'The effect of sex role stereotyped picture books on the play behaviour of 3 and 4 year old children', *Dissertation Abstracts International*, 39.

Ashton, E. (1983) 'Measures of play behaviour: the influence of sex-role stereotyped children's books', *Sex Roles*. 9(1), 43–7.

Association for Science Education, Association for Teachers of Mathematics, Mathematical Association and National Association for Teaching of English (1989) *The National Curriculum – Making it Work for the Primary School*. London: ASE.

Athey, C. (1990) *Extending Thought in Young Children. A Parent–Teacher Partnership*. London: Paul Chapman.

Atkin, J. (1985–8) 'Imaginative play in early childhood education', *OMEP Updates*, 1, 67–9.

Atkinson, S. (ed.) (1992) *Mathematics with Reason: The Emergent Approach to Primary Maths*. London: Hodder and Stoughton.

Ausubel, D.P., Novak, J.D. and Hanesian, H. (1978) *Educational Psychology: A Cognitive View* (2nd edn). London: Holt, Rinehart and Winston.

Barrett, M. (1977) *Thinking about Art Education*. London Borough of Redbridge Education Office.

Barrs, M. (1988) 'Maps of play'. In Meek, M. and Mills, C. (eds) *Language and Literacy in the Primary School*. Lewes: Falmer Press.

Bartholomew, L.B. and Bruce, T. (1993) *Getting to Know You: Record Keeping in the Early Years*. Sevenoaks: Hodder and Stoughton.

Belotti, E.G. (1975) *Little Girls: Social Conditioning and its Effects on the Stereotyped Role of Women during Infancy*. London: Writers and Readers Publishing Co-operative.

Bengtsson, A. (1970) *Environmental Planning for Children's Play*. London: Crosby Lockwood and Son.

Bennett, N. and Kell, J. (1989) *A Good Start: Four Year Olds in Infant Schools*. Oxford: Basil Blackwell.

Bennett, N., Desforges, C., Cockburn, A. and Wilkinson, B. (1984) *The Quality of Pupils' Learning Experiences*. London: Lawrence Erlbaum.

Bereiter, C. and Englemann, S. (1966) *Teaching the Disadvantaged Child in the Preschool*. Englewood Cliffs, NJ: Prentice-Hall.

Beruetta-Clement, J., Schweinhart, L., Barnett, W.S., Epstein, A.S. and Weikart, D.P. (1984) 'Changed lives: the effects of the Perry pre-school programme on youths through age 19', *Monographs of the High/Scope Educational Research Foundation*, 8.

Blank-Grief, E. (1976) 'Sex role playing in pre-school children'. In Bruner, J.S., Jolly, A. and Sylva, K. *Play and its Role in Evolution and Development*. Harmondsworth: Penguin Books.

Blenkin, G.M. and Kelly, A.V. (eds) (1981) *The Primary Curriculum*. London: Paul Chapman.

Blenkin, G.M. and Kelly, A.V. (eds) (1983) *The Primary Curriculum In Action*. London: Paul Chapman.

Blenkin, G.M. and Kelly, A.V. (eds) (1988) *Early Childhood Education: A Developmental Curriculum*. London: Paul Chapman.

Blenkin, G.M. and Kelly, A.V. (eds) (1992) *Assessment In Early Childhood Education*. London: Paul Chapman.

Blenkin, G.M. and Whitehead, M.R. (1988) 'Creating a context for development'. In Blenkin, G.M. and Kelly, A.V. (eds) *Early Childhood Education: A Development Curriculum*. London: Paul Chapman.

Bloch, M. and Pellegrini, A. (eds) (1989) *The Ecological Context of Children's Play*. New York: Ablex.

Bolton, G. (1979) *Towards a Theory Of Drama in Education*. London: Longman.

Brazelton, T. Berry (1969) *Infants and Mothers: Differences in Development*. New York: Delacorte Press.

Brazelton, T. Berry (1977) 'Implications of infant development among the Mayan Indians of Mexico'. In Leiderman, P.H., Tulkin, S.R. and Rosenfeld, E. (eds) *Culture and Infancy: Variations in the Human Experience*. New York: Academic Press, pp. 151–88.

Bredekamp, S. (ed.) (1988) *Developmentally Appropriate Practice in Early Childhood Programs Serving Children from Birth Through Age 8*. Washington: NAEYC.

Brierley, J. (1987) *Give Me a Child until he is Seven*. Lewes: Falmer Press.

Britton, J. (1972) *Language and Learning*. Harmondsworth: Penguin.

Bronowski, J. (1958) *The Ascent of Man*. London: BBC Publications.

Bronson, W.C. (1973) 'Competence and growth of personality'. In Connolly, K.J. and Bruner, J.S. (eds) *The Growth of Competence*. London and San Diego: Academic Press.

Brown, D. (1991) Children's playground culture: a study of children's play area activity with reference to the children and play areas of Asfordby Hill Country Primary School. University of Leicester: Unpublished MA dissertation.

Browne, N. and France, P. (1985) 'Only cissies wear dresses: a look at sexist talk in the nursery'. In Weiner, G. (ed.) *Just a Bunch of Girls*. Milton Keynes: Open University Press.

Bruce, T. (1987) *Early Childhood Education*. London: Hodder and Stoughton.

Bruce, T. (1991) *Time to Play in Early Childhood Education*. London: Hodder and Stoughton.

Bruce, T. (1992a) Keynote Address, Goldsmiths' Association For Early Childhood, 17 October 1992.

Bruce, T. (1992b) Preface to Gura, P. (ed.) *Exploring Learning: Young Children And Blockplay*. London: Paul Chapman.

Bruner, J. (1966) *Towards a Theory of Instruction*. Cambridge, MA: Harvard University Press.

Bruner, J. (1972) 'Functions of Play'. In Bruner *et al.*, (1976) (op. cit.).

Bruner, J. (1976) *On Knowing: Essays for the Left Hand*. New York: Atheneum.

Bruner, J. (1978) *The Process of Education*. Cambridge, MA: Harvard University Press.

Bruner, J. (1980) *Under Five in Britain*. London: Grant McIntyre.

Bruner, J. (1986) *Actual Minds, Possible Worlds*. Cambridge, MA: Harvard University Press.

Bruner, J., Jolly, A. and Sylva, K. (1976) *Play and its Role in Evolution and Development*. Harmondsworth: Penguin Books.

Bryant, P. and Bradley, L. (1985) *Children's Reading Problems*. Oxford: Basil Blackwell.

Butterworth, G. and Light, P. (eds) (1982) *Social Cognition: Studies of the Development of Understanding*. Chicago: University of Chicago Press.

Campbell, R.J. and Neill, S.St.J. (1991) *Thirteen Hundred and Thirty Days: Final Report of a Pilot Study of Teacher Time in Key Stage 1*. Commissioned by the Assistant Masters and Mistresses Association. Coventry: University of Warwick.

Carroll, Lewis (1871) *Through the Looking Glass* and *What Alice Found*. London: Macmillan.

Carvalho, A.M.A., Smith, P.K., Hunter, T. and Costabile, A. (1990) 'Playground activities for boys and girls: developmental and cultural trends in children's perceptions of gender differences'. *Play and Culture*, 3, 343–7.

Children's Learning in Science Project (1993–5) *Summary Reports on Plant Nutrition, Energy, Particles, Heat and Chemistry*. University of Leeds: self-published.

Christie, J.F. and Johnson, E.P. (1985) 'Questioning the results of play training research'. *Educational Psychologist*, 20, 7–11.

Clark, M.M. (1988) *Children Under Five: Educational Research and Evidence*. London: Gordon and Breach.

Constantine, J. (1992) 'An investigation into the sociodramatic play in four year two classes'. University of Leicester: Unpublished MA thesis.

Curtis, A. and Hill, S. (1980) *My World*. Windsor: National Foundation for Educational Research.

Csikzentmihalyi, M.T. (1979) 'The concept of flow in play'. In Sutton-Smith, B. (ed.) *Play and Learning*. New York: Gardner Press.

D'Arcy, S. (1990) 'Towards a non-sexist primary classroom'. In Tutchell, E. (ed.) *Dolls and Dungarees: Gender Issues in the Primary School Curriculum*. Milton Keynes: Open University Press.

Darvill, D. (1982) 'Ecological influences on children's play: issues and approaches'. In Pepler, D.J. and Rubin, K.H. *The Play of Children: Current Theory and Research*. Basel: S. Karger.

David, T., Curtis, A. and Siraj-Blatchford, I. (1992) *Effective Teaching in the Early Years, Fostering Children's Learning in Nurseries and Infant Classes*. An OMEP (UK) Report: OMEP.

Davies, B. (1982) *Life in Classroom and Playground*. London: Routledge and Kegan Paul.

Davies, B. and Banks, C. (1992) The gender trap: a feminist poststructuralist analysis of primary school children's talk about gender'. *Journal of Curriculum Studies*, 24(1), 1–25.

Department of Education and Science (1967) *The Plowden Report: Children and their Primary Schools*. London: HMSO.

Department of Education and Science (1982) *Mathematics Counts*. Report of the Cockroft Committee. London: HMSO.

Department of Education and Science (1985a) *Better Schools*. London: HMSO.

Department of Education and Science (1985b) *The Curriculum from 5 to 16, Curriculum Matters 2*. HMI Series, London: HMSO.

Department of Education and Science (1990a) *Starting with Quality: The Report of the Committee of Inquiry into the Quality of Educational Experience offered to 3- and 4-year-olds*. London: HMSO.

Department of Education and Science (1990b) *English in the National Curriculum (No. 2)*. London: HMSO.

Department of Education and Science (1991a) *The Implementation of the Curricular Requirements of ERA, An Overview by HMI Inspectorate of the First Year*. London: HMSO.

Department for Education and Science (1991b) *National Curriculum Art for Ages 5–14*. London: HMSO.

Department of Education and Science (1991c) *Science in the National Curriculum*. London: HMSO.

Dewey, J. (1958) *Art as Experience*. New York: Putnam/Capricorn Books.

Dixon, B. (1990) *Playing Them False: A Study of Children's Toys, Games and Puzzles*. Stoke-on-Trent: Trentham Books.

Donaldson, M. (1978) *Children's Minds*. Glasgow. Fontana/Collins.

Driver, R. (1983) *The Pupil as Scientist?* Milton Keynes: Open University Press.

Dunn, J. (1988) *The Beginnings Of Social Understanding*. Oxford: Blackwell.

Dunn, J. and Wooding, C. (1977) 'Play in the home and its implications for learning'. In Tizard, B. and Harvey, D. *Biology of Play*. London: Spastics International Medical Publications.

Dunn, S. and Morgan, V. (1987) 'Nursery and infant school play patterns: sex related differences'. *British Educational Research Journal*, 13(3), 271–81.

Early Years Curriculum Group (1989) *Early Childhood Education: The Early Years Curriculum and the National Curriculum*. Stoke-on-Trent: Trentham Books.

Egan, K. (1988) *Primary Understanding: Education in Early Childhood*. London: Routledge.

Eisner, E.W. (1982) *Cognition and Curriculum*. New York: Longman.

El'Kounin, D. (1971) 'Symbolics and its function in the play of children'. In Sutton-Smith, B. and Herron, R. (eds) *Child's Play*. New York: John Wiley.

Erikson, E. (1950) *Childhood and Society*. New York: W.W. Norton.

Erikson, E. (1963) *Childhood and Society*. London: Routledge and Kegan Paul.

Erikson, E. (1965) *Childhood and Society*. Harmondsworth: Penguin Books.

Feitelson, D. (1972) 'Developing imaginative play in preschool children as a possible approach to fostering creativity'. *Early Child Development and Care*, 1, 181–95.

Fensham, P. (ed.) (1988) *Development and Dilemmas in Science Education*. Lewes: Falmer Press.

Fisher, E.P. (1992) 'The impact of play on development: a meta-analysis'. *Play and Culture*, 5(2), 159–81.

Fisher, R. (1990) *Teaching Children to Think*. Oxford: Blackwell.

Fortes, M. (1970) 'Social and psychological aspects of education in Taleland'. In Middleton, J. (ed.) *From Child to Adult*. New York: Natural History Press.

Galton, M. and Harlen, J. (1990) *Assessing Science in the Primary Classroom: Practical Tasks, Written Tasks and Observing Activities*. London: Paul Chapman.

Gardner, H. (1983) *Frames of Mind: Theories of Alternative Intelligences*. London: Heinemann.

Garvey, C. (1976) 'Some properties of social play'. In Bruner, J.S., Jolly, A. and Sylva, K. *Play: Its Role in Evolution and Development*. Harmondsworth: Penguin.

Garvey, C. (1991) *Play* (2nd edn) London: Fontana.

Gentle, K. (1985) *Children and Art Teaching*. Beckenham: Croom Helm.

Goffman, E. (1963) *Stigma*. Englewood Cliffs, NJ: Prentice-Hall.

Grabrucker, M. (1988) *There's a Good Girl: Gender Stereotyping in the First Three Years of Life: a Diary*. London: The Women's Press.

Greenfield, P.M. (1984) *Mind and Media: the Effects of Television, Computers and Video Games*. London: Fontana.

Grenfell, J. (1977) *George – Don't Do That*. London: Futura.

Griffiths, R. (1988) *Maths through Play*. London: Macdonald.

Griffiths, R. (1992a) *Simple Maths: Printing*. London: A & C Black.

Griffiths, R. (1992b) *Simple Maths: Railways*. London: A & C Black.

Gura, P. (ed.) (1992) *Exploring Learning: Young Children And Blockplay*. London: Paul Chapman.

Hale-Benson, J.E. (1982) *Black Children, Their Roots, Culture and Learning Styles*. New York: Johns Hopkins Press.

Hall, N. (1987) *The Emergence of Literacy*. UKRA Teaching of Reading Monograph, London: Edward Arnold.

Hall, N. (1991) 'Play and the emergence of literacy'. In Christie, J. (ed.) *Play and Early Literacy Development*. New York: State University of New York Press.

Hall, N. (In press) *Play and Literacy*. London: Hodder and Stoughton.

Hall, N. and Abbott, L. (eds) (1991) *Play in the Primary Curriculum*. London: Hodder and Stoughton.

Harlen, W. (1985) *Teaching and Learning Primary Science*. London: Oliver and Boyd.

Harlen, W. and Jelly, W. (1989) *Developing Science in the Primary Classroom*. London: Oliver and Boyd.

Hayes, M. (1982) *Starting Primary Science*. London: Edward Arnold.

Heaslip, P., Hurst, V. and Joseph, J. (eds) (1992) *First Things First, Educating Young Children*. London: Early Years Curriculum Group.

Heathcote, D. (1984) *Collected Writings*. London: Hutchinson.

Hillman, M., Adams, J. and Whitelegg, J. (1990) *One False Move*. London: Policy Studies Institute, Report No. 707.

Hohmann, M., Banet, B., and Weikart, D.P. (1979) *Young Children in Action: A Manual for Preschool Educators*. Ypsilanti, Michigan: High/Scope Press.

Holt, J. (1991) *Learning all the Time*. Ticknell, Derbyshire: Education Now.

Hughes, M. (1986) *Children and Number*. Oxford: Basil Blackwell.

Huizinga, J. (1949) *Homo Ludens*. London: Routledge and Kegan Paul.

Hurst, V. (1991) *Planning For Early Learning: Education In The First Five Years*. London: Paul Chapman.

Hutt, C. (1966) 'Play in the under fives: form, development and function'. University of Keele: Unpublished paper.

Hutt, C. (1979) 'Play in the unders 5s; form, development and function'. In

Howells, J.G. (ed.) *Modern Perspectives in the Psychiatry of Infancy*. New York: Brunner/Marcel.

Hutt, S.J., Tyler, S., Hutt, C. and Christopherson, H. (1989) *Play, Exploration and Learning: A Natural History of the Preschool*. London: Routledge.

Isaacs, S. (1929) *The Nursery Years*. London: Routledge and Kegan Paul.

Isaacs, S. (1933) *Social Development in Young Children*. London: Routledge and Kegan Paul.

Ishigaki, H. (1987) 'A comparison of young children's environments and parental expectations in Japan and Israel'. *Early Child Development and Care*, 27(1), 139–68.

Jacklin, C.N. (1983) 'Boys and girls entering school'. In Marland, M. (ed.) *Sex Differentiation and Schooling*. London: Heinemann.

Johnson, J. and Ershler, J. (1982) 'Curricular Effects on the Play of Pre-Schoolers'. In Pepler, D.J. and Rubion, K.H. (eds) *The Play of Children: Current Theory and Research*, Contributions to Human Development 6. Basel: Karger.

Kalvaboer, A.F. (1977) 'Measurement of play: clinical applications'. In Tizard, B. and Harvey, D. (eds) *The Biology of Play*. London: Spastics International Medical Publications.

Karrby, G. (1989) 'Children's perceptions of their own play'. *International Journal of Early Childhood*, 21(2), 49–54.

Katz, L.G. (1992) 'Multiple perspectives on the quality of early childhood programs'. Unpublished paper delivered at the Second European Conference on the Quality of Early Childhood Education, August 1992. Worcester College of Higher Education.

Keliher, A.V. (1986) 'Back to basics or forward to fundamentals?'. *Young Children*, September, 42–4.

King, R. (1978) *All Things Bright and Beautiful?* London: John Wiley.

Kohl, H. (1977) *Writing, Maths and Games in the Open Classroom*. London: Methuen.

Konner, M. (1991) *Childhood*. Boston/London: Little, Brown.

Lally, M. (1991) *The Nursery Teacher In Action*. London: Paul Chapman.

Langlois, J. and Downs, C. (1980) 'Mothers, fathers and peers as socialisation agents of sex-typed play behavior in young children'. *Child Development*, 7, 1237–47.

Lee, C. (1977) *The Growth and Development of Children*. London: Longman.

Le Vine, R. and Le Vine, B. (1963) 'Nyansongo: a Gusii community in Kenya'. In Whiting, B. (ed.) *Six Cultures: Studies of Child Rearing*. New York: John Wiley.

Lewin, R. (1974) *Child Alive*. London: Temple-Smith.

Lewis, A. and Ban, C. (1977) 'Variants and invariants in the mother-infant interaction: a cross cultural study.' In Leiderman, P.H., Tulkin, F.R. and Rosenfeld, A. (eds) *Culture and Infancy: Variations in the Human Experience*. New York: Academic Press.

Lieberman, J.N. (1977) *Playfulness – Its Relationship to Imagination and Creativity*. New York: Academic Press.

Lloyd, B. and Smith, C. (1985). 'The social representations of gender and young children's play'. *British Journal of Developmental Psychology*, 3, 65–73.

McAuley, H. and Jackson, P. (1992) *Educating Young Children: A Structural Approach*. London: David Fulton in association with Roehampton Institute.

Maccoby, E. and Jacklin, C. (1974) *The Psychology of Sex Differences*. Stanford, CA: Stanford University Press.

Manning, K. and Sharp, A. (1977) *Structuring Play in the Early Years at School*. London: Ward Lock Educational.

Martin, P. (1984) 'The whys and wherefores of play in cats'. In Smith, P.K. (ed.) *Play in Animals and Humans*. Oxford: Basil Blackwell.

Masheder, M. (1989) *Let's Cooperate*. London: Peace Education Project.

Matthews, J. (1988) 'The young child's representation and drawing.' In Blenkin, G. and Kelly, V. (eds) *Early Childhood Education: A Developmental Curriculum*. London: Paul Chapman.

Meadows, S. and Cashdan, A. (1988) *Helping Children Learn*. London: David Fulton.

Millar, S. (1968) *The Psychology of Play*. Harmondsworth: Penguin.

Miller, L.B. and Dyer, J.L. (1975) 'Four preschool programs: their dimensions and effects'. *Monographs of the Society for Research in Child Development*, 40(162).

Mitchell, J. (1991) *Play, Representation and Art*. Unpublished MA dissertation: University of London, Institute of Education.

Monighan-Nourot, P., Scales, B., Van Hoorn, J. with Milly Almy (1987) *Looking at Children's Play: A Bridge between Theory and Practice*. NY: Teachers' College Press.

Moore, R. (1986) *Childhood's Domain*. London: Croom Helm

Morgan, V. and Dunn, S. (1988) 'Chameleons in the classroom: visible and invisible children in nursery and infant classrooms'. *Educational Review*, 40(1).

Moss, P. (1990) *Childcare in the European Communities 1985–1990*. Brussels: European Commission Report.

Moyles, J.R. (1989) *Just Playing? The Role and Status of Play in Early Childhood Education*. Milton Keynes: Open University Press.

Moyles, J.R. (1991) *Play as a Learning Process in your Classroom*. London: Mary Glasgow.

Moyles, J.R. (1992) *Organizing for Learning in the Primary Classroom: A Balanced Approach to Classroom Management*. Buckingham: Open University Press.

Moyles, J.R. (1993) 'Just a matter of routine . . . early years classroom organization and management'. *Education 3–13*, 21(1).

Neelands, J. (1984) *Making Sense of Drama*. London: Heinemann.

Newell, P. (1991) *The UN Convention and Children's Rights in the UK*. London: National Children's Bureau.

Niethammer, C. (1977) *Daughters of the Earth. The Lives and Legends of American Indian Women*. New York: Collier/MacMillan.

Osborn, A.F. and Milbank, J.E. (1987) *The Effects of Early Education*. Oxford: Clarendon Press.

Osborne, R. and Freyberg, P. (1985) *Learning in Science*. London: Heinemann.

Paley, V.G. (1981) *Wally's Stories*. London: Harvard University Press.

Paley, V.G. (1984) *Boys and Girls: Superheroes in the Doll Corner*. Chicago: Chicago University Press.

Paley, V.G. (1990) *The Boy who would be a Helicopter*. Cambridge, MA: Harvard University Press.

Pascal, C. (1990a) *Under Fives in Infant Classrooms*. Stoke-on-Trent: Trentham Press.

Pascal, C. (1990b) '4 year olds in schools: rhetoric or reality', Part 1 and Part 2, *Child Education*, June 1990, 13–15; July 1990, 6–8.

Pascal, C. and Bertram A.D. (1991) 'Defining and assessing quality in the education of children from 4–7 years'. Paper presented in September at the First European Conference on the Quality of Early Childhood Education, Leuven: Belgium.

Pascal, C. and Gamage, P. (1992) *Curriculum in the Early Years*. Unpublished paper, University of Nottingham.

Pauling, J. (1991) 'Play and knowledge of the world'. In Hall, N. and Abbott, L. (eds) *Play in the Primary Curriculum*. London: Hodder and Stoughton.

Pellegrini, A. (1987) *Applied Child Study: A Developmental Approach*. Hillsdale, NJ: Lawrence Erlbaum.

Peters, R. (1966) *Ethics and Education*. London: Allen and Unwin.

Peters, R.S. (1981) *Moral Development and Moral Education*. London: Allen and Unwin.

Pfeffer, N. and Coote A. (1991) *Is Quality Good for You? A Critical Review of Quality Assurance in Welfare Services*. Social Policy Paper No. 5, London: Institute for Public Policy Research.

Piaget, J. (1951) *Play, Dreams and Imitation in Childhood*. London: Routledge and Kegan Paul.

Piaget, J. (1965) *The Moral Development of the Child*. New York: The Free Press.

Pirsig, R.M. (1974) *Zen and the Art of Motorcycle Maintenance: An Inquiry into Values*. London: The Bodley Head.

Pitcher, E.G. and Schultz, L.H. (1983) *Boys and Girls at Play: The Development of Sex Roles*. NY: Praeger.

Pollard, A. and Tann, S. (1987) *Reflective Teaching in the Primary School*. London: Cassell.

Postman, N. (1983) *The Disappearance of Childhood*. NY: Comet.

Pramling, I. (1988) 'Developing children's thinking about their own learning'. *British Journal of Educational Psychology*, 58(3), 266–78.

Prosser, G. (1985) 'Play – a child's-eye view'. In Branthwaite, A. and Rogers, D. (eds) *Children Growing Up*. Milton Keynes: Open University Press.

Prosser, G.V., Hutt, C., Hutt J., Mahinaadasa, K.J. and Goonetilleke, M.D. (1986) 'Children's play in Sri Lanka: a cross cultural study', *British Journal of Developmental Psychology*, 4, 179–86.

Rabain-Jamin, J. (1989) 'Culture and early social interactions. The example of mother-infant object play in African and native French families', *European Journal of Psychology of Education*, 4(2), 295–305.

Reid, L.R. (1969) *Meaning in the Arts*. London: Allen and Unwin.

Rubin, K., Fein, G. and Vandenberg, B. (1983) 'Play'. In Hetherington, E.M. (ed.) *Manual of Child Psychology: Socialization, Personality and Social Development (Vol. IV)*. New York: Wiley.

Salmon, P. (1988) *Psychology for Teachers: An Alternative Approach*. London: Hutchinson.

Savage, J. (1991) 'Science education in the early years – some implications from research', in *World Organisation for Early Childhood Education*, OMEP Update.

Schaffer, H.R. (1971) *The Growth of Sociability*. Harmondsworth: Penguin Books.

Schaffer, H.R. (1974) 'Early social behaviour and the study of reciprocity', *Bulletin of the British Psychological Society*. 27, 209–16.

Schwartz, L.A. and Markham, W.T. (1985) 'Sex stereotyping in children's toy advertisements', *Sex Roles*, 12(1/2), 157–70.

Schwartzman, H.B. (1978) *Transformations*. New York: Plenum Press.

Schwartzman, H.B. (1982) 'Play as a mode', *Behavioural and Brain Sciences*, 5, 168–9.

Schweinhart, L.J., Weikart, D.P. and Larner, M.N. (1986) 'Consequences of three preschool curriculum models through age 15'. *Early Childhood Research Quarterly*, 1, 15–45.

Science Processes and Concept Exploration Project (1991) *Electricity*. Self-published by Liverpool University Press.

Scott, P. (1987) *A Constructivist View of Learning and Teaching in Science*, CLIS: University of Leeds.

Serbin, L. and Connor, J.M. (1979) 'Sex-typing of children's play preferences and patterns of cognitive performance', *Journal of Genetic Psychology*, 13(4), 135–16

Serbin, L., Connor, J.M., Burckhart, C.J. and Citron, C.C. (1979) 'Effects of peer presence in sex-typing of children's play behaviour', *Journal of Experimental Child Psychology*, 27, 303–9.

Shahn, B. (1967) *The Shape of Content*. Harvard: Harvard University Press.

Singer, D. and Singer, J. (1990) *The House of Make Believe*. Cambridge, MA: Harvard University Press.

Singer, J. (1973) *The Child's World of Make-Believe: Experimental Studies of Imaginative Play*. London: Academic Press.

Smilansky, S. (1968) *The effects of Socio-Dramatic Play on Disadvantaged Preschool Children*. New York: John Wiley.

Smilansky, S. and Shefatya, L. (1990) *Facilitating Play: A Medium for Promoting Cognitive, Socio-Emotional and Academic Development in Young Children*. Gaithersburg, MD: Psychosocial and Educational Publications.

Smith, P.K. (ed.). (1984) *Play in Animals and Humans*. Oxford: Basil Blackwell.

Smith, P.K. (1988) 'Children's play and its role in early development: a re-evaluation of the "play ethos"'. In Pellegrini, A.D. (ed.) *Psychological Bases for Early Education*. Chichester: John Wiley & Sons.

Smith, P.K., Dalgleish, M. and Herzmark, G. (1981) 'A comparison of the effects of fantasy play tutoring and skills tutoring in nursery classes', *International Journal of Behavioral Development*, 4, 421–41.

Sparrow, L. (1991) 'The airport as one world'. In Hall, N. and Abbott, L. (eds) *Play in the Primary Curriculum*. London: Hodder and Stoughton.

Steedman, C. (1985) 'Listen how the caged bird sings'. In Steedman, C., Urwin, C. and Walkerdine, V. (eds) *Language, Gender and Childhood: History Workshop Series*. London: Routledge and Kegan Paul.

Stevenson, H.W. and Lee, S-Y. (1990) 'Contexts of achievement', *Monographs of the Society for Research in Child Development*, 55(1–2).

Storr, A. (1989) *Solitude*. London: Flamingo.

Strahan, H. (1991) 'Getting from the railway station to the hotel'. In Hall, N. and Abbott, L. (eds) *Play in the Primary Curriculum*. London: Hodder and Stoughton.

Suransky, V.P. (1982) *The Erosion of Childhood*. Chicago: University of Chicago Press.

Sutton-Smith, B. (1971) 'A syntax for play and games'. In Herron, R.E. and Sutton-Smith, B. *Child's Play*. New York: Wiley and Sons.

Sutton-Smith, B. (1972) *The Folk Games of Children*. Austin: University of Texas Press.

Sutton-Smith, B. (1986) *Toys as Culture*. New York: Gardner Press.

Sutton-Smith, B. and Kelly-Byrne, D. (1984) 'The idealization of play'. In Smith, P.K. (ed.) *Play in Animals and Humans*. Oxford: Basil Blackwell.

Swadener, E. and Johnson, J. (1989) 'Play in diverse social contexts: parent and teacher roles'. In Bloch, M. and Pellegrini, A. (eds) *The Ecological Context of Children's Play*. New York: Ablex.

Sylva, K., Roy, C. and Painter, M. (1980) *Childwatching at Playgroup and Nursery School*. London: Grant McIntyre.

Sylva, K., Siraj-Blatchford, I. and Johnson, S. (1992) 'The Impact of the UK National Curriculum on pre-school practice: some "top-down" processes at work', *The International Journal of Early Childhood*, 24, 40–43.

Takhvar, M. and Smith, P.K. (1990) 'A review and critique of Smilansky's classification scheme and the "nested hierarchy" of play categories', *Journal of Research in Childhood Education*, 4, 112–22.

Tharp, R.G. and Gallimore, R. (1988) *Rousing Minds to Life*. Cambridge: Cambridge University Press.

Thomas, A. (1986) 'Patterns of change in an infant classroom', *Language Matters*, 1, London: CLPE.

Times Educational Supplement (1992) Review Section 2: '*A country that couldn't care less,*' 3 November, London.

Tinbergen, N. (1963) 'On the aims and methods of ethology', *Zeitschrift für Tierpsychologie*, 20, 410–33.

Tizard, B., Blatchford, P., Burke, J., Farquhar, C. and Plewis, L. (1988) *Young Children at School in the Inner City*. London: Lawrence Erlbaum.

Tizard, B. and Hughes, M. (1984) *Young Children Learning: Talking and Thinking at Home and at School*. London: Fontana.

Tobin, J.J., Wu, D.Y.H. and Davidson, D.H. (1989) *Pre-School in 3 Cultures: Japan, China and the United States*. New Haven: Yale University Press.

Trevarthen, C. (1974) 'Early attempts at speech'. In Lewin, R. *Child Alive*. London: Temple-Smith.

Trevarthen, C. (1982) 'The primary motives for co-operative understanding'. In Butterworth, G. and Light, P. (eds) *Social Cognition: Studies of the Development of Understanding*. Chicago: University of Chicago Press.

Tyler, S. (1989) 'Techniques of assessment from the past into the future'. Paper presented at the TACTYC National Conference, Worcester.

Tyler, S. (1991) 'Play in relation to the National Curriculum'. In Hall, N. and Abbott, L. (eds) *Play in the Primary Curriculum*. London: Hodder and Stoughton.

Vandenberg, B. (1986) 'Mere child's play'. In Blanchard, K. (ed.) *The Many Faces of Play*. The Association of the Anthropological Study of Play, Vol. 9, Champaign, IL: Human Kinetics.

Vygostsky, L.S. (1962) *Thought and Language*. New York: Wiley.

Vygotsky, L.S. (1978) *Mind in Society*. (translated and edited by M. Cole, V. John-Steiner, S. Scribner and E. Souberman). Cambridge, MA: Harvard University Press.

Webb, L. (1974) *Purpose and Practice in Nursery Education*. Oxford: Blackwell.

Weininger, O. (1988) '"What if" and "as if": imagination and pretend play in early childhood'. In Egan, K. and Nadaner, D. (eds) *Imagination and Education*. Milton Keynes: Open University Press.

Wells, G. (1987) *The Meaning Makers: Children Learning Language and Using Language to Learn*. London: Hodder and Stoughton.

Whalley, M. (1993 in press) *Learning to be Strong: Setting up a Neighbourhood Service for Under 5s and Their Families*. Sevenoaks: Hodder and Stoughton.

Whitehead J. (1989) 'Creating a living educational theory from questions of the kind, "How do I improve my practice?"', *Cambridge Journal of Education*, 15(1), 105–15.

Whitehead, M. (1983) 'Language development and the primary curriculum'. In Blenkin, G.M. and Kelly, A.V. (eds) *The Primary Curriculum in Action*. London: Paul Chapman.

Whitehead, M. (1990) *Language and Literacy in the Early Years*. London: Paul Chapman.

Whiting, B. and Whiting, J. (1975) *Children of Six Cultures*. Cambridge, MA: Harvard University Press.

Whyte, J. (1983) *Beyond the Wendy House*. London: Longman.

Winnicott, D.T. (1971) *Playing and Reality*. London: Tavistock Publications.

Wood, D. (1990) *How Children Think and Learn*. Oxford: Basil Blackwell.

Wood, D.J., Bruner, J.S. and Ross, G. (1976) 'The role of tutoring in problem solving'. *Journal of Child Psychology and Psychiatry*, 17, 89–100.

Woodhead, M. (1987) 'The needs of children: is there any value in the concept?', *Oxford Review of Education*, 13(2), 129–39.

Woods, P. (1983) *Sociology and the School*. London: Routledge and Kegan Paul.

Yawkey, T.D. and Pellegrini, A.D. (eds) (1984) *Child's Play: Development and Applied*. New York and London: Lawrence Erlbaum.

Index

JUST PLAYING?
THE ROLE AND STATUS OF PLAY IN EARLY CHILDHOOD EDUCATION

Janet R. Moyles

Play is a means by which humans and animals explore and learn from a variety of experiences in different situation for diverse purposes. Yet how far is play truly valued by those involved with the education and care of young children? How often is play and choosing play materials reserved as an activity for when children have finished 'work', thus reducing both its impact and its effect on the child's development?

Just Playing explores why we should encourage, promote, value and initiate play in our classrooms, and why teachers should be part of it. Janet Moyles draws on research findings from several countries which provide further evidence for establishing the value of play. She focuses on children between 4 and 8, examining the principles of play in early childhood education, and indicates how these principles can be put into practice. She provides a full justification for including play in the early years curriculum and encourages teachers, through examples of children at play, to review their own thinking on the issues in the light of core curriculum pressures.

This is essential reading for trainee and practising nursery and primary teachers, and nursery nurses; and for all those concerned with the education and development of young children.

Contents
Part 1 – Unravelling the 'mystery' of play? – Play and learning – Part 2 – Play through and with language – Solving problems through play – Play and creativity – Part 3 – Play, curriculum and organization – Play and progress: observing, recording and assessing the value of play – Play and the 'different' child – Play and adult expectations – Play in childhood and adulthood – References – Index.

208pp   0 335 09564 X (Paperback)   0 335 09569 0 (Hardback)

ORGANIZING FOR LEARNING IN THE PRIMARY CLASSROOM
A BALANCED APPROACH TO CLASSROOM MANAGEMENT

Janet R. Moyles

The primary classroom is the context in which a wide range of teaching and learning experiences occur – and not just for the children! What is it that underlies classroom organization, routines, rules, structures and daily occurrences? What are the prime objectives and what influences the decisions of teachers and children? What is it useful for teachers to consider when contemplating the issues of classroom management and organization? What do different practices have to offer?

Organizing for Learning in the Primary Classroom explores the whole range of influences and values which underpin *why* teachers do *what* they do in the classroom context and what these mean to children and others. Janet Moyles draws on several different research findings to examine the evidence in relation to the underlying issues of teachers' beliefs and values. She examines teaching and learning styles, children's independence and autonomy, coping with children's differences, the physical classroom context and resources, time management and ways of involving others in the day-to-day organization. Practical suggestions are given for considering both the functional and aesthetic aspects of the classroom context. Opportunities are provided for teachers to reflect on their own organization and also consider innovative and flexible ways forward to deal with new and ever increasing demands on their time and sanity!

Contents
Introduction: Polarizations and balance – Teachers and teaching: beliefs and values – The learning environment: organizing the classroom context – The children and their learning needs: balancing individual and whole class approaches – Grouping children for teaching and learning: providing equal opportunities and promoting appropriate behaviour – Time for teaching and learning – Deploying adult help effectively in the classroom: delegation and responsibility – Evaluating classroom organization and management – Conclusion: the primary classroom, a place and a time – References – Index.

208pp   0 335 15659 2 (Paperback)   0 335 15660 6 (Hardback)

THE FIRST YEARS AT SCHOOL
EDUCATION 4 TO 8

Angela Anning

This is a practical and reflective discussion of the education of 4 to 8 year-olds based on a sympathetic recognition of the complexities of being an early years teacher. Angela Anning begins by reviewing the historical and ideological traditions of British infant and primary schools, tracing how we have reached the position where teachers are torn between child-centred progressivism and utilitarian demands in educating young children. She then provides a detailed and authoritative critique of accepted thinking about the cognitive, social and emotional development of children; and explores the complexities of teachers' roles, particularly in the areas of language, intervention and expectations. She discusses the organization of the classroom, the structuring of learning in the school day and the content of the curriculum. She tackles the implications of the National Curriculum and national assessment for seven year-olds and their impact on pre-fives and children with special educational needs.

> The book is filled with practice-based knowledge about the curriculum, children, and teaching and learning. As such it should commend itself to all who have an interest in promoting quality education through the management, planning, teaching and assessment of the curriculum for 4–8 year-olds in the 1990s and beyond.

(Christopher Day)

Contents
Histories and ideologies – Children learning – Teachers teaching – The curriculum – A National Curriculum for 4–8 year-olds – Into the new ERA – References – Name index – Subject index.

168pp   0 335 09592 5 (Paperback)   0 335 09593 3 (Hardback)